The HOLLYWOOD SURVIVAL GUIDE

Great to meet you!

Never ever ever give up!

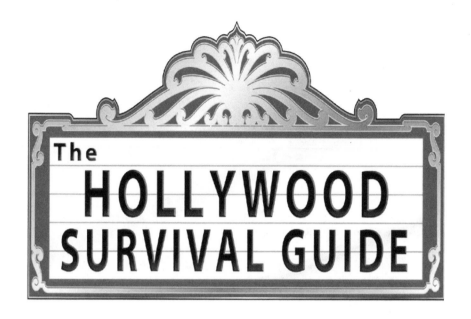

The
HOLLYWOOD
SURVIVAL GUIDE

Your handbook to becoming
a working actor in L.A.

Foreword by Jeremy Gordon, CSA

Kym Jackson

The Hollywood Survival Guide—For Actors
www.TheHollywoodSurvivalGuide.com

ISBN 978-0-9872316-2-8

Book design by SR Desktop Services
Marquee and HSG logo designed by Gaelyn Larrick, GaelynLarrick.com
Cover design by Esteban Oliva, www.be.net/estediablo
Perfict Books™ logo by Gemma Jackson, Gaelyn Larrick, and Nick Lang
Map artwork by Scott Ince, ScottInce.com

Back cover photo by Julian Dolman © 2012 JulianDolman.com—cover image for
The Weekly Review Magazine, November 2012

Published by Perfict Books™

First printing: January 2014

Printed in the United States of America by RR Donnelley

Please address all inquiries to: contact@TheHollywoodSurvivalGuide.com

For Gemma, Mum, and Dad
. . . and the mischief makers: Thomas, Simon, Prissy and Lucky

. . . and for the lost boys, Ash and Mash

CONTENTS

PART I
Down to Business

PART 2

The Filmmakers World
A Sneak Peek on the Other Side of the Camera

PART 3
Surviving LA
The Day to Day Stuff

DISCLAIMER

This book is based on informed opinion in the current market. Hollywood—like life—is not black and white. It is grey. The information will change over time and each person's experience here will differ from those who came before.

The film industry changes constantly so check this edition's publishing date (and the date on any other books you read about Hollywood) to make sure the information is current. Please don't be intimidated by the complex sections of this book or patronized by the basics. This is a comprehensive guide and I hope you will use your own judgment to take what applies to you at this point in your career.

Throughout the book I refer to all casting staff, actors, and characters as 'she', and all others as 'he'. This is purely for ease of reading because many of the examples within the text involve casting directors or actors interacting with filmmakers, agents and managers. Please take this to be the simple literary device that it is.

If your representation or any CD contradicts anything I suggest, follow their advice (within reason). You're in business with them so please trust their judgment. As you read the pages that follow, don't think of this as a textbook and definitely don't consider my opinions to be "rules". Just think of it as you and me sitting down over a nice whisky as I ramble off my thoughts on each of your questions about living and working in Hollywood.

FOREWORD

by Jeremy Gordon, CSA

Jeremy is a member of the Casting Society of America (CSA) and the Academy of Television Arts and Sciences (ATAS), with over fifty feature film casting department credits, including: "The Wolverine," "Think Like A Man," "Horrible Bosses" and "We Bought a Zoo."

The book foreword . . . What to write??? The book foreword . . . Hmmmmm, this is tricky. I want to impart some humorously touching and important words. I want to give you a little insight into who I am so my unending rambling of amazingness about Kym Jackson will seem a bit more tangible and at the same time I don't want to bore you into skipping this section. Judge for yourself and see if I pull that off.

I've known Kym Jackson for many, many years. I first met her when she auditioned for a martial arts film I cast at the beginning of my career. Kym walked into the room in all her Aussie beauty with a weapon. Not some "weapon" in her bag of acting tricks. A real weapon. I believe it was one of those long Japanese fighting ninja sticks. We were auditioning actors who had fighting skills since we were sending them to Shanghai to shoot for a few months and they needed some basic fighting skills. I knew from the moment I saw Kym and her really big stick that she was somebody extremely special.

Years later she's become one of my close friends and an important part of my life. I've been fortunate enough to cast her a number of times and I've sent her to some pretty exotic locations. Kym is one of those people I just KNEW would do great things. She's incredibly talented and auditions like the best of 'em. She's gorgeous but knows how to blend in when needed for certain roles. She does not rely on her beauty to succeed as many LA actors do. Most of all, she's extremely intelligent and savvy about this insane business. It's not just enough to be talented and pretty. You have to know what to do with it all.

Kym knows everybody in this town. Her name comes up in conversations all the time with agents, managers, producers, network executives, investors, PA's and actors from the far reaches of the globe. Kym knows them all and I have never heard a single negative word uttered about her. She's been networking and building these amazing relationships since her first day in LA. She's been all over the world shooting films and television shows and she's constantly booking new projects. She's the real deal. She's the current real deal and she can tell you just as much about foreign sales and distribution deals as she can tell you about Casting Director X.

One of my favorite aspects to Kym's book is that it's not simply a recap of the technical things she learned over the years. She also delves into the life of an actor here in LA and speaks about items some actors may not even think about before making the choice to move to the City of Angels. Topics like marketing tools, networking, the differences between the many types of auditions, day jobs that pay the bills, getting around LA and even production.

Kym intersperses important knowledge with the knowhow of some-body who has been there and done that. She doles out the honest good-ness about things like self-submissions and whether or when they work. She helps you see things from your (hopeful) agent's point of view in order for you to better help yourself and land more auditions.

One of the best parts of this book is that you do not have to read it cover to cover, word for word (although you should—you will learn a whole heck of a lot!) You can use it as a reference. I get calls and messages on Facebook and Twitter every single day from actors with the most basic ques-tions. "Where do I find out about auditions?" "Where can I get the sides?" "What are the important websites to join? There are so many!" Just like Prego, "It's in there!" Kym covers it all. I mean ALL. I am incredibly glad she finished the book. I can't tell you how many calls and emails Kym sent me asking this or that or this or that or this or freakin' that. There isn't much she didn't cover. She even has a section about "Procrastination" and why it sits on your shoulder like a little red man!

Kym has the mindset of an actor, casting director, producer and busi-nesswoman all rolled into one. Like it or not, that's a necessary evil if you want to succeed in this business. In this day and age, you cannot just stroll into town and live the life of an artiste. You must do more. Gone are the days when doing the minimum will get you by. Today you must show the world you have something special. That you have not just that IT factor but that you have the longevity of making the big bucks for you and your team. Kym's section on "Keeping a CD Database" is incredibly helpful and it's what I constantly teach actors at workshops. She will tell you almost word for word what I have been saying for years. She knows what you need to know and she has put it all in this book.

Listen to her. Read her words. Ingest the knowledge. Go out into the world and see what rings true for you. This is not a textbook of how the Revolutionary War started or a step-by-step guide to the defeat of California's Prop 8. It's more like a guide of knowledge that's tested tried and true. Think of Kym Jackson like the Yoda of the acting world. You do not have to live by her every word but Kym, Yoda and I share a philosophy that will help you succeed, "Do or do not. There is no try."

Best of luck to you all!! Xoxo

Jeremy Gordon, CSA

Check out the Facebook groups Jeremy created for actors to network, ask questions, submit to casting calls and post materials: 'Casting Directors for Actors' & 'Jeremy Gordon Casting' and also follow him on Twitter at @JeremyCasts. Combined, there are over 40,000 members [at time of printing]. Go forth and network!

ACKNOWLEDGMENTS

Proofread and edited by Tim McGrath and Hannah Cowley
Computer guy: Dylan Ramsey

Additional notes, contributions, and suggestions by:

Gemma Jackson
Jessie McGoldrick
Trevor Davies
Lee Jackson
Chris Jackson
Nicky Lang
Renee Lim
Rusty Ince
Jeremy Gordon, CSA
Tom McSweeney, CSA
Caitlyn Stasey
Peter Cornwall

. . . and

Nick Krein
Jenna Mattison
Belinda Gosbee
Louise Brownlie
Shane Abbess (special thanks)
Gina Moorley
Sophie King
Kat Randolph
Annette Sym
Todd Leigh
Matthew Wolfe
Claire McCarthy
Ricki Maslar
David M. Lawrence
Brady Romberg
Andy Newton Lee
Rhett Giles

Christian Clark
Brent Bailey
Luke Pegler
Jason Siner
Jack Maxwell
Verity Fiction
Judd Tilyard
Chris Smith
Gayle Max
Ian Paul Cassidy
Tim Maddocks
Brian Holden
Darren Criss
Ron Rogge
Lynn Milano
Jeremy Scott Johnson
Alex Collins
Belinda D'Alesandro
Josh Pyatt
Brian McCabe
Garrett MacGuire
Jeff Kallagheri
Darin Harris
Martin Copping
Kel Dolen
Brandon Henry
Peter Holland
Julia Perri
Dean Kirkright
Tyler O'Neill

INTRODUCTION

After spending a great deal of time answering emails and phone calls from actors moving to LA, I realized that if someone had just told me all this stuff when I first moved out here it would have saved me years of stumbling around blindly.

All too often talented actors with no business sense fail, while mediocre actors succeed simply due to superior networking skills and a clearer understanding of how the industry works. The intention of this book is to answer the fundamental questions for all actors so the business side of the acting game is not the determining factor in the success of an actor.

When starting out in Hollywood, having a strong business plan and marketing strategy can be more important than being able to deliver an Oscar worthy performance. This is because if the Oscar worthy 'artist' doesn't know how to source auditions, nobody who can hire her will even know she exists. Nothing is sadder than an average actor booking a great role because the great actor wasn't savvy enough to get an audition.

There are thousands of talented actors in LA, but the sheer quantity of the competition dilutes the quality of the talent pool. Many of the limited number of audition slots are given to well connected but mediocre actors, which means if you are a strong actor and you can get auditions, you will eventually book jobs.

How do you get these auditions? How do you learn the business and strategy? Who do you market to and how? Well, you have three choices: You can sit at home listening to your agent tell you "It's really quiet at the moment", you can come to LA and spend nine years using trial and error and figuring it out for yourself (welcome to my world), or you can sit down with a highlighter and a pen, and read this book.

Note: *Los Angeles is a large city. Hollywood is a district within Los Angeles. Rather than referring to the district itself, the term 'Hollywood' is most often a reference to the film and television industry within LA, which is dispersed throughout the city.*

In reading the pages that follow, you will learn from my mistakes and the mistakes of my friends. So often it is said "If only I knew then what I know now" . . . well I'm telling you, I know now. It has taken me nine years to learn it and I missed hundreds of opportunities during that time. If you truly absorb the principles presented in the pages that follow, you will understand what it takes to succeed as a working actor in LA.

There are maybe ten thousand working actors in LA. I define the term 'working actor' as actors who are working regularly in films and TV series, and are able to survive solely on acting income. It took me five years of very hard work in LA to finally become one of them. Working actors book roles every few months and are recognized within the industry as being reliable and talented enough to work on a professional film or TV set. Working actors are not necessarily famous. Of those ten thousand working actors, how many could you name? Maybe three hundred?

Fame is a result of a media response or of the emergence and maintenance of an internet following. Fortune is a result of business savvy, inheritance, or dumb luck. Fame and fortune in the acting world is a result of being a business savvy and marketable working actor *with a lot of good luck and timing* thrown in.

Although I will touch briefly on ideas regarding how a person might parlay their status as a working actor towards becoming a celebrity, this is not a book on how to get famous. What I will give you are the tools to make it more likely that when the right roles are casting, you are in the audition rooms. I hope to demystify Hollywood by giving you the necessary insider information and running you through a systematic and logical approach to becoming a working actor in LA. The rest is up to you.

OVERVIEW

Part I—Down To Business

This is the book's main portion, a guide to everything I've learned over the past nine years about the business of acting in LA. It covers where to find your own auditions, how to attain and maintain relationships with industry contacts, audition etiquette, press and publicity, sourcing representation, and much more.

Part 2—A Sneak Peak into the Filmmaker's World

One of the complaints I hear the most from directors is that many actors have no idea what is going on around them on a set. You must be aware of how an industry works if you hope to succeed in it. This section will arm you with a general understanding of the business and on-set portion of filmmaking and television production.

Part 3—Surviving LA: The Day To Day Stuff

This section covers the basic information needed by anyone living in LA. It's a breakdown of things like where to get groceries, how to get around LA, and where to live. You'll learn about fascinating stuff like visas, phone carriers, tipping, and so much more.

Resource Guide

This is the online component of the book. It is a database of resources including acting classes, workshops, casting offices, printing places, and many more. It enables actors to share the experiences they've had with the various companies. The resource guide can be found through the tab at:

www.TheHollywoodSurvivalGuide.com

HSG iPhone App

The HSG app includes all of the information included in this book as a searchable database and reference guide. It offers training systems for improving your industry knowledge, and information from the resource guide, including agency lists and other vital LA information.

Email

I want to make sure this book is accurate and may be doing later editions at some point. If you disagree with anything in the following pages, I would love to hear from you. As the industry evolves I plan to add amendments, so please help your fellow actors out by sharing your thoughts on the website forums, or email them to me at:

Kym@TheHollywoodSurvivalGuide.com

PART I

Down to Business

TRUST ME ... THIS IS GOING TO TAKE SOME TIME

Which actors most frequently book work in LA? The talented ones? The passionate ones? The attractive ones? Absolutely. However, there are many talented, passionate, attractive actors here. The actors who are hired repeatedly are also methodical, consistent, diligent, confident, and professional.

It's often said that the key turning point for most actors in LA is three years. I agree. Allowing a year for visa and Greencard paperwork, let's increase that number to four years for most international actors. Furthermore, it seems to have taken most working actors an additional three or four years before they were able to support themselves financially from acting alone.

Eight years is a long time. How old are you now? How old will you be then? I'm not saying you'll be famous in eight years, or even rich. I'm saying that if you are a talented and consistently proactive actor, four years from the day you arrive in LA is when you will probably have solid mid-level representation, be on the radar of the 'CDs' (casting directors), and frequently doing union auditions. I'm saying that eight years from the day you arrive in LA, with the help of the advice contained within this book, you might just be a working actor. It also takes a whole lot of luck.

An overnight success is a rarity. Lindsay Lohan and Scarlett Johansson were competing for roles when they were (respectively) eight and ten years old. Even Kristen Stewart and Zac Effron were working in lesser-known movies and television for years before *Twilight* and *High School Musical* came out. In the majority of cases, it's not just about having one hit role. It's about having many roles over time so audiences and industry members begin to know and trust your ability to create great characters and engage an audience. It's about building a body of solid credits to help you book that one hit role, and following that role up by attaching to high quality projects.

The reason it takes so long to get into the game is that Hollywood is built on **trust**, or (more specifically) nepotism, familiarity, and referrals. You need to work hard over time to earn the trust of the filmmakers, representatives (agents and managers), and CDs around town. Investors are spending a heck of a lot of money on these projects, so the producers need to know that the people they are hiring can do the job.

Trust takes a great deal of time to earn and prove. Each legitimate film or TV credit on your resume helps convince CDs and filmmakers to trust you, because if you've worked with professionals before, it is likely that you will behave and perform like a professional. Having an agent or manager who is trusted by CD's around town is a vital commodity for up and coming actors, as the reputation they have built for providing solid talent is what will get you into the audition room. When you show your 'demo' (demonstration reel) or do an audition, you're giving the filmmaker evidence that they can trust you to do justice to their character.

Once you gain the trust of the industry and become a public figure, you must earn and maintain the trust of audiences by doing solid performances in well-written, well-produced projects. When an audience watches a film "because *celebrity x* is in it", it's because the audience trusts the celebrity to bring them a story that is worth the cost of the movie ticket or DVD rental. After several bad movies starring the same celebrity, the audience has their trust broken and will be less likely to see the celebrity's next film. This is why stars must be very careful about which films they select and with which directors they choose to work.

Working consistently in Hollywood takes time because earning people's trust takes time. If you're in this business to succeed, make sure you're in it for the long haul.

CHAPTER I

TRAINING

Regardless of how naturally talented you are, you need to train consistently if you want to be an actor. Coaching before important auditions and jobs is essential as it provides another perspective on the character and helps you find stronger choices within a scene. It is often said that acting talent is like a muscle and like an elite sportsperson your muscles must be kept in shape. This is definitely true.

STANDARD AMERICAN ACCENT

For actors moving to Hollywood from other countries and regional areas of America, it is vital to perfect a flawless standard American accent.

There are a variety of American accents: the Northern states (almost sounds Canadian), the East Coast (Boston, Jersey, Philly, New York), the Mid-West (Chicago, Michigan), and Southern accents (Texan, Georgian, Tennessee). All of these accents are different and very specific. The neutral Californian accent spoken by most characters on TV is referred to as a 'standard American' accent.

One in three hundred roles here might require a foreign accent or regional US dialect, and that's probably being generous. Producers are not going to change an entire storyline to explain why the cop with two lines in CSI has a South African accent. Therefore, if you cannot do the accent, it is unlikely you will book work.

An excellent Australian actor who is a friend of mine moved to LA and his American accent (which he had worked on) was terrible. After missing out on several parts, he resorted to speaking in a standard American dialect in everyday life. As the months went by he picked up the nuances and speech patterns. One day I realized his accent had become flawless. It had taken him a year of work. He has since booked several roles, including a lead in a television series, and the rest is history.

Having a standard American accent is more important to you for getting work in LA than those acting classes you're probably taking right now. A bad actor can pass for a good actor to say two lines in a TV show and get away with it. A great actor with a bad accent can rarely pass for an American, even just to say one or two lines.

If your standard American accent is not flawless, you need to **fix it now**. You think it's okay? It's probably not. Go to a dialect coach and get an assessment. You may need coaching or an accent CD (try Bob and Claire Corff or Bruce Shapiro) to understand the fundamental sounds and mouth movements required to perfect the accent.

One way to learn an accent is to watch a movie in which the main character speaks with an accent from that region. Pause the DVD after each line of dialogue then replicate it exactly. Make sure the character is of your gender or else you may mimic the wrong pitch accidentally.

Once you think you've got it nailed, grab a book or magazine and read it out loud, twisting your mouth around words that you otherwise may not think to speak. A widely used elocution exercise is to put a cork between your teeth (holding one end outside your mouth so you don't swallow it) and talk in the accent around the cork. This overworks the muscles and makes it much easier to use the accent after you remove the cork.

If you really want to get crazy with it (because there's nothing weird about the cork thing), speak in standard American when you're out shopping or in a bar. It will force you to maintain the accent during conversations and allow you to work through the little problems.

A standard American accent is hard to perfect, but once you've got it, you will have much more confidence when auditioning in Hollywood.

ACTING CLASSES

Never underestimate the importance of selecting the right acting teacher. An acting teacher should be someone you trust to guide you through the vulnerability and emotional highs and lows that come with honing your skills. When you are considering taking a class, research the instructor. Look at their professional work history and assess whether the projects look like high quality *acting or directing* work. Anyone in LA can have fifty indie film or non-union theatre credits, but this has little bearing on their ability to teach an acting class.

Of course, a great coach doesn't have to be an actor or director so if they are not, research how students from the course have faired in the industry over the years. Look at testimonials from past and present students. If they have celebrity alumni, check how long those actors actually trained at the school.

Find out whether the class is on camera. Many of the better foundation work classes are not on camera, however it is important to take on-camera classes also to know how your performances are translating on screen. Look over the material used in class and analyze how the coach breaks down the scenes to ensure it is compaitble with your preferred style of acting. Ask whether they focus on a specific method and the degree to which they are immersed in the 'technique'. You don't want to end up being force-fed a bunch of theory to which you don't relate.

Most classes in LA allow new students to 'audit' (observe) a session. Take advantage of this and ask the students about the class when it's finished. Make sure the teacher is encouraging but firm. A coach who praises average actors may lead you to false beliefs in your ability. You want someone who will be honest when you do weak work and help you improve, but also compliment you when you've rocked a scene. Beware of teachers who appear to be ego driven because their focus often lies with being right rather than nurturing the students craft and talent.

Aim to be in the bottom half of the class talent-wise. Being the best actor in a class does wonders for your ego but will slow your progression. Most actors perform better when working opposite a great actor, so be selfish and ensure you are always surrounded by more advanced performers. If you can't tell what level your talent is at in comparison to the rest of the class, you're probably right where you need to be.

The skill of your fellow students is important, because if everyone is talented it is more likely that some of you may become successful. This is a key part of networking in LA, because actors often help each other with referrals for representation and auditions. This often evolves into actors writing and producing their own work, which naturally leads to hiring friends.

Scene Study Classes

Be aware of the difference between a scene study class (in which you perfect and finesse specific scenes) and an acting class (where you learn to be a better actor). A scene study teacher will generally have you do the scene once, then redirect you a couple of different ways by making different choices.

An acting teacher will often use scripted scenes, but will focus very specifically on the fundamentals of your work. These include different methods of connecting to your emotions and characters, the physicality within the scene, and a myriad of other facets that go into becoming a great actor.

If you are not a formally trained actor, I advise you to seek out acting classes rather than scene study classes until all of the fundamentals are in place. Once you are trained, a scene study class will keep your talent 'in shape' and hone your ability to analyze and craft each scene you perform.

Don't Lose Yourself at an Acting Center

What I'm categorizing as an acting center is a non-formalized acting school that has more than one teacher teaching classes. Several classrooms allow for multiple teaching sessions to occur at once and students often end up changing teachers as they advance through the levels within the school. Many of the top teachers in LA teach at acting centers.

Don't let the social hierarchy of an acting center distract you from your overall goal. Actors often become obsessed with moving up the levels and impressing teachers. Don't forget that the teachers and other students in this 'world' are rarely the ones who can give you jobs in this industry and are certainly not all knowing beings (if they were, most would be full-time working actors).

Your goal is not to be in the 'super advanced master class' at *Acting Center X*. Your goal is to be a successful working actor. Go to class, work hard, learn as much as possible, then go out into the real industry and focus on your career.

Acting Methods: A Quick History

Acting methods are techniques that help actors create the thoughts and emotions of characters, in an effort to develop lifelike performances. You're going to hear a lot of jargon in LA referring to this 'method' or that 'method'. Each method is a specific way people believe actors should prepare for, cultivate and deliver a performance (i.e. each method is a different style of actor training). Following is a quick history (summarized from *en.Wikipedia.org/ wiki/Method_acting*) of the better-known methods dominating the acting world in the USA.

In the late 1800's and early 1900's, there was this guy called Constantin Stanislavski who was a Russian theatre actor and director. His original technique was for actors to use their actual memories to relive and access emotion. In his later years, he explored other means of accessing emotion, like having an absolute belief in the given circumstances by using your imagination, and the implementation of a physical action (aka: 'business'). Sanford Meisner summarized Stanislavski's later beliefs by saying that an actor should live truthfully under imaginary circumstances.

One of Stanislavski's students Ryszard Boleslawski formed the American Laboratory Theatre in 1925. Lee Strasburg (who studied under Boleslawski) went on to form The Group Theatre (1931–1940), teaching Stanislavski's methods to the members.

One of the members of The Group Theatre, Stella Adler, left to study privately with Stanislavski in Paris and upon her return, informed the group that Stanislavsky's methods had evolved. Other members of The Group Theatre (including Sanford Meisner) supported the implementation of these new techniques but Lee Strasburg refused, and The Group Theatre disbanded.

Stella Adler formed the Stella Adler School of Acting. Sanford Meisner incorporated Stanislavski's new methods into his 'Meisner' technique at the Neighborhood Playhouse in New York (the NY version of Robert Carnegie's highly respected LA school Playhouse West), and briefly taught at The Actors Studio. Lee Strasberg went on to become the artistic director at The Actors Studio.

Two of the main acting methods you'll hear about in LA are 'Meisner' and 'Stanislavski'. These ironically both come from Constantin Stanislavski's teachings. The method called 'Stanislavski' is based on his earlier teachings, and the method called 'Meisner' is Sanford Meisner's interpretation of Stanislavski's later teachings. Stella Adler's teachings are based on similar principles to Meisner's, but without a specific belief in any one method.

PRIVATE COACHING

Most professional actors coach privately before important auditions and jobs to get an educated opinion on the piece and hone the performance. I try to coach at least a day prior to the performance so the advice and direction can sink in overnight. An hour is usually ample time, costing anything from $60 to $200.

A private coach doesn't necessarily need to be a great actor, but does need to be a great director of actors. They should add variance and dimensions to your scene, and help break it down to find the strongest choices.

Don't let a coach pressure you into extreme choices you don't feel fit the character. If you express that you really don't want to play the scene or character a certain way and you are being pushed too strongly in that direction, they may not be the right coach for you. It's a fine line, however, because taking you out of your comfort zone is exactly what a coach should do. Unlike a group class, a private coach has the time to explain in detail why they recommend specific choices and how best to play each moment of the scene.

IMPROV TRAINING

The term 'improvisation' or 'improv' refers to any time during a performance that an actor is saying or doing things that aren't planned or scripted and making things up as she goes along. When people talk about 'improv' in LA, they are generally referring to the performance of unscripted comedic scenes driven by either a game or a suggestion from the audience and performed by groups of actors. In LA, people will often ask if you want to "go to the improv" in the same way people in a typical suburban neighborhood might ask if you want to "go to the movies".

'Short form improv' is when a short scene is performed (or games are played) based on a suggestion given by an audience member.

'Long form improv' is when a series of scenes are strung together and each actor plays one or more characters in different scenarios based on a single theme. This theme is often derived from an audience member's suggestion. Improv is most commonly comedic acting, but show styles can vary from improvised Shakespeare to musical theatre.

At 'iO West' (Improv Olympic) and 'UCB' (Upright Citizens Brigade), the improvisers perform 'The Harold'. The Harold is a long form style of improvisation, created by iO co-founder Del Close, which seems to be the most common style of long form improv performed in LA.

Groundlings, UCB, iO West and Second City are the most well known and respected improvisational groups in Los Angeles. There are other places you could go for this training, but why would you want to go anywhere but the places that are known as the best?

Comedy CDs look for these improv training schools on resumes and often attend improv shows to find new talent. If you look right for a comedic role but don't have a strong credit list, having training from one of these schools on your resume will improve your chances of gaining an audition. The training implies that you have some understanding of comedic timing and gives the impression that your comedy skill level is of the standard CDs expect from students of these schools.

> **INTERESTING FACT:** Many of the cast members of Saturday Night Live over the years are alumni of the top improv schools. Further to that, many of the successful comedic actors working in the industry today are ex-cast members of Saturday Night Live.

ANCILLARY TRAINING

Having a variety of talents to put in the 'Special Skills' section of your resume will make you a more employable and versatile actor. If you are interested in any of the following activities, take classes.

Stunt Training

There is no formalized system of training or official certification required for stunt personnel working in US feature films and TV. Your only qualification is the ability to do the stunt. This means working in stunts results from stunt coordinators and performers knowing you and your work.

Some stunt coordinators teach classes, which are a great networking tool because coordinators suggest and hire stunt performers for projects, often in speaking roles. Stunt coordinators are frequently able to bypass the standard casting process because the focus of the casting is stunt ability rather than acting ability.

Combat Training

Action films and TV shows prefer actors with fight skills. Performers on these projects often undergo months of fight training so if the actor already has martial arts or fight experience, more visually impressive moves can be utilized. Combat classes in LA are often taught by fight and stunt coordinators, so they double as a networking tool.

Singing and Dancing Training

With the success of *High School Musical* and *Glee*, there are roles in the breakdowns almost every day for actors who can sing and/or dance. If you can sing or dance, even at an above average level, it will put you in the running for these highly coveted roles. Specify the style of singing and dancing in which you are trained, and ensure you are at a performance level in each of the listed styles.

Musical Instruments

If a role requires the ability to work with a specific instrument, casting is looking for an actor proficient at a performance level in that instrument. Being able to fake it is not enough because there will be plenty of other actors who are able to play, and you can bet the CD will ask you to demonstrate. If you used to play an instrument, get yourself back up to scratch before adding it to your resume.

Sports

Shows like *Friday Night Lights* or films like *Moneyball* put out breakdowns seeking actors who have experience in the sport around which the project is centered. Stay fresh with any sport in which you have a talent. You don't usually need to be an exceptional player; simply being proficient should suffice.

Keep Your Special Skills Honest

If you are going to put a skill on your resume, make sure you can do it. Skills like surfing, horse riding, and motorbike riding are often falsely added because actors assume they are easy to learn in a short period of time. It is hard to run a testing session for talents of this nature because it involves a separate skill test day. Never tell a CD you can do something if you cannot. It is a lie that may make everybody look bad and prevent that office from bringing you back in to audition.

CHAPTER 2

AN ACTOR'S MARKETING MATERIALS

This section explains how to format resumes, headshots, demo reels, online profiles and actor websites to meet industry standards. Although agents, managers and filmmakers see these marketing tools, they are predominantly utilized by casting directors.

When marketing, think of yourself as a product, consider who you are selling to (the CDs) and figure out what they value most. CDs are short on TIME. This means that every marketing tool must be focused on giving a CD ONLY the information needed to make a decision in as little time as possible.

As you review your resume, demo reel, and other marketing materials, I want you to consistently think about TIME and for each item ask yourself (and several friends) the following questions:

- Is this the most concise, clear way to format this material?
- Am I saying the same thing twice?
- Is the message and information easy to understand as soon as you look at it?
- Is my 'type' immediately clear from this material?
- Am I repeating myself? (sorry, I couldn't resist)

What is a 'Breakdown'?

A breakdown is a list that "breaks down" the roles being cast in a project, detailing the name, age range, and a short physical and personality-focused description of each character. The breakdown also outlines any special skills required or preferred for the role, or unusual requirements like nudity or being "comfortable with snakes".

Breakdown Express Profile

The majority of professional film and television casting directors use BreakdownExpress.com to cast projects. Most theatrical agents in LA exclusively submit through it, so your breakdown profile is your most important marketing tool.

Actors cannot access BreakdownExpress.com, but your profile can be modified through your ActorsAccess.com account. A separate profile exists for each of your representatives so it is important to ensure your demo, headshots, and resume are always updated on each profile page.

WHAT IS MY TYPE?

For the most part your age range, look and body will determine your type. Your personality, energy, and essence will also factor in. CDs, directors and producers will remember you as a certain type based on their first impression.

> **TIP:** Sam Christensen runs a fantastic workshop on identifying your image and type.

Here's an exercise to figure out your type: Ask fifteen people which three celebrities you remind them of and which roles those celebrities have played that would suit you. Ask five industry professionals, five friends, and five strangers. Don't suggest any names, just get three answers from each person. Write down all 35 answers and see which double up to finish with five celebrities to whom you are most similar.

Go to IMDb and look at the types of projects and roles the celebs played *when they were your age*. Are they the bad girl or the good girl? Hero or victim? How do they market themselves? What do their headshots look like? How did they start out? Are their credits in film or TV? Drama or comedy? Find out what sort of press takes an interest in their work. Are they in *FHM Magazine* or *Time Magazine*? What is their BRAND? Emulate their formula to mold your marketing tools around your type.

This is not to say you shouldn't be your own person (you absolutely should), but your individuality will be marketed more successfully if you know what you're selling.

Know if you are too young or old for a type. I spent years pitching myself as the wrong type. I thought that with a strong personality and features I should play Jodie Foster type cop, detective, and strong female roles. I took plain looking headshots with a very un-sexy, serious look. I wondered for a long time why I wasn't getting auditions.

The thing I overlooked was that Jodie Foster is twenty years older than me. If a CD wants a seasoned detective, she is not likely to hire a twenty-six year old actress. However, when casting a strong, smart female in her mid-twenties (even to play a lawyer or cop) filmmakers usually want her to be relatively attractive. I was taking myself out of the running for both types of roles by marketing myself as something I wasn't.

Luckily, a friend of mine showed my website to a VIP in town, asking why I wasn't getting work. The VIP replied something like "In most of her headshots she looks harsh and unattractive. It's easy to make a beautiful girl look plain, but hard to make an unattractive girl look gorgeous. I may not audition her if those headshots were all I'd seen because there's nothing marketable or appealing about her look".

I immediately took all my photos down, and a week later (in early September of 2009) I got a round of new headshots where I said to the photographer "The goal is to look strong and sexy". I went from averaging two auditions a month, to having around ten auditions in late September and close to twenty in October that year. It worked fast and I've hit very few slow patches since!

Hollywood wants to be able to pick your type and know how to sell it, so make it easy for them. Most actors believe they can do every role, but in LA there are so many actors from which to choose.

Some shows won't even hire you to play a few lines as a nurse or EMT unless you actually are a qualified nurse or EMT. For larger roles, obviously, acting chops take precedence over authenticity, but for the smaller roles why wouldn't they hire the real deal?

Don't try to be everything to everyone. Figure out who you are and what you excel at then market yourself accordingly to get your foot in the door. Once it's open, you can show them all of the other amazing things you can do.

Here are some examples of types into which most people will fit. You may be able to 'play' several, but one or two will suit you perfectly.

Child or Teen or 18–24

- Lead (charismatic, cute, smart)
- Sidekick (chubby, quirky, geeky, shy)
- Antagonist (baddie, bully)

25–35 (ingénue) or 36–55 (experienced)

- Lead
- Sidekick (geeky, gothic, comedic best friend types)
- Main antagonist (gang boss, ring leader)
- Low level antagonist (baddie, street thug, gang member)
- Smart, strong characters (detective, doctor, lawyer, stockbroker)
- White collar (accountant, nurse, teacher)
- Blue collar (builder, cop, coach)
- Sex object (hookers, strippers, girls with obvious plastic surgery)
- Parent

55–75

- Same as list above, but add the word 'retired' or 'boss'.
- Young Grandparents
- Mentor, Ex-pro

75+

- Rich 'old person' (board member, guest at society party)
- Poor 'old person' (on welfare, homeless, still working)
- Grandparent

HEADSHOTS IN LA

More expensive doesn't necessarily mean better when it comes to headshot photographers. Check the resource guide and ask your friends and representation to recommend one to you. There are many opinions of how headshots should look in Hollywood, but ultimately, if a photo is getting you auditions for roles that are right for you, keep using it. If it isn't, get a new shot.

> **TIP:** Before reading this section, go to TheoAndJuliet.com, BKHeadshots. com, PaulSmithPhotography.com and DanaPatrick.com, to see the work of some of the top headshot photographers in LA.

Color
Headshots in LA are in color.

Your Headshot MUST LOOK LIKE YOU
If you want glamorous photos, put together a modeling portfolio. An acting headshot shouldn't aim to showcase how attractive you can be photoshopped to look; it should be a 'sample' of your face. You are telling the CD "This is what I will look like when I walk into your office", which allows her to select the most **visually appropriate** actors to audition for each role.

If a CD is casting a twenty-five year old and your headshot looks twenty-five but your face looks thirty-five, she will be disappointed when you show up because you've essentially lied to her.

The actors a CD brings in to meet producers and directors are a reflection on her and how accurate she can be in finding the right actor for each role. If you are wasting a CD's time, she is wasting her employer's time. You will be unlikely to get the part, and the CD will probably not invite you to audition for quite some time. In a town whose currency is founded on relationships and trust, wasting a CD's time is a bad business move.

Size Does Matter
Good framing in a headshot includes from the top of your chest to the top of your head. Including the shoulders gives the viewer a reference point for your body type and overall look.

Ensure your face is between 50% and 85% of the height of the photo. In an 8" × 10" portrait oriented print your head should be between 5" and 8.5" tall. Headshots are displayed as 'thumbnail' size for electronic submissions, so if your face is under 50% of the shot it may be hard to see and less likely to grab the viewers attention. Keeping the size of your head under 85% prevents it from being too overwhelming and allows the viewer to accurately get a feel for your overall look.

High Resolution
Printable photographs require a minimum of 300dpi (dots per inch).

In Focus
A picture that is even slightly out of focus distorts the viewer's connection to the subject. You can test focus by zooming to 100% resolution on your eye in the original proof photo. If each detail in the eye is still crisp and clear, the shot is probably focused well enough to print.

Well Lit and Un-obscured

Your face should be fully visible and un-obscured. Some actors use head-shots with hair or shadows across their face as a stylistic choice. The CD doesn't care about all that jazz; she just wants to see what you look like. You want the CD to see the character she is looking for when she looks at your picture, not the artistic choices of the photographer.

A Good Background is Textured but Not Distracting

A background that is out of focus with a little texture tends to work well for headshots. The background should be something interesting but simple that doesn't distract from the subject (you).

Name Banner for Printed Headshots

It's as important for CD's to see your name repeatedly as it is for them to see your face. Most actors have their name written in a frame-like banner at the bottom of their headshot. The name banner is usually white writing on a black strip or black writing on a white strip. Lining the whole picture with a border is also an option.

The strip at the bottom should be around 2cm to 3cm thick. Font size between 24pt and 40pt is fine for your name. Some actors write 'SAG-AFTRA' in very small writing (8pt to 10pt font) next to their name.

> **TIP: The Moment Two People See Each Other From Across a Room**
> A CD once mentioned to me that a headshot should be a photo of the moment two people see each other for the first time from across a room and smile. Inviting, engaging, and intriguing, it should be an expression that would make someone willing to walk through a crowded room to meet the person in the photo. I always loved that idea.

Photoshop™

All actors should learn how to crop and shrink photos, and incorporate them with other elements to create basic marketing materials. Photoshop-ping is the best and worst thing you can do to a headshot and it should be utilized with care, caution, and **restraint**. Photoshop is great for removing pimples or stains on clothing, reducing (not removing) wrinkles, and fixing makeup flaws or oily skin.

You want the CD to feel a connection to your photo. Lines, moles, dimples, and freckles are what make us human. These 'faults' define us as individuals and help us to look like the interesting, real life characters we're being hired to portray.

Never use Photoshop to make yourself look younger. If you want to fix the contrast to look less washed out, or reduce a wrinkle because the light made it look worse than it really is, that's fine. Just make sure your headshot ends up looking like you look in real life.

Project Your Type

For your theatrical headshot, your clothing, hairstyle, and facial expression should reflect the essence of the type of characters you are looking to play. The color tones, lighting, and textures in the background should also reflect this energy.

Do I Need a Different Headshot for Comedy?

It's not necessary, but some actors use separate headshots for comedy and drama. Comedic headshots should project the high energy and charm required for most comedic shows. Usually the difference is that a comedy shot has more vibrant colors and clothing, and a more upbeat energy than a theatrical shot. Also, in a comedy headshot the actor is almost always smiling or very occasionally pulling a face.

Commercial Headshots

With a commercial headshot, your goal is to come across as trustworthy and open, because these are the traits needed to sell a product. You should be smiling and inviting in your commercial headshot.

Character Photos

If you are at the stage where you are mainly booking lead and substantial supporting roles, you only need one or two main 'theatrical lead' headshots. When you are first starting out, however, it can be helpful to have four or five specific character shots on your breakdown profile to be submitted for small co-star roles such as 'nurse' or 'cop'. All of these photos must be current and you must still be able to replicate each look.

Do not wear uniforms or costumes in character photos; it comes across as cheesy and overdone. Instead, take the energy of each of those characters and use a shot that gives an implication of the part. Examples would be wearing a dark blue shirt for cop roles, or a suit for office worker or lawyer roles.

Dressing with the 'energy' of common support character types will help CDs select your photo from the thousands submitted for each co-star role. Once you have four or five co-star credits under your belt, reduce the number of photos to just a few looks.

Alternative Looks

It's great to have headshots showing alternative looks you have had in the past. This includes beards and moustaches, different haircuts or colors, and anything else you can replicate if required. Try to take a few high quality photos for your files each time you drastically change your look.

Headshots for Men

Keep Your Shirt On

Shirtless profile pictures look unprofessional and sleazy. If you have a great body, show it off by doing a shot in a tank top or t-shirt and jeans, not by posing shirtless. An exception to this is if you have a professional still of yourself in a film, in character with your shirt off or a professional high end modelling shot. If you like, put this up on IMDb or on your actor website in the 'production stills' section . . . but not on your breakdown profile.

How to Shoot with Varied Facial Hair

It's obvious, but here it is: Grow a beard before your headshot shoot. Shoot pics with the beard. Then use clippers and take it down to stubble. Shoot this look. Then shave it all off and shoot the clean-shaven look. Discuss this with the photographer before the shoot. Feel free to throw in a moustache on the way just for fun.

Headshots for Women

Avoid Suggestive Poses

If you pose seductively with cleavage or a sugggestive pout, it may be interpreted that you are not a serious actress. It implies that you have to resort to baiting people with sexuality due to a lack of acting ability. You will rarely be brought in for serious roles, and will probably be called to audition for sleazy producers or for parts requiring nudity.

No Lingerie Photos

Lingerie photos are for playboy girls and porn stars. NEVER display lingerie photos on your breakdown profile. You can get away with a maximum of ONE in your press kit, but ONLY if it's from an article in a high-end magazine discussing your work as an actor, or if it's a professionally shot production still from a studio film, network TV show, or VERY well shot indie.

Use Limited Bikini Photos

Bikini photos are mostly used for models and extras. If a bikini photo is specifically requested when submitting for a role, it is fine to send one through but it's tacky to use a bikini shot for an initial role submission. For your website, one bikini shot as a full length photo with your 'alternative looks' or in a separate modeling section is fine, but do not post a bikini photo on your breakdown profile. If you're adding a bikini photo to your IMDb, ensure it is a professional production still or a VERY well shot modeling photo.

RESUME IN LA

CDs, agents, and managers frequently contradict one another regarding the best way to format or present a resume, but there is a common industry standard used by most working actors.

Ensure that your resume is concise, easy to read, and professionally formatted. Most CDs would rather read a neat and well-formatted resume with two recognizable credits in each section, than try to make sense of a messy page with thirty unrecognizable credits on it.

Quick Resume Rules

Many of these guidelines seem obvious, but you'd be surprised how often people don't do the following:

- An acting resume is NEVER more than one page.
- Print or staple (at the top AND bottom) your 8" × 10" resume to the back of your headshot.
- The resume paper should be cut to the same size as your headshot.
- The text should be printed in BLACK except agency logos.
- All text in the body should be 10pt to 12pt.
- List no more than ten credits in each section until you can list all strong, recognizable network and studio projects.
- Separate TV and film credits.
- Align all of your columns so that each section exactly matches the horizontal alignment of the corresponding section above it. Use the tab function to ensure the alignment is exact.
- Add your reps company logo rather than just typing their information.

Name

Nothing on a resume is more important than your name. Your name should be in 28pt to 42pt writing at the top of the page. Ensure the spelling of your name is consistent on your resume, headshot and IMDb so people are able to easily search for you online. You'd be surprised how often actors use different names or spellings on their various marketing tools. If you are SAG-AFTRA, always include it immediately beneath your name.

The Space Between 'Name' and 'TV Credits'

Direct Contact

Unless you completely trust your representation, list your phone number and email on your resume. It is awful to think an actor might be with rep they cannot trust but sometimes trust is lost over time. When this happens, contingencies must be put into place to ensure you do not lose work.

> **TIP:** When you have worked on independent films with celebrities in the cast, one way to catch the CD's eye is to write the celebs names under the film titles. While the CD may not know the film titles, the celebrities names will imply that you are involved in quality projects. .

If your agent tells you not to list your direct contact details, do as instructed, but make sure your email address is listed on IMDb and on your website. MANY actors I know have lost jobs because their representation did not relay information or due to the CD not being able to reach them directly for a last minute casting.

A friend of mine had a CD contact her ex-agent from an outdated resume in her files, and the agent told the CD my friend had moved back to Arizona to have a baby. My friend was fifty-five years old and living in LA at the time. Luckily, the CD then contacted her directly and told her what had happened. It's a dirty game out here, so you have to cover all your bases and be professional, smart, and always contactable.

Hair Color and Eyes

All headshots are color in LA, so there is no need to put hair or eye color on your resume unless your representation asks you to.

Kym Jackson
SAG / AFTRA

Height: 5'7"
Weight: 116 lbs.
Hair: Blonde
Eyes: Hazel Green

Manager: Christopher Smith (555) 555-5555
@ Vital Entertainment

FILM

Cardboard Boxer	Supporting	Dir: Knate Gwalthy
(2014 - w/Terrence Howard, Thomas Haden Church, Macy Gray)		
Snitch	Supporting	Dir. Ric Roman Waugh / Summit Ent.
(2013 - w/Dwayne Johnson, Susan Sarandon, Barry Pepper)		
Three Pegs	Lead	Dir: Jac Mulder / Muddville Films
(2014 - w/Tom Sizemore, Oz Zehavi, Bernard Curry)		
Retribution	Lead	Dir. Michael Feifer / Feifer Films
(2013 - w/Brian Krause, Frances Fisher, Cynthia Watros)		
Dark Power	Supporting	Dir. John M. Branton / Reinnassant
(2013 - w/Sean Patrick Flanery, Kristanna Loken)		
Iron Sky	Supporting	Dir. Timo Vuorensola / Disney Pics (Fin)
The Victim	Supporting	Dir. Michael Biehn / Anchor Bay Ent.
Richard III	Supporting	Dir. Scott M. Anderson
Scooby Doo	Supporting	Dir. Raja Gosnell / Warner Bros

TELEVISION

NCIS: Los Angeles	Recurring Guest St	Dir. Terrence O'Hara
Carnal Innocence	Supporting (MOW)	Dir. Peter Markle / Lifetime TV
(w/Gabrielle Anwar, Colin Egglesfield)		
Chemistry	Guest Star	HBO/Cinemax
Chuck	Co-Star	Dir. Patrick Norris / NBC
Pregnancy Pact	Supporting (MOW)	Dir. Rosemary Rodriguez / Lifetime TV
Criminal Minds	Guest Star	Dir. Bobby Roth / CBS
The Gates	Co-Star	Dir. Terry McDonough / ABC
Border Patrol	Supporting (MOW)	Dir. Mark Haber / UPN

TRAINING

Ryan Gaul	Comedy / Improvisation	Groundlings, LA
Robert Carnegie	Meisner / Scene Study	Playhouse West, LA
Dave Hill	Comedy / Improvisation	Improv Olympics West, LA
Tom McSweeney	Scene Study / Master Class	Helensvale, Australia

ACCENTS

American (Standard CA, NY, Boston, Texas, West Texas, Tennessee, Georgia, Southern),
Australian, British (BBC & all regional accents), New Zealand, Irish, Scottish, French, Russian,
German, Swedish, Welsh, South African

SPECIAL SKILLS

Firearms, Weapons (swords & knives), Jujitsu, Billiards, Tennis, Poker, Running, Swimming,
Jet Skiing, Rock Climbing, Bike Riding, Horseback Riding, Cricket, Basic Stunt Work
Current USA Green Card, Canadian Work Visa, European, Australian, New Zealand Passports

---

Safety Warning: Keep Your Home Address Info Private
Never put your home address on anything that isn't official paperwork, and especially not online. You want to be contactable, not stalk-able. Do not give it to a producer or director until you have been hired.

Height and Other Measurements
Height is the only necessary measurement. Weight is only needed if you think your headshot doesn't accurately depict your figure (in which case you need new pictures). All other measurements such as dress sizes are unnecessary. **A resume should include the information CDs need to decide whether to audition you, not the information they'll ask for after you're cast.**

Demo Reel Link
If your demo is available at a link that is easy to type out, put it on your resume. You may think a CD wouldn't have time to type in an entire link, but if you look right for a part, you'd better believe she'll type that web address.

Main Resume Sub Headings
- Television
- Film
- Theatre
- Training
- Skills

Resume Sections: Television and Film
The subheadings of 'Television' and 'Film' are always separate on a resume. Under each subheading there should be a list of credits in three clear columns. The columns do not need headings.

List no more than ten of your most recognizable credits under each heading, more than this will look messy. Many actors in LA have done a lot of independent feature films, so **the quantity of credits on your resume isn't important . . . it's the quality that counts.**

"Recognizable credits" are familiar to an average member of the public, like a role on a popular TV show or a film that had a wide theatrical release. Independent short and feature films the CD hasn't heard of add little to your resume except proof of on-set experience (which is important in it's own right if you have nothing else).

Do not differentiate between short and feature film credits. Simply list all films under 'film', and when a CD asks about a particular project let her know (with confidence) whether the project is a short or a feature. Never say it's "just a short film", instead say that it's "a fantastic little short film", and briefly explain why. If it is on your resume, be proud of it.

All CDs want to see is a clean, clear resume that displays all necessary information in a concise and easy to read manner. Please observe the resume sample as you read the following. In three columns, the following should be listed:

Column 1 (far left)—Project Name
Write the name of the project.

Column 2 (middle)—Role Type
The type of role (e.g. 'lead' or 'supporting' in film; 'co-star' or 'guest star', etc. in TV) should be listed. Do not write your character name. A CD cannot tell from a character name what size your role in a project was.

Column 3 (far right)—Director / Network / Studio
List the name of the director, or list the network, studio, or production company if it is more prominent than the director's name. Under TV, one option is to add the director's name in addition to the TV network, e.g. CBS / Dir: Shane Abbess.

Resume Section: Theatre
The subheading 'Theatre' is similar to the prior sections, in that it lists your top credits in three columns.

Theatre Column 1 (far left): Name of Production
List the name of the production.

Theatre Column 2 (middle): Role Played
When listing theatre work, **credit the role under its character name**. The theory is that CDs should be familiar with known plays and the characters. If you were a lead in a lesser-known play, note this in brackets next to the role name.

Theatre Column 3 (far right): Director or Theatre
List the production company, director or theatre (whichever is more notable).

Resume Section: Training

The training section of your resume doesn't need to be extensive. List the top three to six prominent coaches and schools you've trained with. It's fine if you only have training credits from outside LA. Training a CD doesn't recognize is better than no training at all. Suggested columns for training are as follows:

Column 1: Type of Class (e.g. Advanced Scene Study)
Column 2: Name of Teacher
Column 3: Name of School

Resume Section: Special Skills

In this section, list any talents you have that might be required for a film or TV show. The skills should be separated by commas, e.g. "horse riding, motorbike, martial arts, professional baton twirler." This section includes accents and other languages. Be specific regarding which regions your American accents are from.

> **TIP:** Store several resume and headshot copies in your car in a folder (to prevent damage) so you have spares on hand at all times.

Unusual talents may get you an audition if the right role comes up, so make sure the CD knows you've got what she needs. It may seem unlikely, but when a CD is searching for a tuba-playing gymnast who speaks Sanskrit, the lack of genuine competition will be your best ally.

ROLE DEFINITIONS

In film, billing order is negotiable but the size or type of role is not usually specified contractually, which often leaves film credits open to interpretation. In television, the type of role you play is clearly defined in your contracts. The TV credit given to an actor is often a result of contract negotiations between the agent and CD, rather than being purely based on the size or importance of the part itself.

Your credits must be accurate on your resume. LA is a tiny town, and most of the top CDs know each other. Most of them also watch a frightening quantity of TV and movies. If you've said you were a guest star on a show in which you were actually a featured extra, you will probably be found out. TV networks have begun to confirm and modify the IMDB credit lists for each show, so any illegitimate credits are modified to 'un-credited'.

The following defines every acting credit that can be on your resume. All roles can be labeled under one of these categories. Non-speaking roles have the same definitions in both TV and film, so I'll explain them first.

Extra

An 'extra' or 'background actor' plays a non-speaking part that contributes to the atmosphere of a scene. It is not considered to be an acting role, and should be omitted from your acting resume. It is better to have nothing on your resume than extra work credits.

Stand-In

A 'stand-in' literally stands in the place of an actor when the camera department is setting up the framing, lights, and camera movements for the next shot. A stand-in is usually of similar height, build, sex, and skin tone to the actor they are standing in for. On set, stand-ins are referred to as 'second team', while the actors are considered 'first team'.

This role requires a great deal of responsibility and offers you huge exposure to the director of a project. It is a wonderful networking opportunity and a respected job that is usually offered through extra work booking services. Stand-in work should not be added to your acting resume unless you are solely pursuing stand-in work.

Featured Extra / Featured

A 'featured extra' plays a highly visible non-speaking role. A character played by a featured extra could have a name and might even influence the plot of a movie or show. An extra can be upgraded to the role of featured extra if they are heavily featured on screen. Sometimes an interview or audition is required prior to gaining a featured extra part. Roles can occasionally require exceptional acting or a specific skill set (like playing a sport or musical instrument).

Featured extras are usually treated well, occasionally being given a trailer or dressing room on set. If you don't have any TV credits, featured extra work on network TV shows or studio films can be included on your resume (as 'featured') to show CDs that you have worked on a professional set, you understand on-set terminology and are familiar with on-set etiquette. As soon as you have ANY speaking roles in episodic TV or in studio films, remove all featured extra credits from your resume.

TV Speaking Roles

Under 5

A rarely used credit reserved mostly for soaps and Nickelodean shows, an 'under 5' is a role with under five lines of dialogue, separated by periods. Most shows bill roles with under five lines as 'co-star'.

Co-Star

A co-star is a minor TV speaking role that typically features in just one or two scenes of a single episode, though this can vary. Occasionally, a non-speaking role that requires a strong performance is given a co-star credit and pay.

Guest Star

A 'guest star' credit on your resume implies that your character was only in one episode of a TV show. Guest star roles are generally three or more substantial scenes. If you only shoot for one day on a show, you are considered a 'one day guest star'. If you work any more than one day, you are a 'guest star'. Regardless of the number of days worked, your resume should simply read 'guest star'.

When your guest star role appears in more than one episode of a TV show, it should be credited on your resume as 'recurring'. In *Seinfeld*, Larry Thomas, who played the 'Soup Nazi' was likely hired as a 'guest star' because he initially appeared in just one episode of the show. Several years later when his character was brought back, he was hired again (probably under a separate guest star contract) and the credit on his resume could then be upgraded to 'recurring'.

> **TIP:** If you book a large co-star role (at least three substantial scenes) but the CD is unable to upgrade it to a guest star credit, ask your agent to request permission for you to credit yourself as a guest star on your resume.

Top of Show

Most TV shows have a maximum they are willing to pay for an actor playing a guest star role. A 'top of show' guest star is being paid that maximum rate. Many breakdowns will state "We do not break top of show", which is really the CD's way of telling the agents "We will not pay more than our budgeted top of show fee, so don't submit actors who will not work for this amount".

Guest Star / Co Star Switcheroo

For shows using pre-merger SAG contracts (see Chapter 6), an actor hired as a guest star must either be paid to work for one day (as a 'one day guest star'), or for a full production week (as a 'guest star'). This means even if a guest star role only requires two days of shooting, the actor must still be paid for a full production week (usually five days on a half-hour show or eight days on a one-hour show).

To reduce production costs, some roles that are big enough to justify guest star billing are cast under a co-star contract instead. This means a one-day guest star role may actually be smaller than a co-star role that shoots several days.

Conversely, the agent of an actor with a strong credit list may be able to negotiate a guest star credit and paycheck for a co-star role. Shows produced under pre-merger AFTRA contracts allow for guest star roles to be paid per day.

Special Guest Star / Starring / Special Appearance By

These are billing terms negotiated by representation or offered to a celebrity for making an appearance in one or more episodes of a show. These credits imply that the actor is playing a 'major role' and as such, a 'front-end credit' (credit displayed before the episode plays) is usually negotiated.

Recurring

When you play a principal role (co-star, guest star, or other 'major role') that is not a series regular, but appears in more than one episode of a TV show (even if you don't speak at all in one of the episodes), your role is considered a recurring character. You will still be working under a guest star or co-star contract for each episode, but your resume should say 'recurring'.

Recurring credits are highly respected and the character can appear in almost every episode of a show without the actor being put onto a series regular contract. This is a wonderful position to be in, because you are not tied to the show and are free to do other work without approval by the network. Recurring guest star roles are occasionally upgraded to 'series regular' status (like Darren Criss in *Glee*).

An actress who has done a great job taking advantage of the freedom of the 'recurring' status is Jane Lynch (currently a series regular on *Glee*) who, between 2006 and 2009 was sporadically recurring on *Criminal Minds*, *Two and a Half Men*, *Boston Legal*, and *The L Word*. Any of these shows could have called her anytime to check her availability to come back and play her character, but she was not contractually obligated to be available for them.

It seems odd that a co-star role would recur, but it happens quite often. An example might be the receptionist at an office with just a few lines in an occasional episode. It would be odd if the office had a different receptionist in every episode, so the show needs to use the same actor, but the role isn't big enough to justify a guest star billing or paycheck. You can legitimately credit this role on your resume as 'recurring', which looks great, and nobody has to know that it was a recurring co-star role.

Series Regular

When you are put on contract by a network as a series regular, it's usually because your character features in most (or all) of the episodes. In *Two and a Half Men*, the woman playing Berta is a series regular but the three guys are the series leads. In *Bones*, Hodgins and the other main characters in the lab are series regulars but Booth and Bones are the series leads.

Series Lead

Series leads are the regular characters around which a TV series is centered. They appear in every episode (except the odd one here or there in an ensemble show). There are only a few series leads in each show. In *Dexter* the series lead is clearly Dexter, in *How I Met Your Mother*, all five of the friends would be considered series leads because it has an ensemble cast.

Film Speaking Roles

Union contracts do not distinguish between the various speaking roles in a film. Actors are hired as either 'day players' (hired per-day), 'weekly players' (hired per-week), or on a per-picture contract (one set fee for the whole project; this is usually for celebs).

Most working actors simply list their film credits as 'lead' if they're one of the top four to six credited characters, and 'supporting' for any other role.

Day Player / Bit Part

The term 'day player' means the production is paying the talent by the day rather than by the week, so most supporting roles are under day player contracts. When people casually reference a 'day player' role or 'bit part', they are usually referring to a walk-on role that only shoots one or two days. You may see the term 'day player' in contracts and hear of someone booking a bit part, but **neither term should appear on your resume**. Even if you only have one line in a film, credit yourself as 'supporting'.

Cameo

'Cameo' is a term used when a public figure (actor or non-actor) has opted to play a small role (even non-speaking) in a film. This role can be credited as 'cameo' or 'supporting'.

Supporting

In the film section of an actor's resume, any principal role that is not credited as a lead is considered a 'supporting' role.

Lead

A lead credit means either the film is based around your character; you are the sidekick, love interest, or nemesis of the main character; or you are one of several leads in an ensemble cast. A lead credit loosely applies to the top four to six names on the credit list, or (if the list is alphabetized) the six roles with the most screen time in the film.

WWW.YOURNAME.COM

An actor's website is rarely used in the professional casting process. Your profile pages on IMDB.com and BreakdownExpress.com (via ActorsAccess.com) give a filmmaker or CD all the tools needed to consider you for a role.

While a personalized acting website may not make or break your career, it is a great tool to show industry professionals all of your marketing materials in one place. It enables you to guide people towards otherwise hard to find press, like theatre reviews and red carpet photos. To see a clear and simple layout, check out my site at www.KymJackson.com.

If you do have a website, ensure that it is professional, current, functional, and well maintained. There are many companies online that build websites for actors. Others (like Wix.com) allow you to build a site by easily dropping elements and information into pre-designed pages.

> **TIP:** Test all website pages from an independent computer and ensure they work with both Mac and PC.

An actor's website should be utilized as an online 'press kit' (see 'press and publicity' section), referring the user to reviews, articles, film trailers, and other press. The site must be easy to navigate and **all pages must completely download in less than ten seconds**. It is unlikely that a CD will wait twenty seconds for your headshot to display, so if needed, reduce the photo file size. Don't give her a reason to move to the next actor on the list.

A quality actor website will have the following tabs:

- Home
- Resume
- Demo
- Press
- Contact
- Photos

Home Page

Display your name and main theatrical headshot. Perhaps write a bio on yourself and a few career highlights with a small paragraph or two about your recent gigs and upcoming releases. Embed trailers for any current upcoming releases. Include links to your IMDb, Twitter and Facebook.

Resume

Under the resume tab, list the following links at the top of the page then display your full resume on the page below them.

- IMDb profile
- Breakdown profile or Now Casting profile
- Download .pdf
- Print

Your downloadable resume should be in an un-editable .pdf format.

Demo Reel

Your demo can be displayed via a link to a professional site (like Now-Casting.com or ActorsAccess.com), or by embedding a high quality video into your site. If you are using YouTube.com or Vimeo.com for hosting, embed the file into the webpage rather than re-directing users to a public site. Ensure the resolution is high, the file size is small (for fast buffering), and that the picture isn't too big or small (640 × 480 is standard).

Press

Include links to any positive or neutral press written by an **independent** media source (i.e. NOT a production or management company website). These sources include newspapers, magazines, online publications, critic's reviews, and red carpet sites. Scan and upload hardcopy press in .pdf format.

As your press kit grows, separate this section into more specific categories, such as 'articles', 'reviews', 'interviews' and 'event photos'.

Contact

Display contact information for your representation and include their logo for branding. If you have more than one agent, specify the field in which they represent you. Provide your direct email for those rare last minute bookings that occur the night before or morning of a shoot.

Photos

Be selective when adding photos to your website. It is not an appropriate forum for the twenty different headshots you took in one session, or for outdated shots. For models, a modeling tab is great, but ensure none of your shots are too revealing.

Headshots, Alternative Looks, Character Shots

Use thumbnail photos that show a full size version of the shot when rolled over or clicked on. A great example of this is the photo section of your Now-Casting.com and ActorsAccess.com profile. Make sure the larger versions of the photos are easily downloadable and printable (72dpi is a fine minimum resolution), with a print size between 4" × 6" and 8" × 10". Keep this section under fifteen pictures.

Red Carpet / Event Photos

One option is to put direct links to your personal search results page on Wire-Image.com or GettyImages.com. To do this, search your name then copy the url in the browser window above your search results.

Another option is to show a selection of red carpet photos on your website in the same thumbnail format used for headshot photos. Don't worry about the watermarks: they help legitimize the image and prevent you from breaching any copyrights.

Production Stills

Production stills are taken on set during a shoot. Great production stills show crew and camera equipment in the background, the director instructing you, or the other actors dressed in wardrobe on set. Photos of you in character, acting, are also great (these look like someone has pressed pause on a movie).

Production stills taken with a cheap camera or bad lighting infer that the production was cheap. Your production stills should look as good as stills from bigger budget films, implying that you are a professional, working actor. If you don't have great stills, don't resort to using bad ones. It is better to upload no production stills than bad ones.

DEMO REEL

A 'demo reel', 'demo', or 'reel' is a selection of the best clips of footage available to showcase your acting work. Your demo should **NOT be longer than two and a half minutes** (until you've played a substantial role on American TV, or in studio produced or award winning features).

A demo reel is used when a producer, director, manager, agent, or CD is deciding whether to bring an actor in for an audition or meeting. Your demo should show what you look like, what your essence is as an actor, and whether you can act. Scenes should display your ability to portray emotional connection, transitions, comedic timing, and/or just **honest talking and listening**. The footage should show the most genuine and real moments from your best available scenes.

You must have footage to show prospective employers your screen acting ability and how you appear on camera, even if it's just one scene. No excuses. We are all "waiting for footage"; films take months to go through post-production before scenes are released. Your available film footage will almost always feel outdated to you but this is not a good reason to avoid putting a reel together.

A demo is NOT for showcasing how many jobs you have done. Never bulk it up with average scenes to make it look like you've done more work. If you only have enough footage for a one-minute reel, perfect . . . give them one minute of excellent acting and leave it at that. Don't shove another minute of bad footage in there just to make the reel longer.

Most CDs openly admit that while rushing to select actors for auditions, they only have time to watch the first ten to fifteen seconds of a reel. Fifteen seconds is easily enough time for a CD to ascertain whether you're up to scratch for an audition, so make sure your absolute best work (that reflects your type) is the first thing to appear.

Do not add a montage to the start of your reel. EVER. The CDs know you've done ten short films and they really don't want to see clips from them. Even a fifteen second montage may take up all of the time you have to show a CD what you can do. If you feel unbearably compelled to do a montage (please don't), put it at the end.

A title page stating your name is fine, but display it for a MAXIMUM of three seconds. The CD is perfectly capable of pausing the video if she wants your contact info. If a CD is looking at your reel, she already knows your name because it should be in the filename, on the webpage, and/or in the email she received with the demo link.

Study reels from both novice and working actors before you edit your own. You'll find that while your four-minute reel may be fascinating to you, most four-minute acting reels make you lose focus . . . fast. That's probably how other people feel when they watch your four-minute reel. You'll also find that you can usually tell what talent level an actor is at after around fifteen seconds.

The most significant factors to consider when selecting demo footage are:

1. **AMAZING performance.** Truly amazing acting is a rare find. If you are a teenager with no legitimate credits and you have a scene with a phenomenal performance, most people will overlook the presentation. If your playing age is over twenty-five, however, it is vital that you have a reel with strong performances that also takes the following into account.

2. **Recognizable American faces / projects.** Footage of you acting opposite famous people (or in projects the CD knows) adds validity to your work.

It shows that you are in the same league as (and can hold your own opposite) professionals. This principle also applies to footage with a **network watermark** in the bottom corner. CDs associate network watermarks with footage from professional actors, so prioritize any footage that has a network logo when compiling your reel.

3. **Quality of the footage.** A pixelated or poorly lit image, badly recorded or inconsistent sound, or dodgy camera work will make the piece harder to watch and distract from your performance.

4. **Production value.** 'Production value' refers to the quality of the image and sound, and how much it appears to have cost to shoot the scene. High production value is gaged through elements like intricate set decoration, impressive camera movements, extras, or special effects. These factors imply that you are working in projects with substantial budgets, which adds value to you as an actor.

5. **Performance of the actor opposite you.** If you are in a scene with an actor who sucks, the implication is that you are working on sub-par projects. Bad acting is distracting, and it is hard for viewers to ignore the other actor's bad work and focus on your amazing performance. One way around this is if you can edit out all of the other actor's lines except those that are absolutely necessary. Only cut to the other actor for short moments, bringing the focus back to you and your reactions whenever possible during their lines.

Compiling Your Demo

Weighing the various factors from the points above, find **up to five** of your best scenes. Cut each scene to between ten and forty seconds. Put your best scene first, followed by your second best. Scenes should be displayed in order of quality except when a change in the order allows for a variance of performance styles. For example, if your best dramatic scene is first, put your best comedy scene second. It is also important that your first scene reflects the type of character you are most likely to be cast as, so avoid opening with a scene in which you play an obscure character.

If you have scenes using different voices or accents, put a scene using a standard American accent first... but only if you can do the accent flawlessly. One of the biggest issues for CDs when auditioning foreign actors, or actors with thick regional US accents is to trust that they can do a flawless standard American accent.

Opening with a scene in which you use an accent will cause the CD to listen for you to slip up when she hears your standard American. If the first time she hears your voice is in a standard American accent, and she believes it, you've got her.

For someone starting out, I recommend cutting a full-length demo between one and 2.5 minutes. Then cut a sixty-second speedreel from the best moments of that demo footage. Post your speedreel to the casting websites for CDs to watch, then post both your speedreel AND your full-length demo to your website and other online reference pages like IMDb. You can title them 'Demo' and 'Speedreel'.

> **TIP:** Learn to use video editing software NOW to save thousands in demo editing costs throughout your career.

. . . But What if All My Footage Sucks?

If you only have scenes with bad production value opposite average actors, don't let everything you just learned put you off assembling a reel. If you don't have the cash to pay someone to film a scene, just use the best of what you have according to the guidelines above, and add to your reel each time you get better footage. All that ultimately matters is that YOU are acting well and your accents are perfect. If your *acting* isn't strong in any of your scenes, don't cut a demo. It's better to have no reel at all than one that stops you from getting auditions.

Comedic and Dramatic Demos

Working actors sometimes create separate comedic and dramatic reels. A busy CD booking talent for a show like *Two and a Half Men* needs actors with excellent comedic timing. Watching your amazing dramatic work won't give her any sense of your comedy chops. If your demo starts with dramatic footage, she has to scan through the drama to see if you have any good comedy scenes. If there is no comedy within the first two scenes, she might guess that all of your work is dramatic and move on to the next actor in her very long submission list.

Likewise, when casting *Criminal Minds*, a CD needs actors who can connect to complex, intense characters and seem completely real. Seeing footage of you performing in the heightened reality of sitcom may not help her assess whether you are right for a CBS drama. It may, however, make her think your performance style is too "big" for the show.

Keeping each reel specific allows CDs to view the genre and style of acting they are seeking.

Should I Include Commercial Scenes on My Demo?

If you don't have ANY network TV or studio film scenes, it's fine to put ONE exceptional commercial scene **in which you are speaking** towards the end of your theatrical demo, especially if it showcases your comedic timing.

Once you have any network TV (or well-produced film) scenes, remove **all** commercial footage from your demo. Everyone knows that most actors do commercials to pay the bills when they are starting out, but when a director is considering you to be the leading man in the next Mila Kunis film, it's best not to remind him you're the guy from the toilet cleaner advertisements.

One exception is if you are in a very high profile ad for a respectable product from which you are frequently recognized, like Justin Long in the Mac vs PC ads or 'Flo' with Progressive. . . but even then, the footage probably shouldn't be on your theatrical reel.

ONLINE DEMO REELS

DVD demos have been completely replaced by demos posted online. If you want someone to view your demo, email the link.

Demos online should play at a high resolution, but with a small file size for a clear picture and fast buffering. Some actors upload a separate video for each major role they've done.

If you've done a scene on TV that's longer than twenty seconds, you might like to upload that footage (labeling it with the name of the show) so CDs can opt to watch only that scene. Only do this for truly exceptional acting footage from shows or films with very high production value. It's best to have less than five videos on any casting website as too many options can be overwhelming.

Where to Upload Your Reel

Other than your acting website, your reel only really needs to go onto professional breakdown sites (ActorsAccess.com, NowCasting.com) and IMDb (if you like).

Speedreels.com

If you send your full length demo, Speedreels.com will create a one-minute speedreel for you (for a fee) and host it on their site.

Public Video Sites

While CDs should all have the software 'players' required to play videos on the professional breakdown sites, you'd be surprised at how many independent filmmakers do not. An easy way to ensure that people you meet around town are able to see your demo is to post it on YouTube.com or Vimeo.com. This also allows you to easily embed the video into other websites.

If you have acquired footage from an unreleased project, get the producer's permission before you post it on a public access site as it may cause issues with securing distribution for the project. Vimeo and YouTube each have an option that allows the video to be un-searchable and require the user to have a direct link and/or a password to watch the video (only do this if absolutely necessary).

OTHER VIDEO OPTIONS

Actor Slate

An actor slate is a one-minute video of you introducing yourself to the camera: your name, hobbies, sports, special skills, favorite color, and a short anecdote. This is intended to be an online equivalent to a general interview. To put together an actor slate costs around $200.

I have yet to meet a professional actor who has an actors slate. If you're just starting out and you don't have any acting footage at all, I recommend investing in a service that tapes actual scenes for your demo reel instead.

Services for Taping a Scene for Your Demo Reel

There are companies that will tape a scene for your reel that looks like part of a film. This is a brilliant way to showcase your talent at the start of your career. Avoid filming a scene from a produced film or TV show as the CD may recognize the dialogue.

Your scene must be well written. You can only act as well as the scene is written, so the material should reflect your ability and range. If you can't find these features in an unproduced scene, ask the taping company whether they write original scenes for actors. Ask any writers you know if they have a strong original scene that matches your type . . . or write something yourself (though if you're not a strong writer, get help from someone who is).

Another option is to get permission to use a scene from a very modern play with great dialogue. Check the resource guide for a rundown of the various companies who offer this service.

AirCheck

For a fee, a company called Edit Plus will record the entire episode of almost anything aired on TV in America. For an additional fee, this footage will be sent to Breakdown Services and the AirCheck editors will search through the footage to find your scene(s) and cut them together. The footage is added to your Actors Access (Breakdown Express) profile within days, which saves you having to do it.

Edit Plus keeps a catalogue of almost every TV show that has aired in the past few years, which helps to track down old footage. The link to the AirCheck forms is at the bottom of the ActorsAccess.com home page.

IMDB.COM

I'd be surprised if you're unfamiliar with the website IMDb. IMDb stands for Internet Movie Database, and it's exactly that . . . an online database of movies and TV shows that has a wealth of information about almost every project that has ever had legitimate distribution. The site also lists many films and web series that have only been screened at film festivals or online. If a project isn't on IMDb, it is either really old, wasn't released, doesn't exist, or the producers may not have listed it.

IMDb is used by almost every industry professional in the film and TV business, especially in the USA. If you chat at length with someone at a party, film festival, or premiere and share your name, it's likely they'll search IMDb to find out what you've done.

In saying this, information listed on IMDb should be taken as a guide rather than fact, as the site can be inaccurate. Many executives prefer to use a site called 'Studio System' for project and actor info. CastingAbout.com and NowCasting.com are more current than IMDb for casting and production status info. Regardless, it is imperative to keep your IMDb profile up to date and post your current headshot.

There is a 'links' section under which you can list your website and press. A biography is always nice to give people a little background but make it short, clear, and have someone else (perhaps your agent or manager) post it for you.

IMDb Resume and Pictures

If you don't have any credits on IMDb, post your pictures and add a resume. This will create a profile for you. If you have more than two or three credits on IMDb, it's best not to worry about the resume section and just let your few credits stand-alone. ALWAYS ensure a headshot is visible on your IMDB home page.

NEVER Add Your Birth Date to IMDb

Once a birth date is added to IMDb, the IMDb administrators will NEVER take it off. I get it, you're in your twenties, you're proud to be in your twenties and you're not worried who knows how 'old' you are. Well, in a few years time when you hit thirty, you're going to find yourself with a little problem called ageism. Adding your birthday to the site does nothing for you. If you don't add it, they won't have it on file, so why do it?

Your date of birth cannot be removed from the IMDb 'Personal Details' tab on IMDBpro, however, you can remove your DOB from your IMDBpro *home page*. Simply set up an IMDb resume account and click the following tabs:

- Edit Your Resume
- Control My Details
- Uncheck the box for 'Age, Birthdate'

IMDB PRO

IMDBpro stands for 'Internet Movie Database Professional'. The site lists the contact information for the majority of the companies and individuals in the entertainment industry.

Another significant benefit of IMDBpro membership is that you're able to see which companies represent other actors. You can also view the box office earnings for various films, see which production companies have films in production, and in which country those projects are being shot. Every actor should have access to IMDBpro.

IMDBpro Starmeter

IMDBpro.com allows you to view an addictive little thing called the 'Starmeter', which gives a weekly numerical ranking of the 'popularity' of every person on IMDB. It is based on a top-secret and ever-changing algorithm that may incorporate factors like the number of "hits" on an actor's IMDb page, or the ranking of projects to which they are attached.

It is known in Hollywood that a starmeter ranking on any given week is not an accurate system by which to gauge the success or marketability of an actor. Some very famous and bankable Asian, Australian, and European celebrities have rankings in the tens of thousands. Most CDs don't even look at the starmeter (much less take it into account) when deciding which actor to bring in or cast in a role.

> **TIP:** Hitting 'refresh' on your IMDB page will not improve your starmeter ... but nice try! ☺ Apparently, the starmeter algorithm only records hits from each IP address (computer ID) once every 24 hours. According to this theory, after you have clicked on your page, any subsequent hits that day from your computer will have no impact on your rank.

In saying this, perception is often reality. The starmeter is hard not to look at it, and for American celebrities it does tend to be vaguely accurate. If an actor maintains a starmeter 'above' (numerically less than) a thousand for several months, they are probably a recognizable personality in the USA.

Some indie film makers will even tell CDs not to audition anyone with a starmeter worse than '*x*' for certain roles.

Ultimately, studio and network execs don't give it a second thought because if an actor doesn't have a tangible 'Q score' or theatrical bankability (proven ability to draw various paying audiences) for international or domestic sales, they're just another actor.

> **TIP:** Add production stills to the IMDb page **for the film** rather than adding them to your personal page, then link the pictures to your personal page by noting that you were in them. This gives users of the site the impression that the filmmakers (rather than you) added the photos, which makes you look just that little bit more professional.
>
> ———
>
> **TIP:** If you are in an indie short or feature film project, and the producers are having trouble convincing IMDb to approve it for addition, suggest entering it into an IMDB eligible festival through WithoutABox.com. In most cases, once the film is received by the festival organizers, the project will be immediately approved for an IMDb listing.

OTHER COMMON MARKETING TOOLS

Business Cards

Business cards are an efficient way to give your information to a contact without having to hand over a full headshot and resume. Make it simple with just a tightly cropped headshot, your name (with 'actor' written beneath it), phone number, email, website, and union status if you are SAG-AFTRA.

Wikipedia™

Once you have substantial credits on IMDb, you can create your own Wikipedia page. What does this do for your career? Pretty much nothing . . . but it is kind of cool to actually be in an encyclopedia.

It's also helpful to foreign actors when applying for the O1 visa. Almost every celebrity in the world has a Wikipedia page, so if your tactic for tackling LA includes giving the impression that you're a celebrity overseas, a well-written wiki page may help.

Facebook Page

Being friends with filmmakers, CDs, and rep on Facebook is a great casual way to stay in touch. If you are a big partier, be aware of the image you are putting across through your page and avoid posting status updates that imply anything unprofessional about your work as an actor.

The rule of thumb tends to be that you can 'friend request' people you've met socially or while working on a job, but avoid friend requesting CDs you've met in auditions. Producers and directors are usually more open to maintaining contact through Facebook than CDs.

Facebook Fan Page

A fan page enables you to post production stills and screening dates when you have a project coming out, but other than people who are already your Facebook friends, who is going to look at it? You're going to look a little silly asking a top producer to become your Facebook fan so he can stay abreast of your low budget independent film career moves.

If you think a hundred people . . . okay, no, let's even just say fifty. If you believe there are fifty people in the world (NOT including your friends, family, and school buddies) impressed enough by your acting to search Facebook for a page to express their undying fandom to you, then definitely make a Facebook fan page. If not, it is merely an unproductive ego stroke.

Start a fan page on Facebook when you are a regular character on a TV show, if you play a decent role in a popular film, or have fans from doing a successful web series. You'll know it's time to create a fan page when you receive friend requests, emails, or messages from strangers who specifically say that they've "seen your work", and are a fan. It can be good to respond to these messages with a link to your facebook and twitter pages.

If you do have legitimate fans of your work or if you are a musician getting your work out into the public and building a fan base, Facebook fan pages and groups are important marketing tools.

It is vital to have a way to let fans know where and when they can see your next project without having to become actual friends with them. If, however, your fan page exists for your three hundred best friends to support your acting dream, you can probably hold off on creating one.

Twitter

Even if you have no fans, it's important to have a twitter membership running. Twitter followers are becoming a vital marketing tool for films and TV shows and **the number of real followers you have can affect your desirability as an actor.**

Twitter enables fans and friends to keep up to date with your movements and feel connected to you between projects. **Your twitter profile should be linked in with your IMDb page**, allowing new fans to easily find you online. Ensure that your 'tweets' imply nothing that could negatively affect your image as a professional actor.

Note: IMDb and Wikipedia both create Facebook fan pages for the actors and public figures in their databases.

Other Social Media

If you want to get really crazy with social media, the next level down from Facebook and Twitter are: LinkedIn, Google Plus, Instagram and Tumblr. MarketMeSuite.com will help you to manage many of these profiles at once.

MAILING AND EMAILING CD's AND REPRESENTATION

This section covers postcards, representation submissions, and self-submissions for roles.

The first rule of 'mail-outs' is to personalize, which means including the recipient's name in the greeting line and mentioning something specific pertaining to that recipient. How often do you respond to impersonal mass mailings? People do not respond to spam. If your message is not personal, CDs, agents and managers will not give it a second thought. Most LA office interns are told to throw away anything that doesn't start with "We met at" or "I was referred by" and any postcard that isn't hand written.

That doesn't mean that CDs and agents *will* give personalized marketing material a second thought, it simply means a personalized message is more likely to actually be seen by the intended recipient.

It is important to spend your time **nurturing pre-existing relationships** rather than trying to forge new ones via emails or letters. Contacting CDs you haven't met or agents you haven't been referred to rarely garners a response. Is spam more effective when your name is at the top? No.

On the other hand, when personalized mailings referencing specific news (like watching you on TV or in a movie) are sent to a CD you **have** met they can be effective and I've gained several auditions this way.

Sending personalized mailings seeking representation to agents and managers you **have** been referred to (and following up with a phone call), is a necessity for gaining representation in LA.

Seeking Representation

While seeking representation from *agents* you have not been referred to is rarely effective, seeking representation from *managers* you have not been referred to can be successful. There are more managers than agents in LA, so there is less competition for each manager. Gaining quality management this way is a rarity but it can happen, and I think there's something to be said for putting it out there. You never know, you could be exactly what one manager is looking for . . . and it only takes one.

The best way to contact potential representation is to write a short cover letter or email (under 200 words) with links to your IMDB, demo, website, and Actors Access profile. Attach a headshot and resume, and use the cover letter guidelines on the next page to format your email. If you cannot find the agent or manager's address, call them and ask where to send a letter or email seeking representation. If you are being referred, make sure you write "REFERRED BY [referrer's name]" in the subject line or on the envelope.

For hardcopy, send only a cover letter with a headshot and resume. Include a link in the cover letter to your online demo rather than sending a DVD. Unsolicited DVD demos aren't welcome and will rarely be watched.

Cover Letters Seeking Representation

A hardcopy cover letter should be on an A4 page, typed, and in standard letter format with justified typesetting. Include the date at the top of the page and a formal address bar at the top left with the name and address of the recipient.

> **TIP:** Hollywood manager Mitch Clem once shared a great piece of advice with me. He said the purpose of a cover letter is to show forward motion without the recipient having to hunt for it in your resume. Take a couple of things from your resume and highlight them. Avoid cliche statements like "I know I can book"; focus instead on recent career activity, training, specific skills, and unique traits which you have to offer.

For both email and hardcopy, the body of the letter should be less than two hundred words. Don't let the important things you want to say end up lost in a sea of ancillary verbiage. Keep it short and to the point: most of the following paragraphs should only be two or three sentences. The reader should be able to scan the letter or email in under thirty seconds and see all of your key points.

Paragraph 1: Intro

Introduce yourself and say that you're looking for representation. If you've been referred, mention your referrer and highlight their name in bold. If you have a fan base from previous work or any substantial press, mention it early on to catch their attention. This is also where you briefly list the names of any additional references (e.g. filmmakers or CDs willing to put their name behind you) who may or may not know the recipient.

Paragraph 2: Your Previous Work

List only **two or three** of your most recognizable film and TV jobs and whether you have anything coming up to shoot. If you've done any theatre, list one or two of your most recognizable productions. Tell them where you've trained or are currently studying, and mention if you have improv or stand up comedy experience.

Paragraph 3 or 4: Describe Your 'Type'

An example of describing your type might be: "I am often cast as strong, thuggish characters". If you have the time to make it more personalized, mention something specific about the agency, and why you would be a good fit. An example might be "Your agency doesn't represent any women in their mid-twenties who have curly red hair like I do" or "Many of your actors have worked recently on one-hour dramas and gritty dramatic work is my strength", something that gives a reason as to why you've singled them out.

Paragraph 3 or 4: Mention Any Unique Special Skills
If you excel at martial arts, singing, stunts, or any other unique skill, mention it in a short sentence.

Paragraph 5: Closing Statement
Add a link to your IMDB and a demo or some acting work that the recipient can see online. Add a closing sentence like "I look forward to hearing from you", or something of the sort.

Add "Kind Regards" or another friendly but formal sign off, then leave enough space for a signature (for hardcopy) and add your name at the bottom in bold. Put your telephone number and email under your name for their reference, and website link if you have one.

Follow up in two weeks with a phone call to every agent and manager you've mailed via hardcopy, and in one week to every agent and manager you've emailed. Be prepared to get a lot of rejections but remember, all you need is for one person to say yes.

Mailing a Headshot and Resume to CDs
If you have decent theatrical representation (getting you out monthly), DO NOT submit yourself for parts directly to CDs. If you are well represented, all communication with CDs (except those you know VERY well) is best put through your agent or manager. Actors have been dropped by their representation for this.

Mailing or emailing CDs directly is only for actors with no other option but to take matters into their own hands . . . if you are unrepresented or if your rep is not sending you on enough theatrical auditions, this means you. Also, hardcopies are being phased out, so the notes that follow regarding hardcopies may only be relevant for another few years.

It doesn't matter how proactive you're feeling or how bored you are, sending your picture and resume to CDs you haven't met is a complete waste of time. Do not do it. CDs have hundreds of headshots sent to them every week from eager actors who've just arrived in town. I'm not saying sending your headshot to a CD will never work . . . heck, for all I know it might get you famous, but that's like saying entering the lottery might make you rich.

Mailing a "pic and res" (picture and resume) is really only appropriate when submitting yourself for a specific role. Only submit to CDs (and associates) you **have met** before at an audition, showcase or workshop and who have seen your acting work.

At workshops, CDs may say to mail them when you have updated your pic and res, or when you have seriously upgraded your representation. While many of these updates probably hit the trashcan, some CDs do keep hardcopy workshop files of actors they like, which means updated copies may be easily added to the file.

If you are sending an updated pic and res, include a formal cover letter, but don't ramble. Remind the CD where you met and when, then detail what work you've done since you last met. Keep the letter in 12pt font and **under one hundred and fifty words**, which is around two short paragraphs. There should be a lot of white space on the page so the CD can read the whole thing in less than twenty seconds. In most instances, a postcard detailing any updates you have will suffice.

Sending Postcards to CDs

In LA, some actors create a postcard-sized version of their headshot with information written on the front, and a standard postcard format on the back. When (and only when) something *interesting* happens in your career, it can be useful to send a postcard to all of the CDs you've met professionally. Do not do this more than once every two months.

The purpose of mailing postcards is to remind CDs you've met of who you are and let them know you're booking work, so when they see your face in the submissions, they are more likely to recognize and select you.

The message on the back of the card should be either hand written or printed in 12pt to 14pt font and should total no more than forty words. If you know less than fifty CDs, take the time to hand write a personal note. On the FRONT of your postcard, make sure you include all of the information you want them to see. A postcard I mailed on June 9th, 2011, is shown on the following page.

Even if she doesn't flip the card over, the CD can see my name and face, what the project is, the airdates, times, and my representation. I stacked all the writing to the right so the reader's eye would be drawn to my face before anything else, and I intentionally added the logo for *Lifetime* rather

than writing "Lifetime" in normal typeface. This was to give the reader an association between a major cable brand and me.

The postcard isn't perfect, nor is it how you must design your postcards, but it is one way to get all your information across in a five second glance.

Only send a postcard to a CD if you are playing a speaking role. If your character doesn't have an actual name, simply write "Appearing on *Criminal Minds*" rather than "Appearing as 'Guard 2' on *Criminal Minds*". If it is a guest star, write "Guest Starring as '*character x*' on *Criminal Minds*", as a guest star is a well-respected credit.

Mail your postcards five business days before the show airs. This allows time for them to arrive, get through studio mailboxes and interns, and be read by the recipient. Show airdates change constantly, so order the cards close to the mailing date. Epguides.com and IMDB are good reference guides for air times and dates, or simply call the TV network and confirm.

Mailing Labels

Mailing labels for producers, directors, and CDs are readily available in LA.

CastingAbout.com and NowCasting.com

The best and cheapest way to get up-to-date mailing labels is by printing them at home through Now Casting.com or CastingAbout.com. They track every major film and television project casting in Hollywood, along with each project's current mailing address, casting staff, and updated production status. Researchers update each site every day, which is essential as CDs relocate offices constantly.

The services allow you to easily select CDs and print your own labels from those selections, saving you time, money, and wasted labels that can result from purchasing pre-printed label packs.

Other Label Sources

You can download lists to print from other sources or buy expensive label sheets in hardcopy at Samuel French or other bookstores. Some of the addresses tend to be outdated, so check address details on IMDb before sending. Another time-consuming option is to keep your own CD address database or spreadsheet and print your own Avery labels.

PRINTING MARKETING TOOLS

Headshot Printing

To print quality headshots, go to an actual storefront (rather than online) so you can see proofs and discuss formatting. Additionally, many printers can design the layout for a small fee. Print options are generally lithographic or photographic, then matte or glossy. The most professional looking is matte photographic, but it's more cost effective to do a matte lithographic run.

A hundred headshots should last you around a year. Smaller runs of ten units are useful for character shots. Hardcopy headshots are being replaced by electronic submissions, so soon you won't need to print pictures at all.

Postcard / Business Card / Promotional Printing

The cheapest way to print promotional items in America is online for delivery. I used to get the '100 free postcards' deal that Vistaprint.com still frequently offers to members. Add charges for shipping and file upload, and a hundred postcards cost around $10 to print with a color front and B&W back. Check the resource guide for a full list of online printers.

TIP: Website Vouchers

When purchasing anything online, always search Google for a 'discount voucher' or 'coupon code' first. You'll almost always find 10% to 40% discounts for US retail websites.

CHAPTER 3

REPRESENTATION

Whenever I mention 'representation' throughout this book I am referring to theatrical representation, which is either an agent who represents you for film and television work, or a manager who represents you for everything. If voice-over, commercial, or other representation is being discussed I will specify it clearly.

There seem to be two main ways most actors come to LA. Either with fantastic representation getting them out on several studio and network auditions and general meetings each week (this is mainly foreign celebs), or with no representation and little more than a visa and a suitcase. If you are lucky enough to be accepted by solid representation, only some sections of this chapter apply to you. If you're coming out here with a suitcase and a dream, read on to learn the basics about representation in Hollywood.

It is important to know the companies with whom you are ultimately striving to work. Most LA actors know who the top agents and managers are, and most well established actors here know who the top law firms and publicists are. If you meet a director who is 'repped' (represented) by CAA, you're going to want to stay in touch. How will you know this if you're not aware of the significance of him being represented by the biggest agency in Hollywood?

Selecting representation is always going to be on a case-by-case basis. An agent at a top agency might get some actors out every day, but other equally skilled and qualified actors on that agent's books may not have gone out in months. This is where each actor's personal and working relationship with the agent or manager comes into play. Selecting representation is not just about which agency you're with, or even which agent. It is about how strongly the specific agent or manager who is representing you believes in you and your work, and how high you are on their priority list of actors to pitch for each role.

Note: The 'TMA' (Talent Managers Association) and the 'ATA' (Association of Talent Agents) are the two unions with which some American managers and agents are affiliated.

How to Gain Representation

The following list is pretty self-explanatory:
- Mail or email the rep directly (see previous chapter).
- Have your manager refer you to an agent or vice-versa.
- Attend a representation showcase (explained later in this chapter).
- Get a referral from a mutual friend or colleague.
- Get a referral from a CD.
- Meet an agent or manager socially and pursue a business relationship.

Referrals

In the representation arena—more than any other arena in Hollywood—nothing is more important than a referral. I know many actors who are represented by top agencies who have fewer credits or are less talented than other friends of mine who can't even get a bad agent. **It's all about who you know and how marketable you are.**

If an agent gets a call from one of their colleagues, clients, or friends saying "You have to meet this actor", the agent will be more likely to meet the referred actor than an actor whose picture and resume was submitted with no referral.

Of course, the referral just gets your foot in the door. You need to be talented and marketable enough to keep that door open long enough to get through it.

Look at which companies represent your friends, but be realistic about who you may be able to sign with. Make sure all of your marketing tools are at a professional standard, then ask your friends and contacts to refer you.

Referrals are a valuable commodity in Hollywood, so never be upset if someone won't refer you to one of their contacts. Any person referring you is putting their name on the line for you. Giving a contact one bad referral raises doubts, but is forgivable. Giving two bad referrals may make the contact wary of your suggestions.

If a friend who has the power to refer you doesn't think you're at the right level, that you'd make a good match, or that it's the right time, accept this and move on. You will do more damage than good being upset or expressing annoyance over it. There may also be factors involved that your friend is unable to share with you.

Be realistic about your salability. If you are not in SAG-AFTRA, or even if you are in SAG-AFTRA but you do not have USA TV credits or some level of celebrity overseas or online, you are unlikely to be seen as a viable commodity for a higher level agency. Exceptions to this are if you can play a teenager, your look is rare, or if you have a specific and commonly sought after talent (such as singing or martial arts).

CD Referral into Representation

Occasionally you will come across a CD in a workshop or class (this is inappropriate at auditions) who seems particularly impressed by your work and will go out of her way to chat with you. If you are getting the right vibe, this may be an opportunity to ask if she knows any agents or managers she thinks would be a good fit for you. If she does, ask her if she would mind referring you or if you can use her name as a referral.

Meeting With Potential Representation

Breathe. Relax. This is when you need to play the role of the most confident version of you there is. You don't need to sell anything. The agent or manager has read your resume and they have seen your demo, so they already know whether you will potentially fit into their client list or not.

If the rep is interested in signing you, the meeting is to find out whether you 'vibe' together. **They want to like you** but are watching out for warning signs of desperation, neediness, overselling, and poor communication skills. You should be looking for the same. This is someone you're meeting to discuss a potential business partnership. As equals. You may say no to them just as they may say no to you. So get a feel for whether they are someone you trust with your dreams and your livelihood.

Make it a conversation, not an interrogation. Don't try to control things, but let the conversation flow. Ask questions about their interests in the industry eg. "How did you get into being a manager?", "What kind of films do you like?" even "Where are you from?" get a feel for who they are. Most importantly, find out where they see you fitting in the industry: what type of shows, projects and roles they see you working on, and which strategy or path may get you there.

Many meetings in LA are taken as favors. It would be rude of the rep to say no to an actor referred by an important industry member without meeting with the actor first. If the rep has no intention of signing you, there are few things you can say to change their mind.

What is a 'Development Client'?

Before discussing the details of representation, it is important that you know exactly what type of client you are. It varies, but generally once you have played two or three guest star roles, or one recurring guest or series regular role on American network TV or a major cable TV network, you are unofficially considered as a working actor. An actor would probably be seen as a working actor after playing a substantial role (two or three good scenes) in a film that gained a **wide** theatrical (more than 2000 theatres) release or major critical acclaim.

When you are already in the system as a working actor, it is much easier for an agent or manager to procure auditions for you. This is because many casting offices are familiar with your work (or at least with the projects you have worked on), and you have already gained the TRUST of many of the CDs around town. Substantial recent credits give your agent something to pitch you with to help gain auditions.

Until you are a working actor, you are a 'development client'. Your network and career is under development because you still need to be introduced to the casting offices around town. This is why even after coming from playing a series regular role on a TV show overseas, you would still be considered a development client in LA (though having a series reg credit does make you much easier to pitch).

When an agent takes on a development client, that agent must use his reputation to ask CDs to trust him enough to audition this new actor. The agent must work with his connections rather than utilizing connections the actor is able to bring to the table. This means much more work is required by the agent to get each audition. It also usually means the actor is booking smaller roles that pay less, so the agent is earning less money for putting in more work. This is why some agents and managers prefer not to take development clients above a certain age bracket.

What's the Difference Between a Submission and a Pitch?

When **submitting** on a role, your agent or manager clicks on the character name in the breakdown list, and is brought to a screen that displays thumbnail sized pictures of each client who fits the physical parameters set by the CD for the role. These parameters may be defined by characteristics such as sex, age range, ethnicity, and height. For this reason, you must ensure your age range and other attributes are accurate in the computer system at BreakdownExpress.com (you can edit via your ActorsAccess.com profile).

Your rep then selects clients who fit the physical description, personality, and special skills of the character (e.g. "Strong cop type", "Surfing ability required", or "Pale and quirky looking") and have the talent to pull off the role. If you fit all requirements, your rep 'submits' you by clicking the checkbox under your photo.

There is the option to include a short note with each submission (these are extremely effective), and to submit a 'video' (this is vital as submissions with videos attached are ranked first for the CD). The whole submission process takes less than a minute and is much faster than the days when agents had to mail a hardcopy photo for each role.

Even if your rep is awful, they are still probably submitting you daily for roles. What a great agent or manager does, is follow up on select submissions with a 'pitch'. When your rep is **pitching** you for a part, they call or email the CD or associate at the casting office, saying something in the vein of "Jesse, you gotta see Thomas for this role, he's exactly what you're looking for because *x, y, z*".

That x, y, z could be anything from having a Russian accent to martial arts experience, or being willing to work as a local hire in South Africa. There are thousands of factors that an agent or manager could pitch you on: special skills, physical features, or simply the fact that you're an exceptionally talented actor and the CD HAS to see you for this "Just trust me" says your rep . . . and that's where it's at with pitches: how much each CD trusts your representation. This is why the quality of your representation and their relationships is so important.

Can You Get Work Without Representation in LA?

Yes . . . but it's really limited. I know many talented, marketable actors with a SAG-AFTRA card who don't even have a decent manager let alone an agent. Not having representation sucks, but it is sometimes unavoidable and you can procure work without it.

Casting workshops enable actors with no representation to gain direct access to CDs. Many unrepresented actors book legitimate work by maintaining direct relationships with CDs after meeting them at workshops or showcases.

Many indie film projects are posted on the breakdown sites each day that specifically ask actors to self-submit. Most of them are non-union or SAG-AFTRA Ultra Low and Modified Low Budget indies, which are great credits for actors building their resume and network. Actors also commonly get work from knowing producers or directors socially.

While you can get some work in LA without representation, there are limits to what you can do alone. To be a legitimate working actor in Hollywood, you must have an agent or manager working with you.

Once you have spent a year or two in LA building up your demo, getting into SAG-AFTRA, and getting a few American credits on IMDb, you should have secured a manager and commercial agent at the very least. If you have not, put all of your energy into finding solid representation.

Mentioning Roles to Your Rep

Agents and managers spend all day looking at the breakdowns and submitting their actors for roles. Many agents and managers feel that when an actor sends them the breakdown for a role that is casting, it is an implication that the actor feels they aren't capable of doing their job.

If your friend is reading for a role you're right for, it is tempting to contact your rep and ask why you aren't going in for it. It's likely that your rep has already submitted you and casting has chosen not to bring you in.

In saying that, sometimes your rep may submit you but overlook calling to pitch you on a role for which you are perfect. The only time it's really acceptable to send your representation a breakdown is when you have a specific skill required for the role, or if you have a good relationship with the casting director. It is important to bring the agent or manager's attention to these facts as it gives them something unique to lead a pitch with. Never call with this type of information. Email is invariably the preferred method of communication with your rep.

Acknowledge that this is a unique circumstance, for example: "I know you've probably already pitched me for this, but they're looking for a professional tightrope walker, and I am one". Or "I just met this casting director in a workshop and we got along great". Avoid doing this more than **once a month** unless you are regularly booking well-paid work, otherwise your rep may feel distrusted and harassed.

No Representation vs Bad Representation

An agent once said to me that it's better to have no agent than a bad agent. It is generally better to be represented, but there are some low level agents and managers who are so bad at their job that their unprofessionalism and miscommunications can hinder your career and tarnish your reputation.

An agent or manager is your conduit to the CDs. Information must travel very quickly from a CD through your rep to you and vice versa. I've had agents and managers forget to tell me about network TV auditions, or tell me that it's a cold read (little or no advance time with the dialogue) when in actual fact the sides were emailed out days earlier (for a three page audition for *Avatar*, of all things). I've heard of representation losing work for their actors by simply not doing the daily submissions on the breakdowns, forgetting client's names, not doing phone pitches, not checking voicemails, and worse. These reps are probably not actively trying to be bad at their job. Agents and managers are people too, and just as some people are disorganized or unfocused in their job, so too are some reps.

If you have major trust issues with your representation, it is better to interact with the CDs directly. Until you have amazing rep, make sure your direct contact information is listed on IMDB.com, ActorsAccess.com, your website, and your resume.

Keep in mind that if your agent seems sleazy, abrasive, or somehow socially awkward, the CDs have probably noticed. A CD's job is to read people and figure out their character and essence. If your agent comes across as offensive, the CDs probably don't enjoy dealing with them any more than you do. Many CDs have certain agents or managers that they avoid working with due to negative past experiences. If CDs around town don't like your rep, the fact that they have to deal with him in order to get to you could deter them from bringing you in for roles.

Querying Representation Practices

If your agent is breaching their contract and they are 'SAG-AFTRA franchised' (SAG-AFTRA doesn't franchise managers), SAG-AFTRA may be able to help you. To assess your options, contact the TMA or ATA to find out whether your rep is a member and which guidelines they are expected to follow according to their respective union. If your agent isn't with a union, you could find out the guidelines laid out according to their agent's license. Managers do not require a license, so if your manager is not with the TMA, you are probably stuck with the contract you signed with them.

Leaving Your Representation

A lot of actors leave their rep only to find it's harder than expected to get new representation. When dropping your representation, it's best to already have new rep lined up so you don't end up with noone. You don't need to mention to the new company why you are seeking new representation, but if they ask, avoid telling a negative story about your current team.

If you are seeking a new agent, discuss it with your manager first and ask him to obtain the meetings, and vice versa. As long as you have a clear and justifiable reason for leaving, people will generally understand.

As an actor, you are running a business. You need to be surrounded by the most efficient, well-positioned team possible. That doesn't mean forgetting the people who help you along the way, but it does mean moving up the ranks as quickly as possible and upgrading your representation if necessary.

I had a talented, loyal friend who stayed with the same representation for ten years. In the first few years, he was auditioning constantly and booking some extremely high profile jobs. He took three years off and when he came back, he returned to the same agent. At that point his agent wasn't able to get him into any audition rooms. He stayed with the agent for another three years and barely went out once a month. My friend finally left and signed with a boutique agency in Beverly Hills. Within one year, he had gone on over fifty auditions and booked guest star roles on two top network shows.

If you're not making them money, most of the agents in this town will keep you for a year or two at most before dropping you from the client list. I'm not saying you shouldn't be loyal. I'm saying to treat your career as business and only work with people who are helping that business succeed.

Loyalty is important in life, but you must always stay aware of exactly how much that loyalty is holding you back because when it gets to a certain point, you must cut the dead weight and move forward. This is your life and your career. None of us know whether we get a second shot, so make every day count. You don't want to look back in twenty years and say, "I could have had a great career, but I gave it all up to make that one manager feel like I was loyal".

Breaking Your Contract

Any contract you sign with an agent or manager is a legally binding document involving your money. Do not take signing paperwork lightly.

If you are a development client with little income, most reps will let you terminate the agreement early. It wouldn't be worth chasing you down for the few hundred dollars in lost commissions. If you're making real money, there is a high likelihood that the agent or manager you are trying to leave will expect their full commission until the end of the signed agreement and may take you to court if they are not paid.

If your theatrical agent is SAG franchised, you have grounds to break the contract if you do not work at least ten days in any ninety-one day period. If your theatrical agent is with the TMA, the contract may be broken if you have not been offered employment within an excess of four consecutive months.

To officially terminate an agreement with your rep, send a letter (you can get a form letter from SAG-AFTRA) by certified mail or attached to an email stating that you're terminating the agreement.

Wherever possible, avoid signing contracts with your representation. Many managers in LA work on a verbal agreement (loosely termed as a 'handshake deal') rather than paper contracts. If you are asked to sign a two or three year contract, it is wise to request a three-month trial period first.

NEVER sign a contract with representation lasting longer than three years. Also, be aware of any auto-renew clauses; make sure you are able to terminate the contract when it expires.

Should I Pay My Rep if They Didn't Get Me the Job?

The answer is almost always: yes. If your manager gets you a job, you must still pay the agent who represents you in the department under which the job falls, and vice versa. In most cases, you are contractually obligated to pay your manager a commission on any job, irrespective of project type, source or location. Throughout your career you should procure your own paid acting gigs, and for these you must pay your rep.

If your regional agent gets you a local hire job outside of LA, you may not be obligated to pay your LA agent. It is a nice gesture to pay your LA agent for non-LA jobs, however be aware that this may set a precedent inferring your LA agent is entitled to commissions on all out of town bookings. Of course, if your LA agent gets you a job out of town you must pay them.

If you are going to cut your representation a commission check, make sure it is always for the full standard commission amount in ratio to your gross paycheck. If you can't afford to give your rep a full commission on something you don't officially owe money on, a nice birthday or Christmas present will be less potentially offensive than a partial commission check.

Never Pay to Sign with Representation

A final and extremely obvious note about agencies and management companies anywhere in the world: NEVER PAY A FEE TO AUDITION FOR OR JOIN AN AGENCY OR MANAGEMENT COMPANY (showcases with several reps attending are an unfortunate exception).

This especially applies to children, as scam youth agencies often take advantage of well-intentioned parents by charging signing fees and making them pay for photos.

Agents and managers should earn money from the commissions they make by getting their actors work. If they need to charge new actors to join, it means they are not getting their talent enough work to stay afloat solely on commission. Remember, it is better to have no agent than a bad one.

Does +10% Factor into the Gross?

Most deals are negotiated as union scale +10%, which means the production is paying your agent the anticipated 10% commission. The gross pre-tax total upon which both your agent and manager's commission is based should exclude this 10%.

Some managers may include the 10% as part of the gross total upon which their commission is based. Unfortunately, if your management contract states that their commission is based on all monies earned by you, the manager can legally expect a commission on the 10%. This is because the 10% is paid as part of your gross earnings, but it's pretty dodgy of them.

Where Do My Paychecks Go?

Your paychecks go to whichever address you provide for the production payroll company. Usually, your agent will provide the production company with a check authorization form (signed by you) that allows them to accept checks on your behalf. In an emergency (eg. if your rep turns out to be untrustworthy), you can re-route these payments to your home address by giving production a signed letter from you overriding the 'check autho'.

Your paychecks are usually mailed to your agent, who takes a cut (of the pre-tax gross total) then forwards the original pay stub and a photocopy of the original check to your manager along with a check for the remaining amount.

Your manager takes their cut (of the pre-tax gross total) and forwards your original paystub plus a copy of your original paycheck, a copy of the check your agent sent to them, and a check for what little remains of your paycheck.

Some agents will send the check directly to you after taking their commission. You are then expected to mail the commission check to your manager, along with a copy of the paystub. Your representation (or you) should forward the money within ten business days of receiving it.

Where Do My Residual Checks Go?

Each production company forwards residuals to SAG-AFTRA rather than directly to actors. SAG-AFTRA sends all residuals to the residual routing address provided by you. If this address is a non-franchised agency, residuals will be forwarded to the primary address you have provided to the union.

Does My Rep Get Paid on Residuals?

Yes. SAG-AFTRA franchised agents are only contractually entitled to residuals on prime-time re-runs. **All other managers and agents should receive full commission on the gross total of all residual paychecks for jobs procured while you were working with them.**

This means if you are still being paid residuals on a job your ex-representation negotiated, you must send them commission. **Your current representation should only be paid residuals on jobs procured since you signed with them.** Always pay your commercial agent commission on residuals, as this is where the bulk of income is made in commercials.

THEATRICAL AGENT

A theatrical agent represents talent predominantly in the fields of film, television series and webisodes. A standard agent's commission is 10% of your gross (pre-tax) paycheck. As mentioned, an actor's fees are often negotiated to x dollars 'plus 10%', which means the production is paying your agent's fee. Most states require talent agents to be licensed by the city, state, or an appropriate governing body.

Being represented by one of the top agencies in town can be the golden key to the city . . . as long as your agent is passionate about you. While a top agent is backing and pitching you, they have the capacity to get you out on huge auditions several times a week, and sometimes several times a day. This is partly because the top agencies also represent celebrities, so every CD in town wants to maintain a strong relationship with these agencies and will happily see the agent's new development client for almost any role. In many cases, a smaller boutique agency would have to pitch like mad to get a client that same audition.

If you can sign with a top agency with an agent actively pushing for you, go for it. Many celebs from other countries arrive in LA, sign with a great agent, and are introduced to the top CDs and VPs of casting at this studio or that network. If you don't book work in the first year or two, however, the agent will probably move onto the next big development client with 'star potential'.

If you look older than 25, aren't a working actor, and don't have a pre-existing fan base (even fans from a popular webisode or reality show can get you signed), it is unlikely that a 'top ten' agent will take you on as a client. The bigger agencies expect new adult clients to already be working actors, so you need to build your credit list before you aim for the big guys.

If a top agency is not passionate about you, aim to sign with a strong boutique agency that has one agent (with an assistant) for every fifty or so clients on their theatrical client roster and no more than two other actors who fit your casting type (age, look, etc.).

The question is: how do you find these agents?

There is a list of SAG-AFTRA franchised agencies at SAGAFTRA.org. These are agents who work within SAG-AFTRA guidelines. While the list is a good place to start, the fact that an agent is not franchised has absolutely no bearing whatsoever on the quality of the agency . . . in fact many of the best agencies in LA are not SAG-AFTRA franchised.

The best way to figure out which agencies are getting their actors work is on IMDBpro.com. Look up the TV shows that you would most like to work on, click on a recent episode of each show, then go to the page of each actor who has played a recent strong co-star or guest star role in that show (guest star characters usually have a full first and last name). The actor will have representation listed on the page, so click on the agent and manager names and find out a little bit about each company.

To research an agency on IMDBpro, look up how many clients they represent. Click on the clients with top starmeters to see if they have current credits or work listed in production. The credits you want to see are guest star or co-star roles on network TV shows and studio films within the past year. This indicates that the agency has a working relationship with the casting office that runs each show.

What to Expect from Your Theatrical Agent

An agent is not a manager and until you're earning decent money, your agent is not your best friend. He is not around to make you feel better about yourself or pep you up when you're down, so don't call your agent to gripe. Your agent's role is to source auditions and negotiate contracts.

If you haven't heard from your agent in three or four weeks, send an email to stay fresh in his mind. Think of an excuse to reach out (preferably with career news), though just "touching base" is perfectly acceptable.

It's hard to say how often an actor in LA should expect to audition because it varies according to the actor's resume and type. The general consensus among LA agents and actors is if an agent gets a development client out for film or TV auditions at least twice a month, he is doing his job well. If he sends the actor out once a month, he is doing his job adequately.

Some months you may have ten auditions (heck, some weeks you may have ten!), other months you may have none. If your LA rep has gotten you out theatrically less than six times in the past six months, you may want to consider finding new rep.

If you are with one of the agencies on the list below, you will probably audition a lot. During pilot season some actors (mostly those with the top agencies and management firms) go out several times a day.

Top Agencies in LA

The list below is oh-so-debatable and will change as time goes by, but it shows the agencies currently at the top of the Hollywood totem pole.

The Top 2
- CAA (Creative Artists Agency)
- WME (William Morris Endeavour)

The Second Tier of Top Agencies
- Abrams
- APA (Agency for Performing Artists)
- CESD (Cunningham, Escott, Slevin, & Doherty)
- Gersh
- ICM (International Creative Management)
- IFA
- Innovative
- Paradigm
- UTA (United Talent Agency)

MANAGER

Unlike agents, managers do not require a license to operate a management company. People who are new in town may tell you that you "don't need a manager until you're famous". Actually, you do.

A manager, by definition, is someone who literally 'manages' a working actor's career. As a working actor, your manager should help you find or select an agent, work with your various agents to decide which projects to select, work with your publicist to decide which press ventures and endorsements would be the most beneficial or lucrative, and help you ensure nothing is missing from your marketing tools.

Your manager helps you make educated decisions on how to move your career forward in the most productive way possible. Think of a manager as a shield between you and your business dealings, taking calls from your other representation and dealing with all the details so that you primarily have to deal with one person rather than five.

According to the above definition, most developmental actors do not need a manager, but fortunately you do.

Most of the managers in LA do not act as managers in the purest sense of the word. Here are the tasks that a 'manager' in LA is unofficially expected to take care of when dealing with a development client:

- Submitting you on breakdowns
- Calling CDs and pitching you to procure auditions
- Looking over and negotiating contracts on your behalf

Sound familiar? That's because most managers in LA essentially act as agents. This means an aggressive manager might source more auditions for you than your agent. The best part of this is that it is easier to get a manager than an agent.

Once you secure a manager they can help you get an agent, who (if needed) will eventually get you a better manager, which is how you move up the chain to be with the top companies and forge a career. The hope is, of course, that you will sign with a manager who is savvy and capable enough for you to stay with them throughout your years as an actor.

You will only ever have one management company at a time. Unlike with agents (see section: 'Other Representation'), you cannot get a 'voice-over manager', 'hosting manager' or a 'commercial manager'. Your manager represents you in all areas and consults with all the agents and other representatives that you have working for you. Your manager also takes commission on the jobs you get in all areas, including peripheral sources of income like appearance fees, endorsements, and work out of state.

What You Should Expect from Your Manager

A standard management fee is 10%. When working with development clients, some managers charge 15%. People may balk at this figure, but the reality is it takes a lot more work to get a development client into each audition room than a working actor. Most managers should be open to adding a clause in the contract allowing for a fee reduction to 10% after the actor earns over a certain amount (around $50k is reasonable) in a year.

Once you've begun to book jobs through your manager, they should be willing to help you find an agent. A manager should also help you select and plan out what type of headshots you need, what hair color or style works best for you, and which workshops or classes you should be attending. They will help format your resume, and work with you to select roles that are more likely to lead your career in the direction you would like to take it. Try to make the easy decisions for yourself, but if you do ever need advice on something, your manager is the person you contact. As a development client, expect your manager to procure a similar number of auditions as your agent: between six and twelve every six months.

A manager guides your career in the right direction. Don't call your manager when you're depressed about where your career is at; call a friend. A manager is an educated advisor, not a shoulder to cry on... their time is valuable. Email where possible rather than calling, as it enables your rep to think about the answer and respond rather than having to rush a quick answer on the phone.

Top Management Companies in LA

- 3 Arts
- Anonymous Content
- Brillstein Entertainment Partners
- Evolution
- Leverage Management
- Lubler Rocklin Entertainment
- Management 360
- Principato Young Management
- Roar Talent
- Silver Lining
- The Collective
- Untitled Entertainment
- Zero Gravity Management

ENTERTAINMENT LAWYERS

Hiring an entertainment lawyer isn't a necessity until you're at an advanced stage in your career. An entertainment lawyer's function is to read and modify (when needed) your contracts and paperwork, and to negotiate the financial deal and other specific requirements you may have on a project. The large agencies have entertainment lawyers in-house for clients to utilize.

Most high-end entertainment lawyers are very well connected. This can help you gain access to the bigger agencies, managers, and to funding sources for films and pilots, which is helpful if you end up producing.

Incorporating Yourself as a Business

When regularly earning more than $100k(ish) per year from acting, most actors become their own corporation for tax purposes. This will allow you to expense things like car leases and other business-related purchases that are hard to claim as an employee. As a corporation, any work-related law suits are held against the corporation rather than you as an individual.

Some of the Many Top Entertainment Lawyers in LA
- Zifferen
- Loeb & Loeb
- Sheppard Mullin
- Ohmelveny and Meyer
- Stone, Meyer, Genow, Smelkinson and Binder
- Bloom, Hergott, Diemer, Rosenthall, Laviolette & Feldman
- Lichter, Grossman, Nichols, Adler & Feldman
- Hirsch, Wallerstein, Hayum, Matlof & Fishman
- Barnes, Morris, Mark, Yorn & Levine

OTHER TYPES OF REPRESENTATION

You may have one agent that represents you 'across the board' (in all areas), or several agents, with one representing you in each field of expertise. Having several allows each agent to focus on one area and is a solid "don't put all your eggs into one basket" approach.

Voice-over Agent

The main thing a voice-over agent wants to hear is your ability to convey truth in your readings and the essence of your own natural voice. Securing a voice-over agent is similar to getting a theatrical agent in that you put together a demo and submit it to agents around town.

A voice-over agency should have a recording studio or sound booth, however, most prefer you to record the auditions at home and email them.

David Lawrence, one of LA's top voice-over artists has put together an introduction to voice-over work in LA. Details are in the resource guide, and I recommend you check it out and learn how to get started in this lucrative side of the acting world.

Some of the many top voice-over agencies are also theatrical agents who represent actors in several areas. The top voice-over agencies in LA include:

- APA
- CESD
- DPN (Danis, Panaro, and Nist)
- Imperium 7
- Independent Artists
- WME (William Morris Endeavor)

Commercial Agent

Getting a commercial agent is less difficult than getting a theatrical agent, but that doesn't mean it's easy. Most commercial agencies are open to talent without any credits and will often take on actors who don't even have enough footage for a demo reel. To make yourself more appealing to a commercial agent, take a class in commercial auditioning to show that you are taking commercial acting seriously. Getting a commercial agent is often the best place to start with representation in LA (even if your goal is purely to get into film and TV), because it shows other agents that someone is willing to represent you.

Some theatrical agencies have a commercial division. Once you've been with the commercial division for a year, booked a job, and spent some face time in the office, it's not unreasonable to ask your commercial agent if you can meet with the theatrical division. If the agent says no, don't be perturbed. Simply wait six months, then ask again.

Expect to get at least three commercial auditions a month on average. Some months you may have no auditions and other months you may have twenty. If you're getting at least fifteen commercial auditions every six months, you should feel comfortable that your commercial agent is working for you. If your commercial agent is SAG-AFTRA franchised, and you have not earned more than $3500 in the past 91 days, you have grounds to terminate your agreement.

The major agencies almost all have commercial talent departments, some of which (like Innovative and Abrams) are at the top of the commercial field. Here are a few of the top commercial agencies in LA:

- AKA
- Brady, Brannon, and Rich
- CESD
- Coast To Coast
- Commercial Talent
- Commercials Unlimited
- Daniel Hoff
- Diverse
- Don Buchwald & Associates
- JLA
- KSR
- Pantheon
- Reign Agency
- Sovereign Talent
- Venture IAB

Hosting

A hosting agent works with you specifically for hosting gigs. This includes live gigs at venues and hosting on TV shows or infomercials. You'll need a hosting demo. These can be anything from one to five minutes long so people can get a feel for your style and how you lead an interview.

If you want to do hosting work, it's best that you get an agent who works specifically on hosting gigs because your main theatrical agent isn't likely to be aggressive in this area (although it is a very lucrative market).

Stunt

When hiring stunt actors, stunt coordinators don't usually use an 'agency' system. Most coordinators pull from the group of stunt actors they already know or have had referred. The best way to get to know the stunt coordinators and other stunt men is by training with them at gymnasiums or at the few stunt schools around town. The top schools are expensive so most stunt actors in LA just get together and train for free.

One of the places a number of stunt performers train is Bob Yerke's backyard in Van Nuys. Alternatively, LA Valley College holds open floor nights in the gymnastics building where you can train freely for a couple of dollars, or they also offer classes with trainers.

When you get to LA, ask everyone you meet whether they know any stunt actors. Arrange an introduction and ask those actors where they train and whether they can bring you to training sessions. You may hear "no" a few times before you hear a "yes", but networking on the ground level is rumored to be the most effective way to solicit stunt work in LA.

Stunt Agencies
- Stunts Unlimited
- KSR (has a stunt department)
- Bobby Ball (has a stunt department)

Stunt Work Calling Services
- Stunt Phone
- Missy's
- Joni's
- Teddy's

Stunt Training Centers
- Rick Seamen's Driving School
- Bob Yerkes Backyard
- Gymnastics Olympia
- Tempest Free running Academy

Hustling
Stunt work is also often acquired through 'hustling'. Some stunt coordinators allow stunties to visit set during the coordinator's downtime on a shoot and introduce themselves. It's a forced 'meet and greet' where you literally just show up to a film shoot that you've heard about, have security radio the stunt coordinator to give you permission to go on set, then hand the coordinator your headshot and resume. While some stunt coordinators are not fans of hustling, it's common practice in LA and many stunt actors get work this way.

SHOWCASES

I'm not a huge fan of showcases. I don't like the idea of paying to audition for an agency, BUT if no one will refer you to decent representation, showcases are the easiest and most effective way to get in front of representation to show them what you can do.

I know many people who have gained rep through showcases. It's a timing and numbers game. If the agents or managers happen to be looking for someone of your type and you happen to do great work at a showcase, they might happen to sign you. The odds are slim but they do exist, so why not give it a shot?

What is a Showcase?

A showcase is an event at which several actors perform for industry members. Although there are many different types of showcases in LA, I'm going to discuss the ones where twenty or thirty actors perform a series of two to three minute scenes for an audience of agents, managers and/or CDs in order to gain representation and work.

> **TIP:** Never attend a paid showcase that has just one agent attending; this is essentially the agent charging for actors to submit to the agency, which is illegal. If you hear of anything like this, it should be reported to SAG-AFTRA.

In Hollywood, there is usually a fee (between $50 and $100) for the actors to attend, though SAG-AFTRA does occasionally run free showcases for members. Some acting schools put together regular showcases for students. Sometimes a showcase audience will include general 'industry members', including studio execs, CDs, and filmmakers.

At a typical representation / CD showcase, guests are given the headshot and resume of each actor. If the audience is just three or four agents, the showcase may begin with a Q & A where the actors are able to ask questions of the guests. With a bigger audience, there is generally a welcome announcement and then the scenes begin. The actors may work in pairs, or with a reader (simulating a real audition). Scenes should be capped at a three-minute maximum, preferably most should run closer to two.

At some showcases, guests are asked to fill out feedback forms for the actors. If an agent or manager liked your work, they will call you. The showcase organizers often say not to contact the agents and managers after the showcase, but I see that as a bad business strategy. Try to put in a phone call around six business days later to follow up the meeting.

Showcase Guidelines

When selecting a showcase to participate in, make sure:
- There are no more than thirty actors performing
- An audition is required to get into the showcase or into the group running the showcase

- The scenes are capped at three minutes
- The location has comfortable audience seating (you want the audience focused on you, not their back pain)
- The performance portion of the showcase is sixty to ninety minutes max
- The location is in a good, central area of town (preferably West Hollywood, Hollywood, Beverly Hills, Burbank, or Studio City)
- The location has substantial parking for guests
- It starts after 7PM and before 8:30PM, and ends by 10:30PM (agents, managers and CDs work late)

Diversity Showcases

Diversity showcases are for individuals with ethnically diverse backgrounds or disabilities. NBC, ABC and CBS hold diversity showcases for actors and stand up comics. SAG-AFTRA contracts include diversity incentives, so it's beneficial for the networks to find diverse talent. If you qualify and pass the audition, performing in these showcases is a fantastic way to be seen by network executives. Information on diversity showcases can be found on any of the network websites.

Making Showcases Work for You

Select a Strong Scene

Make sure your scene highlights your strengths, and is the most dynamic, well-written scene you are able to perform at your skill level. Don't perform an average scene expecting your talent to shine through; find a great scene and do it brilliantly.

If comedy is your strength, don't just perform a comedy scene. Perform the funniest scene you can find . . . as long as you can do it justice. Make sure you know your level of talent. Select the best material that you can perform well.

Play Your Strengths and Your Type

There is absolutely no reason to play 'against type' in a showcase. What types of moments or characters reflect your strengths? Moments like arguments, love scenes, or witty banter? Are you best with characters who are cute, strong, or victims? Select a scene in the genre in which you are the most skilled, with a character that is perfect for you.

Don't Butcher the Classics

Avoid scenes performed by the masters. Novice actors repeatedly destroy once-great scenes by butchering the masterful dialogue in classes and showcases. If you perform a scene from *The Godfather*, audiences are likely to cringe even if you do it well, because people have an emotional attachment to the scenes in their original form. Almost every 'green' (new) actor performs the bedroom scene from *Good Will Hunting*. Please don't.

Find a scene with which people are not as familiar. Use a scene that isn't in every actors 'scene box'. Go for obscure films. The scene I do in a pinch is from *True Romance*, which is a familiar film to most industry members, but it is not as well known as say, pulling a scene from *Heat* or *LA Confidential*.

CHAPTER 4
CASTING DIRECTORS (CDs)

For an actor, casting directors are the gatekeepers of Hollywood. While CDs are rarely the final decision makers, their opinion is usually a very strong factor regarding which actors are cast in a project. They also decide which actors the director and producer see. Frequently an audition session with over thirty actors will be cut down to a shortlist of ten or twenty before the director even sees the audition footage. The director can't invite you to a call back if the CD doesn't show him your audition.

CDs are the most vital people for an actor to get to know in Hollywood. Directors are focused on things like the script, shot list, and storyboard. Producers are focused on budgets, locations, and everything else on the film. CDs spend all of their working hours thinking about actors and keeping ever growing databases filled with talent. While a producer or director may do one or two films a year, a CD might cast ten or fifteen over the same time period.

In Los Angeles, there are over two hundred commercial CDs. These CDs work a little differently and they are not the folks we're here to discuss.

The union for CDs is called the 'CSA' (Casting Society of America) and has over two hundred and eighty casting directors and associates registered throughout LA in over a hundred and fifty offices. CDs in LA are constantly searching for new talent, which is fantastic because that's exactly what you are. So . . . you need to get to know the CDs.

CASTING OFFICE STAFF

The staffing structure varies a great deal between casting offices. Following is a breakdown of the various job titles in the field of casting.

CDs as Film Producers / Executive Producers

It is much easier for a producer to find investors to finance a film if name talent is attached to the project. Often a CD will work on an unfinanced project 'on spec' (for free) or for a small fee, trying to attach celebrities. Due to the fact that the majority of projects in development will never be green-lit, a CD on working on spec will often be given a 'producer' or an 'executive producer' credit. This credit is to compensate the risk the CD is taking by spending her time on a project that may never go into production.

Note: *When I use the term 'CD' throughout this book, I am also re-ferring to 'casting associates' (detailed below), and any other person who is involved in making decisions regarding talent in a casting office.*

Powerful CDs in Hollywood are often able to negotiate producer credits even when they are being paid their full rate. This is simply because the film-makers are lucky to be working with CDs of this caliber and to have access to the celebrity connections they bring to the film. A producer credit is also often given because the CD actually did produce the film.

President or Vice President of Talent or Casting

Each studio and network has an in-house casting department: A team of casting executives who hire, oversee, and work with outsourced casting of-fices to cast the projects being produced by the network. Although the hired office is the one officially casting the show, the casting executives will still suggest actors for roles, watch the audition tapes, and approve the cast that has been selected. If there is a particularly large guest cast or for some reason the outsourced office can't run a casting session, the in-house executive CD may run auditions.

Owner / CD

Most CDs own the casting company for which they work. This is made clear by the fact that most casting offices are named after the head CDs. In larger offices, there are some CDs who are not the owners of the company. An example of this is UDK, one of the largest casting offices in LA. Ulrich,

Dawson, and Kritzer are all CDs and owners of the company, plus they have several other casting directors and associates working for them as employees.

Casting Director (CD)

A CD is in charge of sourcing and auditioning actors for a project. Most CDs are members of the CSA. CDs decide or collaborate with the producers and director on which actors are called back, and are often part of the decision making process regarding who gets the part (though ultimately the director and producer decide).

CDs remember and re-use talented actors they meet and *like*. They have both the authority and motivation to find new actors because most CDs truly enjoy finding undiscovered talent.

Casting Associate

CDs working in TV or working regularly in film usually have a casting associate working for them. The associate aids the CD with organizing and running the sessions, pulling sides, delegating work to the assistants, and dealing with paperwork when actors are booked. Casting associates are generally more accessible than CDs, so establishing a relationship with them may help you source auditions from some of the impenetrable big offices. Associates are usually only a few years away from becoming CDs, so meet them early before they get that big promotion.

Associates are often assigned the task of finding much of the talent for supporting roles in projects, which is one reason many of them attend showcases and workshops. Just because they are paid to be at a workshop (they usually are) doesn't mean they aren't actively looking for talent. On many TV shows, the associate is often responsible for selecting actors for the co-star audition sessions.

Associates frequently do the initial selection from the submissions received online. Out of a thousand submissions an associate might choose a hundred actors from which a CD then selects the final thirty who are invited to audition.

Casting Assistant

Many casting offices in LA don't have a specific 'receptionist'. The person you meet at the front desk is often a casting assistant, though it can sometimes be the associate or even the CD. A casting assistant is usually a paid employee. Assistants help the CD with sessions, answer phones, and work with the interns sorting through the piles of mail received on a daily basis. They don't usually make selections, but if an assistant finds an amazing actor, you can bet she'll pass that actor's info to her bosses.

Intern

Interns are usually university students, people wanting to get into casting, or actors who are looking to learn more about the casting process and hoping to network with the CDs. An internship is an unpaid position with little power beyond possibly having the ear of the people in the office and VERY occasionally suggesting an actor for an audition. Interns sort through mail, make copies and coffee, and anything else the paid office employees are too busy to take care of. Interns may not have much influence, but they are people who care about their goals enough to give their time freely for their career, which means they deserve your respect just as much as any other staff member in a casting office.

GETTING INTO THE ROOM

I discussed the importance of being trustworthy, now here's where being that trustworthy person people are willing to put their name behind comes into play. Just as the overriding goal of this book is to teach you to become a working actor, the immediate and very real goal that you must focus on each day in LA in order to get each job and to keep getting jobs is to GET INTO THE ROOM.

Of course the room I'm talking about is the audition room and the person who controls that room is the CD.

The producer hires the CD, who is held responsible for the talent, behavior, and professionalism of all actors on the set. The most dreaded phone call a CD can get is the one from the producer of a film saying they must replace an actor who is being a diva, hasn't learned her lines, or isn't acting well.

To reduce the likelihood of this, CDs prefer to mostly audition actors they already know and those who are 'referred' to them. This doesn't mean CDs don't audition actors they don't know, but when casting a substantial role top CDs prefer to audition actors they trust, even if that trust is by association.

Here's a list of middlemen (referrals) and ways to get onto a CD's radar so she is more likely to bring you into the audition room:

Representation: Agent or Manager

When an agent or manager takes on a new client, he is putting his name behind that client. If the CD knows and trusts the agent or manager, they will in turn trust any actor referred (i.e. submitted or represented) by him. This is where having a quality agent's name displayed underneath your headshot thumbnail in the submissions helps you get auditions.

Representation: Top Ten Agent or Manager

A large percentage of actors auditioning for most major roles are with the top ten or so agencies and management firms. In most cases, this is simply because the CD trusts the top agent because she has witnessed his ability to sign strong talent over the years.

Another reason the top reps easily get their clients into the room is because by auditioning and hiring lesser-known actors from an agent that represents celebrities, the CD is doing the agent a favor (giving him an opportunity to earn money). This nurtures the CD's relationship with that agent and agency. This makes it more likely that the agent will return the favor by listening when the CD is pitching new projects or roles for one of the many celebrities represented by that agency.

Directors / Producers

On almost every project, the producer or director refers a few actors to the CD. These are actors the director or producer has worked with before, knows socially, is related to, has had referred, or has seen in something. As an employee of the producer and director, the CD will always audition these actors. On most indie films, the director and producer are free to hire any actor they like without even auditioning them. This isn't the case on many studio films or network TV shows where studio and network execs prefer to see audition tapes to approve most or even all of the talent after the director makes a selection.

Other CD

Most CDs are friends with at least a few other CDs. If a CD refers an actor to another CD, that actor will be likely to get an audition. A CD referral would generally happen without your knowledge. For instance, if a CD is casting a unique role and asks her CD friends for suggestions. This is not something you can control (asking a CD to refer you to another CD is inappropriate).

Casting Associate or Assistant

A casting associate or assistant will often refer actors to the CD with whom she works. It is then at the CD's discretion whether to audition those actors. On some projects the associate may organize a session and is free to bring in any actors they feel are right for the role.

Network TV / Studio Credits

It looks great if you've worked on a network TV show, studio project, or with a director or producer that the CD knows. Having a familiar credit gives you a stamp of approval because if you were good enough for a network or studio to hire you at almost a grand a day, you're probably good enough for the CD to give you a shot.

Knowing You Socially

If a CD knows you socially over the years from parties or events, she probably trusts you more than an actor she doesn't know, especially if you know her through (were referred by) a mutual friend.

Knowing You Professionally

When I say this I'm referring to the CD knowing you from an audition, workshop, showcase, general meeting, or watching your demo reel.

Knowing Your Work

Most CDs view as many TV series as possible and watch the guest roles to find talent they haven't met. I know a few who even fast forward through the main storyline and just watch the guest spots! Most CDs also watch films, local theatre, and comedy CDs watch live improv and stand up comedy shows to find new talent.

Nepotism

If you are related to, or know anyone who is related to, a CD or filmmaker, when the exact right role comes up . . . USE IT! The reason nepotism runs so rampant in Hollywood (and in any industry) is exactly what we've been talking about: TRUST. If you were casting and you only had one interview spot left and a choice between strangers or someone referred by a trusted friend or family member, who would you see?

Special Skills / Unique Look

If a role requires a rare skill, language, or physical attribute, the CD may have trouble finding the right actor in her existing pool of talent. This means she must take a chance and audition mostly actors she doesn't know. If you have specific special skills, this can be enough to get you an audition without a referral.

What If I Don't Have Access to Any of the Above?

The number of actors a CD will take a chance on varies dramatically between offices and depends a great deal on the type of role and project. For most roles in bigger budget projects and lead roles in low budget projects, casting will mostly see actors with substantial resumes and/or strong representation. For low budget projects and day player roles in bigger budget projects, most CDs widen the net and take a chance on some actors with less impressive credits and representation simply because their headshot and reel indicate they may be right for the part. This is where you can get your foot in the door. This is why it's imperative that you secure the best possible representation, and develop relationships with filmmakers and CDs throughout Hollywood.

MEETING AND MAINTAINING CONTACT WITH CDs

Remember, if you have solid representation and are getting frequent auditions, you should not submit yourself directly to CDs on studio, network, or bigger budget indie projects. An exception is if you have a strong personal relationship with a CD, but even in this instance it's best for your rep to make the call.

The tips below are for actors **without strong representation** who have no choice but to take their career into their own hands.

Timing

Time is a CD's primary concern, but what else matters to her? A CD meets many actors, so her memory is constantly holding thousands of names and faces. Even when a CD knows you well, if you are expecting her to remember you at the exact moment that the right job comes up, you're being a little hopeful.

Think of those times when you've run into a friend who said: "Oh, I'm glad I ran into you, there's a party tonight . . . want to come?" The fact that your friend hadn't already invited you doesn't mean that he didn't want you to come to the party . . . it's just that you weren't in the forefront of his mind until seeing you jogged his memory.

You must get your marketing materials in front of a CD at the exact time she needs them: when she is casting a role you are right for and/or when you are in a project she can watch. This gives us a secondary goal of TIMING.

THE HOLLYWOOD SURVIVAL GUIDE

The two things you need to focus on any time you communicate with a CD in a professional capacity are TIME and TIMING.

Each time you reach out to any business contact you must first ask yourself this question: "Is this the most potentially effective (aka: likely to produce results) time for me to send this marketing material?"

Sending your pic and res to a CD when she is not casting anything is a complete waste of time. Whereas, if you send your pic and res as a specific submission when a CD you've met is casting a role you're right for, she may give you an audition.

If your rep calls a CD to pitch you for a role at 1:30PM, I would consider this bad timing. Why? It's lunchtime. Avoid dropping by a casting office on a Monday or a Friday because they are busy days. Never visit before 10:30AM or after 5PM. Avoid dropping by between 12:30PM and 2:30PM because lunchtime in LA runs from 1PM to 2PM.

Relationships, business, marketing, everything in this world is timing. Never underestimate the benefits of being in the right place at the right time. That means having your marketing materials and/or yourself in front of the right person at the exact time that he or she has an opportunity to give you.

Note: The only time you should personally visit a casting office is to drop off a 'thank you' gift or to drop a hardcopy headshot in when submitting for a role. When you are there, be conscious of their time and don't force a conversation, just drop off the submission or thank you gift, say a quick hi, then leave.

How to Get to Know a CD

I keep talking about referrals and relationships . . . but how on Earth is an actor new to LA with no referrals supposed to get the casting staff around town to know them?

Luckily the answer is short, sweet, and attainable. If you don't have representation or a referral the best way to meet a CD is in an audition, workshop, or showcase. Once you **have met** a CD, maintain contact through self-submissions (if they have given you their email address) when a role comes up, and postcards whenever you are in a TV show, film, or play. Try to see each CD once a year at workshops, showcases, or auditions in order to stay fresh in their memory.

If you **have not met** a CD, do not send any mail to them. I know it's tempting, but it's a complete waste of time. This includes sending invitations to plays, postcards promoting TV appearances, or introduction letters.

The Rule of Three

It is a known marketing rule that most consumers must be exposed to a product's brand three times before they remember it. Likewise, I believe that in life you must meet (or be seen on stage or screen by) people three times before they remember you long term.

The first time you meet a person, they're just one of maybe a thousand new people you meet each year of your life. The second time you meet someone, you draw on the memory of the first meeting and a little association is born in your mind, but again, you meet many people twice in your life.

The third time you meet someone seems to be the winner. Once that third encounter happens, it's like your brain tells you "This is someone who is part of our tribe". Perhaps it's a limbic response of some sort. Upon the third positive encounter a person usually becomes someone with whom you are now familiar, no longer a stranger, and someone you remember . . . at least for a year or two.

Almost every time I meet a CD for the third time they know my face and often remember my name. If it was in a workshop I would frequently get an audition with the CD in the few weeks that followed.

The transient nature of people in LA causes folks living and working here to have short memories for professional contacts they haven't seen in a while. For this reason, you must continue to remind each CD that you are still in town.

If you maintain your network over the years, your career will thrive. If you start assuming that CDs should remember you because you've got a strong resume or have met them once or twice before, you are likely to be left behind.

Thank You Gifts for Casting Directors

CDs work hard and often push for you to get a role. It's good business to send a thank you card when you book work, to acknowledge their part in the process. It's nice to include a token of your appreciation, like a gift card or movie tickets.

Giving an actual gift to a CD when you book a role is unnecessary, but it is a smart business move and is usually appreciated. NEVER SEND CASH TO A CD as it is completely inappropriate. Appropriate presents are booze and other consumable items. Perhaps call the casting associate and ask what they think the CD would like. Avoid fatty snacks like cakes and chocolate, as most CDs receive a number of these.

Mention the name of the project and the role you booked in the card. CDs cast so many actors that they may have trouble remembering who you are from your name alone. Some actors say to enclose a headshot or business card, but I think the best approach is to deliver the gift personally. If the CD's office is on a studio lot, call the associate to arrange a walk on pass at the gate.

SELF-SUBMISSIONS

Your goal should be to get to a stage where you know your representation is getting you into every room possible. If you feel that your agent and manager are picking up phones and pitching you for all roles, **there is no need to submit yourself for projects**. If, however, you aren't happy with the number of auditions you're getting, you can work to obtain your own auditions.

As a development client, it is important to submit yourself daily for those roles that are intentionally made available to actors online through NowCasting.com, ActorsAccess.com, etc. This section, however, refers to roles on the breakdowns that are only accessible to agents and managers.

A common complaint heard amongst the rabble of noise in acting circles is "My agent isn't getting me out", and I often wonder "Are you getting yourself out?" Here's the deal: if your agent has sixty clients, his time is divided into sixty pieces. So, if your agent works an eight-hour day from 10AM to 7PM, he should have around eight minutes a day to focus on YOUR career.

Now, factor in the time agents spend considering new clients, negotiating contracts for their working actors, sending emails, having peripheral conversations while pitching, fielding phone calls from clients, and the other fifty tasks they undertake on a daily basis. This probably leaves your agent around four minutes per day for each client, which he is unlikely to spread evenly across the roster. The four minutes usually consists of the time between reading a breakdown, scrolling down to your face, and clicking the 'submit' button to put you up for a job (with an occasional pitch thrown in for good measure).

How can you expect someone to get more auditions in four minutes than you're getting yourself, when you have the entire day to focus on your career? You can't.

How and When to Self-Submit

Firstly, find out whether your rep is submitting you for co-star roles or SAG-AFTRA Ultra Low and Modified Low Budget projects as some agents and managers don't. Once you figure out which areas are being covered by your representation, you can start doing submissions for those that aren't.

Self-submissions are most likely to garner results when seeking roles in independent films rather than studio films or TV series.

TV CDs work very quickly, often posting a breakdown then setting up audition sessions a few hours later to see actors the following day. By the time you hear about a TV co-star or guest star casting notice, it's likely the audition timeslots have been allocated to other actors.

The most effective time to self-submit is when you know a filmmaker or CD well enough to contact them directly when they are casting a role that suits you. This is why you must broaden and maintain your network at every opportunity. This takes YEARS and will continue throughout your entire career as you enter each new level of the industry.

If you do not have a pre-existing relationship with a CD, self-submitting is a long shot but can occasionally result in auditions. Check the breakdowns every day and when a film role is right for you, submit.

If you have the CD's email address, send a short email that simply says "We met at *x* and I would love to be considered for the role of *y* in project *z*". Include your headshot and resume, plus a link to your demo, IMDBpro.com profile, and online press kit.

While almost all CD's prefer online submissions, most flick through the few hardcopies they receive for film (rarely for TV) projects. Write the project name and role you're submitting for on a post-it, stick it on the front of your headshot with your resume attached (never self-submit with a post-card), and mail or drop it to the CD. If you have previously met the CD but don't know them well, attach a separate post-it saying: "We met at *x*" to jog their memory.

Look, the truth is the majority of CD's prefer not to get submissions directly from actors, and yes, there can be something a little needy about it . . . but most CDs also understand that LA can be an absolute dogfight. They get that actors without decent rep have no choice, and they know that talented actors sometimes can't get decent rep . . . so if the CD knows you, she will probably give your submission the same consideration she gives to all of the others.

The bottom line is: **ONCE YOU'RE IN THE AUDITION ROOM, NOBODY CARES HOW YOU GOT THERE.**

When they're not looking for names, all the CD and filmmakers care about is whether you are the best choice for the part and whether you will be professional and pleasant on set.

CASTING WORKSHOPS

CDs working in episodic television need to actively seek out new talent on a weekly basis, as they may cast as many as thirty co-star and guest star roles per episode. Film CDs must audition many actors for each role to give the director options. To find strong actors for so many auditions, every CD must constantly get to know new actors and assess their skill level.

Casting workshops are not for beginners. They're not for 'green' actors who are still fumbling their way through a scene. A number of the actors who perform at the workshop I used to attend have previously played recurring or series regular characters on American TV shows.

One potential issue with workshops is that most don't require an audition. Because of this, you may find yourself working with an actor so unfathomably bad they drag you down with them as you try to rescue the dying scene.

If you can't get into an audition entry workshop, you shouldn't be performing at workshops. This doesn't necessarily mean you are a bad actor, it could simply mean you are not practiced in your cold reading skills. Take a class, work on your cold reading skills at home and audition again in a few months. Once your acting is at a standard where you are extremely comfortable with your work (and preferably in an advanced class at your chosen acting school), you are ready to perform.

Note: If you are auditioning theatrically more than four times a month, you probably don't need to attend casting workshops.

A Typical Casting Workshop

Between fifteen and twenty-four actors attend an average casting workshop. The CD will talk about herself for around ten minutes, discussing how she got into casting, who she works with, and what she is currently casting. Take notes. It's important to know the background and preferences of each person with whom you're planning to do business.

After the introduction is a quick Q & A, then the CD will 'cast' each actor in a role from her catalogue of 'sides' (audition scenes). These are mostly two to five page audition pieces she has used to audition actors for actual projects in the past. Some workshops use prepared scenes, and some CDs prefer improvisation to find the 'essence' of each actor (rather than having actors play a role that may not best reflect their strengths).

At a typical casting workshop you're paired up with another actor, which is why the skill level of the other actors is important. When the actors are not paired, you'll play your scene either opposite a reader or the CD (depending on how the CD prefers to assess talent).

The actors are given around fifteen minutes to work on their scenes. Aim to be familiar enough with the dialogue that you are only glancing at the page momentarily once every two or three lines. This gets much easier with practice, so work on memorizing a page of scripted dialogue in under ten minutes every day at home as preparation.

The actors head onto the stage to perform the scenes. Each scene is performed once, then the CD will either: give notes, a redirect, and have you do it again (most common); give notes and not have you do it again; or simply thank you and you'll sit back down. Listen closely, as your ability to proficiently apply the redirection is a skill that is often just as important to the CD as your ability to perform the scene.

Selecting Casting Workshops

Be aware of the genre and type of show or films the CD works on before you head to a casting workshop. This will give you an idea of how to dress and the style of acting the CD is likely to be looking for. For example, if you're an attractive girl and the CD for 'Two and a Half Men' is coming in, wear something sexy. If you are meeting a Sitcom CD and you're bad at comedy, it's probably not a relationship you want to spend $40 per class to build.

There are around twenty casting workshop facilities in LA. The main factors you want to look at when selecting a workshop are:

Quality of the Other Actors

It is hard to act well when you're opposite a bad actor, especially in comedy. If possible, audit a class and check out the resumes of some of the regular attendees.

Quality of the Guests

Never pay to meet an intern or an assistant. The majority of guests at CD workshops are casting associates, so if you're on a budget select them on a case-by-case basis. Try to meet all of the casting directors who work on projects that interest you.

Cost

Around $45 per class is standard but some high level CDs can cost up to $70. Never pay more than $80 no matter how important the CD appears to be. Most workshops have discounts if you pre-purchase multiple classes.

Location and Presentation of the Room

When you're sitting in a room for two hours a night, you'll appreciate reasonably comfortable chairs and flattering lighting. If the room is well decorated and clean, the CD will subconsciously feel that it's a less desperate group than workshops held in dirty, dingy facilities.

KEEPING A CD DATABASE

Every time you meet a CD or casting associate, whether you are at a workshop, a social event, or an audition . . . make a note of it.

Each casting office is different. Each CD expects different levels of formality, preparation, and even has different preferences regarding choices like props and miming. Some expect you to be word perfect on the dialogue, and others prefer it when you improvise. You need to know what you're walking into when you arrive at each casting office.

After you've spent a few years doing workshops and auditions, you should have met around a hundred or more CDs. In that same period of time, each CD will probably meet several thousand actors. Believe it or not, you probably won't remember them all by face and name . . . but they might remember you.

If a CD can remember your face out of thousands of actors, you can bet that she is expecting you to remember her out of a hundred or so CDs. It's about respect, so be professional and keep a CD database. Try to make note of the following:

- Name of the office.
- Mailing address (check CastingAbout and NowCasting for updates).
- Email address (if available).
- Date and location you first met.
- A physical description to jog your memory.
- Likes, dislikes, and anything you remember about what she said.
- What scene you performed and with whom (if applicable).
- How your scene went and her comments.
- What project and role you auditioned for and if you were called back.

Casting About

CastingAbout.com is a fantastic CD database through which you can find current information on the casting office working on each TV show and film in LA. It lists the casting directors, associates, and assistants for each office and what projects they are currently working on. It also allows you to make notes next to each CD and associates name, which is a great place to copy and paste your database notes.

CHAPTER 5

AUDITIONS

HOW FILM AUDITIONS ARE BORN

A producer 'locks in' the financing to make a film. If he hasn't already chosen a CD, he sends the script to the various CDs he has previously worked with, would like to work with, or who are referred to him. He also provides an intended budget for 'above the line' (celebrity) and 'below the line' (non-celebrity) casting.

Note: *Producers often attach celebrities early to attract financing. In some cases the film may be financed without stars attached, but this financing is usually 'cast contingent'. This means the investors have approved a list of celebrities and agreed to finance the film "only if any of these celebrities plays the role of x". In this case, each CD may discuss how well she knows the listed celebs and their respective representation, the pros and cons of casting each celebrity, and who is the most suited or likely to sign on.*

When financing is not cast contingent to specific actors it usually still requires celebs bankable enough to recoup the money being invested. In this case, each CD compiles a list of name actors she might be able to attach to the project given the appeal of the script and the above the line budget.

The filmmaker selects a CD, whose first task is to send the script and the offer of money (and possibly 'points' (profit share)) in the film, to the actors (via their representation) on the offer list. This is termed as having an 'offer out' to the various actors. Occasionally the *script only* (without an official offer) will be strategically sent to several actors reps at once. This is to create competition for the role and more bargaining power for the CD. The CD and filmmakers will usually meet with each of the interested celebs, then discuss which of them is the most appropriate for the project before the filmmakers make the final casting decision.

For the large supporting roles in the film, most CDs (and associates) compile a list of the actors they know or who have been referred for each role. For these (and most of the smaller supporting roles) the casting office also releases a character 'breakdown'. Sometimes the breakdown is sent directly to a pool of agents and managers the CD prefers to work with, but most breakdowns are released to all representation.

Note: *When a CD is looking for names, she may put out a breakdown requesting suggestions for certain roles (yes, even celebs are pitched for parts). The breakdown will go out with "Star names only" written beside the role. This doesn't always mean they will not audition non-celebrities; sometimes the statement is just there to let the major agencies know that there is money available for negotiation should they want to submit name talent.*

Once the breakdown is released, agents and managers immediately start submitting actors for the roles listed. Within hours the CD will have received thousands of submissions.

Moments after the breakdown is released, the CD receives potentially hundreds of personalized phone and email pitches from agents and managers. The purpose of a pitch is to sell and draw attention to one (or more) of the submitted actors. While pitching you, your agent or manager may email the link to your Breakdown Express or Now Casting profile page, IMDb profile, headshot, resume, press, and demo reel/s to the CD.

After submissions start coming in (sometimes immediately, sometimes weeks later), the casting office selects actors to audition. Electronic submissions are displayed to the CD similarly to computer photos in 'thumbnail' viewing mode. For each role, the CD can choose to view twenty, sixty, or a hundred 2" × 3" (thumbnail) headshots at a time. The actor's name and any comments attached to the submission are displayed beneath the corresponding headshot.

Beneath each photo are three checkboxes labeled 1, 2, and 3 on BreakdownExpress.com and Y, N, M on NowCasting.com. Each casting office goes through the list in their own unique way, checking the boxes. An example might be if the associate selects an initial group by marking actors as '2' then the CD selects the '1's from the '2' pile. In some offices, the CD or associate makes all selections without collaboration. Whichever method each office has, the result is the same: a selection of actors is invited to audition for the project.

The CD schedules an audition session by choosing a date and time range for each role and the time required for each actor (the Breakdown Express system defaults to 7.5 minutes per actor, but this can be changed).

When the session is created the person who submitted you (agent, manager, or yourself) is notified by email that you have been given an audition appointment. This notification should include all audition information: address, date and time of the audition, CD and filmmaker names, character description, and the 'script code' (password) for the sides and script.

The initial recipient of the audition notification must click 'confirm', 'unavailable', or 'reschedule'. If there is something very specific to discuss with the casting office, your rep may call or email the CD directly. Your rep will then download the script and audition scene, and email them to you along with the audition information. Most agents and managers will also call to let you know you have an audition.

Actors not invited to audition through an online breakdown service (for example, actors the CD brings in from her workshop files or hardcopy submissions) are invited via phone or email. This is a lot more work for CDs, which is one reason they prefer actors to be submitted electronically.

FILM AUDITION PRE-REQUISITES

Following is an attempt to give you an idea of which actors are most often selected to audition for each type of project and role. This is impossible to define as it varies so vastly between projects, but I want to show you a 'typical' scenario for each type of project.

Short / Webisode / Under $100k Feature Film

Filmmakers working on micro-budget projects generally use one of their producers or a friend to cast the film. A CD working on projects of this nature rarely has the budget for names or even to hire the working actors they know, so almost all of the actors auditioning are selected from the submissions (which generally posted online for actors to self-submit).

Agents and managers rarely submit or pitch actors on projects this small. The actors are selected to audition based on how much their submitted headshot looks like the character and on the quality of their demo and re-sume, though at this level, previous credits are a bonus rather than a necessity.

SAG-AFTRA Feature Film $100k to $650k / Full Scale SAG-AFTRA Paid Short

CDs at this level are usually indie pros. These projects can afford to cast one or two recognizable DVD level names or current TV series regulars in the lead roles. The next three or four roles on the credit list are usually given to actors with at least a few familiar feature films and TV spots under their belt, and all other roles tend to go to the best actor, regardless of recognizable credits.

SAG-AFTRA Features Over $650k

For the lead one to five roles in films budgeted over $650k, the producers need to lock in name actors bankable enough to ensure the level of distribu-tion required to recoup the budget. The level and number of names required depends on the genre and budget of the project. The CD will pull from a list of celebrities approved by the producers for each role and send out offers.

For major supporting roles, a CD at this level will have a large pool of very talented working actors she has previously worked with or audi-tioned. If the budget is over $2.5 million, it is even harder to get an audi-tion for strong supporting roles because most actors in LA will likely be interested in the project. Even so, most CDs try to see new talent, so some auditions may be given to new actors pitched by agents and managers the CD trusts.

For the smaller supporting roles, many directors tend to prefer unfa-miliar faces to aid the audience's suspension of disbelief while in the 'world' within the film. This gives CDs the freedom to bring in newcomers, which is where being 'referred' to a CD can get you into the room. Even so, on studio films the big paychecks and substantial residuals attract working ac-tors to audition, even for roles with only a few lines. Occasionally, these roles are offered to actors who auditioned for larger roles and didn't book.

On films that are shot in another state, the day player roles are usually cast by a regional CD who has their own pool of local actors.

HOW TV AUDITIONS ARE BORN

Casting a TV episode is similar to casting a film, but much faster. While a film CD may cast thirty roles in a month, a TV CD has just over a week to do the same. Most shows hire between three and fifteen guest cast members (guest star and co-star roles) per episode, but some hover upwards of thirty.

Each show has a budget per episode (and per season) allocated to casting, and the CD must find actors to fill all roles without going over budget.

Usually, the production 'week' for a half-hour show is five business days and a one hour show 'week' is eight business days, but some shows have production weeks of four, six, seven, nine, or even ten business days. With the exception of shows on a five (or ten) day 'week', TV shooting schedules often don't match a typical calendar week, so "day 1" of each week could fall on any weekday.

Most TV shows shoot consistently and tape a new episode every production week. For example, episode 1 may be filming while episode 2 is 'prepping' and episode 3 is casting.

A standard network TV season is twenty-four episodes, and a standard cable TV season is thirteen. Since networks usually order TV shows in twelve episode 'blocks', many shows shoot twelve episodes (or thirteen for cable) in three to five months, then take a break for a couple of months. When a TV show is not shooting, it is considered to be on 'hiatus'.

Any time days or weeks are referenced in the example that follows, it refers to production days or weeks, which exclude weekends. When I use the term 'CD', it may actually be an associate or assistant at the casting office. Here is an example of how some TV shows are cast:

The casting office receives the script for the new episode. On some shows, a table read will be done with producers, director, execs, and (occasionally) series regular actors to get a feel for the tone. Updated copies of the script will be sent to all cast (and key crew) every few days leading up to (and during) the shoot.

The CD compiles a list of co-star, guest star and recurring characters to be cast, allocates a portion of the budget to each character, and decides which (if any) roles need to be offered directly to known actors.

Based on the script, the CD (or staff at breakdown services) creates a character breakdown, which describes and defines each character. Offers go out to celebrities, breakdowns are released online, and thousands of actor submissions arrive within minutes.

Most CDs begin selecting actors to audition within hours of releasing the breakdown. If the office is holding 'pre-reads' (first round auditions that the

---

Note: Hiring a celebrity in a television guest role or small film role is loosely referred to as 'stunt casting'. Though this is a standard and necessary practice, some CD's feel that the term has a negative tone.

producers don't see) for the role, they are usually within two days of the breakdown being released.

After pre-reads, a 'producers session' is scheduled (this is just a fancy term for a callback). The producers and director may be in the room, but it's also common for the CD to tape each actor and send the best audition tapes to producers. If the producers are attending, audition sessions for all characters are usually held on one day to accommodate the producer's schedules. Producer's sessions for guest cast are usually held within five days of the initial character breakdown being released.

Some actors are invited directly to the producer's session without a pre-read. Going "straight to producers" is a big deal (it's like going straight to a callback) and is most likely to happen if the CD knows and trusts you, your work or your representation. Some offices don't do pre-reads, in which case all actors go straight to producers.

In most cases, casting decisions for each role require approval from the network. So even after the CD, director, writers, and executive producers have chosen you, the network casting executives also have to approve you. This is because executives must balance casting across all the shows on their network, watching factors like avoiding having the same actor appear on different shows within a certain period of time.

The selected actor is notified as soon as the casting decision is made so that production (especially wardrobe) can get to work, and casting can ensure the budget is correct. It is usually only a week or two from the date you are cast to the date you shoot.

Prior to the shoot, you attend wardrobe fittings and there is usually an "optional" (always attend if invited) 'table read' (seated reading of the script by actors). These table reads are often viewed by the producers, writers, executives, department heads, director and casting department.

Sitcom Shooting Schedule

The shooting schedule on a sitcom differs from the above explanation. Sitcoms rehearse throughout the production week and tape all interior locations within just a few hours on a soundstage, in front of a live audience. Any non-soundstage shots are taped throughout the week. Also, some sitcoms shoot three [production] weeks on and one week off.

Types of TV Shows

In American television, narrative TV shows fall under very specific genres. Even if you know nothing else about a series, you MUST know which genre it is prior to auditioning. It is also very important that you watch at least one or two episodes, as the style of acting greatly varies between shows.

A TV episode must provide viewers with an entire story arc in a limited amount of time, so keep the pace up when you are auditioning for TV. Aim to keep your timing at around one minute per page, as this will be close to the intended pacing of the scene.

Note: *It's a great experience to watch a sitcom taping and it's a must for any actors who have just arrived in LA. There are free tickets available to become a live audience member at tapings for shows on most TV networks through a company called 'Audiences Unlimited'. Call them on (818) 506-0067.*

One-Hour Drama

Shows like *NCIS* and *Breaking Bad* fall under the one-hour drama category. The tone of these shows is often similar to dramatic films, but since performances on TV require faster pacing, the actors tend to tighten up most of the potentially long, drawn out dramatic moments.

Dramedy

Comedic TV shows with dramatic undertones like *Shameless* or *House of Lies* often have a heightened reality, but (while keeping up the comedic pace) performances tend to be grounded in sincere emotion and connected moments.

Situational Comedy (Sitcom) / 'Multi-Cam'

Half-hour shows like *How I Met Your Mother* and *Big Bang Theory* are sitcoms. Sitcom scripts are usually double-spaced. Each episode is thoroughly rehearsed and each take is usually a performance of the entire scene. Multiple (usually 4) cameras are used so several actors can be filmed at once. This allows the director to catch great moments from every angle without messing with the pacing or having to re-enact improvised scenes.

Sitcom acting is fast paced, larger than life, and scripts are riddled with set ups and punch lines (research the comedy 'rule of threes'). How 'big' the performances are depends upon the style of the show.

Mockumentary

Mockumentaries have become popular in recent years due to the success of shows like *The Office* and *Modern Family*. The last time I auditioned for a mockumentary, a message came from casting before the audition asking actors not to try to "play the comedy". It's most often a dry type of comedic pacing that is best learned by watching the shows to see how the characters interact.

Soap / Daytime Drama

Almost every narrative show that screens five days a week (except reruns of old shows) is considered a 'soap opera', 'daytime drama', or 'soap'. Consider a soap audition to be the same as any dramatic TV show audition. Don't 'overact' because that's what you imagine soap actors do. If you can see past all the stylized music and overdramatic storylines in soaps, you'll find that many of the actors on these shows are actually doing some solid acting work.

Audition Pre-Requisites

As with the film roles, this is a very general overview of what **some** CDs take into account when selecting actors to audition for each type of role. For roles under 21(ish), previous credits are often not as important as the quality of the actor's demo footage and representation.

TV Co-Star

This is the entry-level position for TV shows. For co-star roles, CDs are willing to take risks and pre-read actors with few or no credits. The shows need new faces and the pressure of saying two or three lines isn't all that huge, even for an inexperienced actor. Many CDs and associates will pull headshots from their workshop and showcase files for these auditions, and will try to see between ten and thirty actors for these roles.

TV Guest Star / Recurring

Most offices read between eight and thirty actors for each guest star role. To be called in for a guest star role, an actor usually needs to have a few co-star or (preferably) guest star credits under their belt. Recognizable film credits also factor in. On network shows, the main guest star role in each episode is often cast by an offer to name or industry-known talent before auditions are even held.

TV Series Regular

Ironically, it can be easier to get a series regular audition than a guest star au-dition. CDs are given more time to cast series regular roles, so they're often able to see literally hundreds of actors. These auditions are mostly given to actors with solid representation, but if your rep has a good relationship with the CD and pitches passionately, most CDs will see you (or at the very least request a self-tape).

When a series regular role isn't cast with a celebrity, live audition sessions are held and casting watches hundreds of self-tapes received from top agents around the world. Often, even well-known actors still need to audition, as the competition is fierce.

HOW COMMERCIAL AUDITIONS ARE BORN

Let's say the CEO of *Company X* wants to make a new commercial for *Product X*. The marketing department of *Company X* puts out a brief, inviting advertising agencies to have their creative writers pitch a campaign for *Product X*.

Within each advertising agency, there are a number of producers working full time. Once a campaign is selected, the chosen ad agency assigns a producer to the project who hires the director, crew, and CD.

The producer gives the 'storyboard' (like a comic book strip) for the ad to the CD, who then puts the breakdown out to agents and managers. The CD figures out what type of actor the director, producer, advertising executives, marketing department, and owners at *Company X* are picturing for each character. She then goes through the headshots and selects the most suitable actors to audition.

Usually, hundreds of actors are auditioned for each role, so the producer and director of most commercials look through the auditions almost as though they are a pile of headshots. As you 'slate' (state your name and height), the producer and director decide whether you look and sound right for the part and whether you have the essence they're after. If you don't, many of them skip to the next actor before they even watch your audition.

The structure of the commercial casting process means that auditioning for commercials is even more of a numbers game than auditioning for TV and film. It's about being called in for the right role at the right time and being exactly what each of those five or ten aforementioned decision makers had pictured. It's then also about doing a strong audition on the few occasions you are actually right for the part.

WHO MAKES THE FINAL CASTING DECISION?

Independent Films

The producer hires the director on most film projects. A director makes many decisions throughout the production process, but as an employee of the production company, these decisions can almost always be overruled. How much authority a director wields on a project is subject to many variables: past experience, celebrity status, involvement in writing the script, contribution of investors to the project, the social status and relationship dynamic between the producer and the director, and lastly how much the producer chooses to micromanage each aspect of the film.

When it comes to casting, a collaborative discussion usually occurs between the CD, the director, and the producer regarding which actor fits best for each role and how various actors would fit with others in the project. For independent films, the director usually makes the final decision on which actors are cast. Most producers will give the director freedom in this area but can at any point dispute or simply overrule the director's casting decision.

Often, casting decisions can be a case of bargaining between a producer and director, for example if the director and producer have strong opinions on two different actors for each of two roles, they may say "I'll let you have *actor x* for *role a* if we hire *actor y* for *role b*".

Occasionally, investors will interject on casting decisions and if their financial contribution is substantial enough, the producer and director might do what they say. If celebrity attachments are required, sales agents, distributors, and investors may need to approve bankable name cast attachments.

Studio Films

On a studio film, the freedom a director has with casting often depends on his notoriety. Lead roles are cast from a list of celebrities pre-approved by the studio and financiers. For the support roles, the director makes a selection for each role, then the producers and studio executives watch the audition tapes, discuss, and review the decisions. If the studio disagrees with a casting decision, they can overrule the director. They may ask for the next few choices, or simply decide who must be cast.

Network TV

In network television, a different director is hired for each episode of the show. This means that as a guest employee of the show, he does not hold the same level of authority as the producers, executive producers, writers, and network executives who work on it full time. While the network does try to give the director freedom to make casting decisions, a director's choice may be overruled by any of the aforementioned permanent decision makers attached to the show.

WHERE TO FIND AUDITIONS ONLINE

Breakdown Express

BreakdownExpress.com is the main casting service in LA, where top CDs list almost every professional film and TV role. It is used to notify agents of projects that require both electronic and hardcopy submissions, and averages between forty and ninety new breakdowns (projects) per day. These breakdowns include feature films, shorts, theatre, webisodes, TV episodes, and commercials. Breakdown Express is inaccessible to actors, and can only be viewed by registered managers and agents for around $450 per month.

The Breakdowns

Any time a role is listed on any casting service, it is referred to as being released on "the breakdowns".

The term "the breakdowns" is also used in reference to a rumored .pdf document illegally sold and emailed to actors around LA each night. This document apparently contains a comprehensive summary of all projects and roles released on BreakdownExpress.com that day.

Showfax.com

A Showfax.com membership gives you free submissions through the Actors Access section of Breakdown Services, plus the ability to download audition sides and upload e-cast audition videos for free.

Self Submission Websites

On the following sites, professional and amateur breakdowns are listed for projects that encourage actors to submit themselves. There are always many short films, webisodes, and lower budget feature films listed. Don't submit on ANY projects if you are unable to attend the audition. **Especially not if you are outside of LA or overseas without a USA work visa.**

ActorsAccess.com

Actors Access is part of Breakdown Services. When listing a project on Breakdown Services, the CD is offered the option of listing the breakdown on Actors Access. If the CD selects this option, the breakdown becomes available for all actors to submit through the Actors Access website, rather than it just being available for agents and managers. You can submit to an unlimited number of projects for free on Actors Access if you have a paid up Showfax.com membership.

NowCasting.com

Now Casting is an online casting service on which breakdowns for a number of independent projects are listed. The site also lists some bigger budget film and TV auditions. I obtained the majority of my auditions when I first came to LA through this site.

LaCasting.com

LA Casting is mostly utilized by commercial CDs, but many indie films and TV series are also listed on the site. Some actors and CDs find the interface a little tricky to use, and it costs money every time you change your main profile photo or add additional photos. Commercial actors are all expected to have active profiles on this site so their representation can submit them on the listed projects.

Backstage.com

Backstage lists auditions in LA and is mostly used by independent filmmakers who aren't using a CD to cast their project. The 'Backstage West' section of the Backstage.com website lists projects on the 'West Coast' (California).

LetItCast.com

Let It Cast is an audition submission website that allows you to tape and upload your own auditions for roles that match your type..

Cazt.com

Cazt is an audition facility that gives casting directors free space to run audition sessions. In return, they enable actors with memberships to watch and share auditions and upload a replacement audition if they aren't happy with it. The Cazt website also lists auditions for projects casting at the facility.

CastingFrontier.com

Discussed in the commercial section, Casting Frontier allows actors to self-submit on commercial and print castings.

WHERE TO GET YOUR AUDITION SIDES

CDs either email audition sides to your agent or post them online to be downloaded. Represented actors should never pay to download sides because it is free for registered agents and managers. However, if it is after hours and your rep hasn't gotten the sides to you (or if you are unrepresented), you may need to download them yourself.

Showfax.com

Showfax.com is one of the main resources for audition sides because the website is part of Breakdown Services (the parent company for BreakdownExpress.com). You can search for sides either by project type and name, or by using the 'sides code' (which should be in your audition email and on the original breakdown). Sides cost anything from a dollar to ten dollars per download, but are free with a current Showfax membership.

SidesExpress.com

Using Sides Express requires a username, password, and (if applicable) a 'sides code'. It's expensive to get sides from this site, so always check Showfax.com first.

ScreenplayOnline.com

Scripts on this site require a 'script code' to download. This is partly to ensure TV plotlines and feature scripts are not revealed to fans by bloggers. If you are not a member, it costs around $10 to download a film script. Ask your representation or (if you are unrepresented) the casting associate to email you a copy rather than paying the fee.

A TYPICAL HOLLYWOOD AUDITION

There is no 'typical' Hollywood audition. What I am about to describe is an amalgam of the common denominators that have recurred throughout the hundreds of auditions I've attended in LA.

An audition is like a first date: everything is amplified. Filmmakers imagine if you're great in an audition you're going to be AMAZING on set, and if you're nervous in an audition you're going to be a total wreck on set.

Firstly, you MUST keep your sides in your hand during an audition. Even if you know all of your lines, hold the pages anyway because in Hollywood there is rarely time to start over if you lose your place. The CD won't offer for you to do a line run prior to the audition. You must be ready to tape when you walk into the room, and know that you'll probably only perform the scene once.

You'll usually have one or two days to prepare for TV auditions, and two or three days for film. The amount of prep time varies with every audition. Sometimes it can be as fast as your agent saying "You have an audition . . . now. Pick up the sides when you get there", which is why you ALWAYS answer the phone when your agent or manager calls. Other times, you might have a week or more to prepare.

If the audition is on a studio lot, **you'll need a valid ID** to get past security. The security guard at the gate will give you a guest pass and a map and tell you where to park and where the audition is being held. You may be given a 'walk on' pass (rather than a 'drive on' one), which means you must park outside the studio lot and walk through the gate on foot. On some studio lots, the audition room is a solid ten-minute walk from the parking area through a maze of sound stages. When budgeting your time, assume that it will take twenty minutes to get from the studio entrance gate to the casting office.

When you arrive at an audition, check how many actors are ahead of you on the sign-in sheet. It doesn't matter if you need to run lines or do makeup touchups, check first, as the wait time can sometimes be over an hour. If you need more time and there's no wait-time, you can always choose not to sign in until your allocated time.

Always bring a headshot with you. Often, the associate or assistant will ask for your headshot before walking you into the audition room. Don't be surprised if you get to the room and it's tiny; most audition rooms in LA are the size of a small bedroom.

Once inside (if no one introduces you) introduce yourself, but don't offer to shake hands unless they reach for yours first. Some casting offices don't use a camera, but most do. Walk to your 'mark' (a piece of tape on the floor about two meters in front of the camera) as soon as you're in the room . . . the CD is just going to tell you to do this anyway. Any conversation you have can be had from there while the camera operator frames the shot. If there is no mark, walk to where it should be. If there is a chair on your mark, but you were planning to stand, simply ask "Would it work for you if I stand, or would you prefer me to sit?"

There may be anywhere from one to ten people in the room watching your audition. There are usually two casting staff members running each session: an associate, and either the CD or an assistant, depending on the size of the role and the structure of the casting office. From this point on I'll refer to the senior casting staff member as the CD (although it may be an associate).

At a callback or producers session, the director and/or producer(s) might be present. On some projects, the director and producer are in the audition room during the first round of auditions. The CD usually asks whether you have any questions, and may have you 'slate'. When you slate, there is no need to say anything more than your name unless the CD specifically asks you to. After you slate she'll say something to the effect of "Whenever you're ready", and you'll go into the scene.

After your first read, the CD may simply thank you and that will be it. Say a sincere and general "Thank you" to the room with a smile and leave. Don't take it personally if the CD doesn't redirect you or ask anything further after your audition; often there isn't time. Most actors I know have booked roles just as often from auditions in which they were not redirected as auditions in which they were. I know that only doing one take feels anti-climactic after working on an audition piece for so long, but sometimes the decision makers only need to see it once.

When you leave, make sure you have everything with you; it's never fun having to go back into the room to get your handbag. I usually leave my belongings in the waiting room with the other actors or the assistant at the desk. Stay confident until you are in your car and driving away as some casting offices have a view of the street.

Here's the most important step of all: You've done the audition, now FORGET ABOUT IT. It's done and there is nothing you can do to change it. Definitely analyze and learn from it. If you want to run it over in your mind or talk it through with a friend do it on the way home, but before you get out of your car take a deep breath, accept that what's done is done, and let it go.

AUDITION ETIQUETTE

The problem with writing about audition etiquette in LA is that each CD has different (and often conflicting) opinions about auditioning. The CSA (Casting Society of America) has no rules (nor should they) for audition protocols in LA, so every casting office has unique expectations.

The goal in any audition room is always to get in, do your job, and get out. That's it. You don't have time to waste and neither do the CDs. You want the people in the audition room to remember you for your acting, rather than for that lengthy excuse you gave for being late. Be relaxed, friendly, charismatic, confident, brief in your responses to any questions, show them your take on the character, thank the CD, then leave.

Some of the suggestions that follow may seem arbitrary or obvious, but each is important. It is not worth going through all of the trouble of moving to LA, getting a visa, getting an agent, getting to know the CDs, submitting for auditions, learning your lines, and working the character only to walk into the audition and make some basic etiquette error that could lose you the job. Your goal is to come across as a focused professional who understands appropriate behavior on and off set.

Audition Do's

Book the Room, Not the Part
Auditions are as much about forming long-term connections as they are about getting the part. The odds of booking each role are slim, and many factors come into account that have nothing to do with your acting ability. Many working actors do thirty or forty auditions for every role they book.

Most casting directors cast thousands of roles throughout their careers, and part of their job is to remember talented actors. At each audition, show the CD you are prepared, professional, and talented so they see that even if you aren't right for this part, you are a reliable actor who may be right for future roles.

Learn Your Lines

Some actors say it is unnecessary to know your lines for each audition. This is ridiculous and unprofessional. If you have more than a couple of hours before your audition, why on earth wouldn't you know your lines? Do you think when they were starting out Cate Blanchet or Meryl Streep would go to an audition without knowing their lines? I doubt it. I have run audition sessions, and the professional actors almost always know the words. The actors who consistently book jobs are those who put in the work. No one is going to look at you fumbling through the scene and think "I can picture her being really good at this if only she knew her lines".

When you audition, treat it as though you are going to work on set. The performance should be as polished as you can get it in the time you have. Anything less and you are wasting everybody's time. I've heard actors say "I'll learn the lines when they are paying me." Good for them. Let those actors waste their lives doing sub-par auditions for a few years, and watch as they leave town empty handed. Don't let lazy actors influence you to throw away your opportunities.

> **TIP:** When you get an audition, tape the other character's lines into a voice recorder (e.g. the 'voice memos' function on your phone), leaving silent gaps long enough for you to say each of your lines. Then you can use this virtual scene partner to run lines with you as many times as you like!

Be Prepared: Do Your Homework

The most important thing to a CD is that actors prepare for every audition. More than just learning the words, being prepared means you have really thought about the scene, the character, and the character's intentions. Make strong choices about how the character would behave in this situation. Find out the pronunciation (at HowJSay.com) and meaning of words, phrases, or names you don't know.

For film auditions, you are expected to have read the full script unless you only have a few lines. For TV auditions the script is rarely available, but you should have watched a few episodes of the show (most are available online). Read the crossed out and 'FYI' sections of your sides (if any exist) to understand what happens before and after your scenes.

Know the Style of the Piece

After reading the script, watch previous works of the writer, director, and attached celebrities to get a feel for the tone and pacing. When you watch previous episodes of a TV show, analyze the energy, intensity, and pacing of actors in roles similar to yours.

With comedy, see if it is the series regulars or the guest cast who have all the punch lines. In watching the show, you may find that most of the guest roles are simply there to set up jokes for the series regulars without drawing attention by being too funny. Or it could be the opposite, with the lead character as the 'straight man' and the guest cast as quirky caricatures.

Know Who You're Reading For

It's rude to apply for a job when you don't know whom you're asking to hire you. Know the CDs name. Look them up online. If possible, look up the director, writer, and producer so you are familiar with their previous work. If an opportunity arises, mention if you liked one of their past projects or enjoyed reading the current script. Say this briefly and honestly so it doesn't sound like sucking up. When it is sincere, recognizing and complimenting a fellow artist on their work is a sign of respect and professionalism.

Bring a Headshot and Resume

I know the CD has your headshot on file. I know your agent sent her one when he submitted you. I know you're famous in South Africa. Does that mean the CD always has your resume handy when you come in to read? No. Hardcopy headshots are being phased out, but for now, unless you are told otherwise, always bring a stapled headshot and resume for the CD.

Often, the associate will bring your resume to the CD prior to your audition to review your credits. CDs and filmmakers often spread out the headshots of the strongest contenders after an audition session while they discuss who felt right for each part. Without your shot, how will they re-member to pick you? Your headshot is your main marketing tool so make sure you have it with you at all times.

Play Well with Others

Be nice to the assistant, reader, camera operator, receptionist, and other ac-tors at the audition. Often the person you are reading with will actually be a CD. On low budget films, it may be the producer or director. The person at the front desk answering phones may not be an assistant; she could be an-other CD in a shared office, or the partner or boss of the CD you're reading for. If you're disrespectful to her (or to any of the other actors in front of her) you can be sure she'll mention it to the CD.

Be nice to everyone . . . they're all just doing their job. So if you have to wait or if there's a mix up, don't take it out on the girl walking people into the room. Understand that she is doing the best she can, and be nice!

Keep the Accent of the Character

I have learned this lesson too many times not to enforce it as a rule. When auditioning with an accent, NEVER talk in your real accent until your audition is finished. ALWAYS SLATE IN THE SAME ACCENT AS THE CHARACTER. This is NOT negotiable.

Never lie about where you are from. If they ask, say you're from Australia (or wherever) IN YOUR CHARACTER'S ACCENT (preferably with a cheeky smile).

If they specifically ask to hear your 'normal' accent, it is (of course) fine to oblige them and talk in your real accent. It would be odd for a CD to ask this prior to the scene, especially with filmmakers in the room.

Once the audition scene is done, it is your choice whether to keep the character's accent or drop back into your natural voice . . . many actors and CDs disagree on which is the better approach but most agree that you should always keep the accent until you finish the scene.

Read the Vibe of the Room and Let the CD Lead

There is no standard for how long the conversation should be before you perform your audition. Each room will be different, with a different CD, director and producers... all of whom have had a different day today than the last time you read for them. When you walk in, be acutely aware of the tone of the room.

You're there to work, not to make chit chat or entertain the audience, so let the CD lead the conversation. If she asks you questions, pay attention to the energy with which she asks. If she seems rushed, get straight to the point. If she seems relaxed, be more conversational in your responses. Either way, try to be friendly, engaged, and BRIEF.

Be Directable and Open to Change

Following direction is one of the most important skills an actor needs. Don't rehearse the scene the same way too many times, otherwise you may get stuck in the 'choices' you've made and have trouble being redirected in the room. Often a CD will redirect an excellent audition simply to test whether an actor is able to take direction.

One way to be open to direction is to play the scene at home a few different ways: once happy, sad, angry, laughing, and any other way you can think of. Even doing a 'speed run' (where you say the lines as quickly as possible) can help. This will prevent you from being stuck in one reading, and can often surprise you by revealing new ways to say a line organically.

Keep Your Sides in Your Hand

Even when you know the scene or only have a few lines, hold the sides. CDs have countless stories about actors who think they know the lines, so they don't bring the sides into the audition. When the actor subsequently forgets the words, it becomes a time wasting debacle to find the pages.

Also, when some directors or producers see an actor audition without sides, they think they are seeing a polished performance and that it is the best the actor can do. When the actor holds sides, it reminds the filmmaker they are watching an audition that is a fraction of how good the actual performance could be. Besides... when there are no props, it's nice to have something to hold onto.

Only Ask a Smart Question

Most CD's ask whether you have any questions before you begin the scene. If you have a smart question, ask it. If it's a question with an obvious answer, find the answer before you go in there. Try to stick to just one question.

Questions that reveal you have not researched the role include: the pronunciation of words that are in the dictionary or the series regular character's names, querying the style of a TV show (unless it is a pilot), anything that implies you haven't read a feature script, and any other questions that you could have found the answer for. Of course, if you haven't done the work and need to know the answer to one of these questions, ask . . . just know that it may imply a lack of preparation.

Smart questions include the pronunciation of oddly spelled names or things you couldn't find online, or for TV auditions "What happens next?" or "What happened just before this?" Questions about the director's image of the character are fine, or even "Does my character turn out to be the killer?" Most questions are okay as long as they imply you've done your homework and really thought about the scene.

If you're not sure which accent they're after or how strong it should be, have your rep find out prior to your audition. Often this information can be diluted in translation, so it's fine to confirm accent details in the room.

Be Easy to Work With

How personable and easy to work with you appear can be as important as your acting ability. The director will be on a film or TV set with you for days, weeks, or even years, so he will ask himself "Is this someone with whom I could spend three months of my life?" In the words of Tom Mc-Sweeney "Just be cool" and put a likeable, confident energy into the room.

Smile When You Come Into and Leave the Audition

When you smile at someone their brain releases endorphins, which makes them feel happier and drop their defenses. People who smile appear to be friendly and easy to work with. Remember, there's a big difference between a relaxed, confident smile and a desperate grin.

Schedule Ninety Minutes for Each Audition

If you are scheduling several auditions in one day, allocate ninety minutes from the time you park your car to the time you get back into it. This will prevent those awful times when the session is running behind and you have to ask to be bumped ahead so you can get to your next audition. That isn't fair on the ten other actors patiently waiting their turn.

If you have two auditions scheduled close together and are not able to change either, the sneaky approach is to just show up to the first one a little early (no more than thirty minutes without approval). CDs usually audition in order of who signed in first, not who was scheduled first, and most CDs won't mind if you're a little early.

If possible, have your rep find out what the 'window' is (what time the session runs from and till) so you know how early (or late if approved) you can show up. If you do need to arrive more than thirty minutes early or ten minutes late, please call your rep so they can notify the CD.

Audition Don'ts

Don't Smoke Before or Wear Strong Perfume to an Audition

This is the number one 'pet peeve' mentioned by CDs in LA. Casting spaces are often small. Respect that the audition room is the CD's working environment and she has to be there all day. If you wear strong perfume or smoke before you go in, it will stink up the room and the CD will not appreciate it, especially if she is allergic. In the same vein, be aware if you have BO or bad breath and remedy the situation.

TIP: Avoid wearing black, white, stripes or bold patterns to an audition as they do not look good on digital footage.

Don't Dress in Costume, But Do Dress 'To Suggest'

Dress in the vein of the character, not as the character. Do not audition for a fireman role in a fireman uniform, but at the same time don't wear gothic clothing. Wear something a fireman would wear (like jeans and a t-shirt), not the actual uniform. Seriously . . . why would you have a fireman uniform if you're not a fireman? It's odd. Just dress with the energy of the character and let your acting speak for itself. This applies to doctors, cops, and any other uniformed characters.

Don't Bring Props

Feel free to bring a (switched off) cell phone, pen, folder, glasses, or any small item you might already have with you to auditions. Anything else is not okay. You would not believe the things actors bring into auditions: entire kits of props to 'create' a scene. It's a complete distraction from your acting, and it takes time to set them up. DO NOT BRING PROPS!!! Definitely NEVER bring weapons of any form, not even fakes.

Don't Shake a CD's Hand Unless She Offers

Don't initiate any form of physical contact. This is not because CDs think they're better than you. It's because after a CD has caught a cold every single month for a year or two, she begins to realize that people's hands are not always clean. CDs see hundreds of people a week and the chances are pretty good that a few of those people are either sick or coming down with something. The CD is not being rude; she is protecting her health. If she offers her hand, shake it. If she doesn't, don't offer to shake hers.

Don't Say You "Just Got the Sides"

Most of the actors I know in LA (including myself) can memorize four or five pages of dialogue in an hour or two. You are going up against professionals who audition several times a week and are always off-book. If you cannot get off book in the time allocated, your 'cold reading' skills should get you through.

If you have more than twenty minutes with the sides, you should be familiar with each beat in the scene and have made specific choices for the character. Limited time with the material is no excuse. There is no handicap in this business. **What you do in the room is your audition.**

Giving excuses implies to CDs you are not a professional actor and you can't work on your feet. On soaps, the writers often appear with a rewritten version of your scene twenty minutes before you shoot. On one film, I was given seven brand new pages of emotional, intense monologue at 9PM and told the scene was to be filmed at 7AM the next day. This sort of thing happens often. You must come across as someone who can adapt quickly to changes. An actor who complains that she "only got the sides this morning" does not project that level of confidence.

Don't Apologize

If you were late, the CD probably doesn't know about it. If you don't think the scene went well, don't tell the people in the room! People are very easily convinced. If a director liked your work, but you say "Sorry, that wasn't very good", you may cause him to rethink his opinion. To apologize for your work isn't ever going to help you and it certainly won't make anyone think you can do better. Don't apologize. Once the work is done, let it be.

Don't Say "I've Prepared the Scene Two Different Ways".

This implies that when you're on set you may not be able to make a clear choice about what you want to do with the part. In television, the director doesn't have time to talk you through the scene; you need to arrive on set ready to perform. MAKE A CHOICE, be confident and strong in that choice, and show them what you can do. The director or CD will tell you if they want it done another way.

Don't Try to Sell Yourself

In many industries, pressure selling works. Not in an audition room. If the CD doesn't have any questions when you finish an audition, thank them and leave confidently. You either got the job or you didn't. Any credits or special skills you want to brag about should be on your resume. It's easy to talk yourself out of a job, so don't risk it by trying to make conversation.

Don't Touch the Reader

If there is a kiss or a fight component within an audition scene, ask the CD "How would you like me to play the action?" The reader is there to deliver your dialogue, not to be threatened, punched, kicked, scared, kissed, or in any way manhandled. Keep your hands to yourself.

Don't Show Any 'Naughty Bits' Unless Forewarned
It is inappropriate for a CD to request to see you topless in an audition unless the actors were warned in advance. Even if the project requires full nudity, they should only need to see the top half nude; the rest can be seen in underpants.

Ensure the CD has previous casting credits. Avoid nudity in auditions that do not come through your representation and for non-union projects. If it seems legitimate, the assessment should only take a couple of seconds, and if the director or producers are there, there's no reason for them to run the camera. For females, a woman should be present in the room at all times. NEVER sign a release form at an audition, but this is even more important if they somehow record you topless.

Even if you agreed to do it prior to the audition, **you can still always say that you'd rather not.** You never have to do anything you don't want to do until it is written into your signed contract (and even then there are exceptions). If you don't want to strip down in an audition, you are not being difficult or obstinate you are simply respecting your own boundaries. Any CD worth working with will respect this and wont hold it against you.

NEVER Talk About Anything Bad That Happened to You
Before the Audition
Nothing that happened before the audition matters once you're in the room. Don't mention that you're paying six dollars an hour for a parking spot that it took you thirty minutes to find, and that you've been in the waiting room for an hour after sitting in traffic for two. The CD certainly didn't plan it that way just to ruin your day so there is really no need to mention it to her.

If you come into the room with a negative attitude, the CD may think you will complain on the job and bring down the tone of the set. I mean, really, if you can't wait an hour in an air conditioned waiting room without complaining, how are you going to wait around for twelve hours a day on a noisy, busy, uncomfortable film set? If you really have to vent, call your best friend after you leave the audition, I'm sure they'd love to hear all about it.

The Fine Line Between Professional and Desperate
See the fine lines in the approaches? Dress LIKE a fireman but not AS a fireman. Use available props (like pens or glasses), but don't bring a whole

prop kit. Learn all your lines but keep your sides in your hand, because a professional actor knows that sometimes you forget a line no matter how well you know them, whereas a novice tries to impress the room by showing she doesn't need her pages.

All these things are about walking the fine line between putting in enough effort to be a professional, and putting in too much effort by dressing up the performance because you don't have faith in your ability.

The more effort you appear to be putting into the external stuff, the less faith you appear to have in your talent. When you arrive with props, costumes, and too much conversation it can feel like you're trying to distract from a sub-par performance . . . like your acting talent isn't enough.

When auditioning, there is a point at which preparation and hard work end, and desperation begins. I believe this point is when you focus too much on anything other than THE ACTING WORK. If you believe in the quality of your work, you won't need all the bells and whistles.

Trust your talent and let the work speak for itself.

Actors Who Won't Audition

When actors have done a substantial amount of work, there are certain jobs they will not do, and some jobs they will not audition for. Some actors only accept certain roles if they are 'offered' the part without auditioning. This is a tactic commonly used by actors with substantial credits in order to seem less 'available' and more of a valuable commodity.

Refusing to audition and claiming to be "offer only" causes many actors to lose perfectly good roles. Even if the actor is a celebrity, the director often needs to see their take on the part before offering it to them. If you want a part, be willing to audition for it. Directors are appreciative and humbled when a reasonably well-known actor is willing to come in and audition. This show of respect can often be the deciding factor when a director is choosing between two 'known' actors for a role.

When *Lord of the Rings* was casting, Elijah Wood was a known working actor and celebrity. With his childhood fame, he was most likely an 'offer only' actor for many projects. When he heard about the role of Frodo Baggins in *Lord of the Rings*, he is rumored to have gotten a camera and a hobbit costume and gone up a mountain to film an audition for the part. They had the audition sent to Peter Jackson, and the rest is history. No matter who you are, it sometimes takes a little humility and effort to get yourself to the next level.

NETWORK TESTING

When auditioning for series regular roles on TV shows in the USA, there are several levels to the audition process.

- Pre-read
- Audition
- Callback
- Producer's Session
- Network Test
- Chemistry Read

At any point, new actors may be added who have not attended previous stages of the audition process, similarly, some actors may skip some levels. Actors who send tapes from other countries are typically flown in directly to the network test or chemistry read stage.

A Typical Network Test

Prior to testing, you will have already negotiated and signed your 'test deal', which is your contract for the pilot and subsequent episodes of the show.

There isn't really a 'typical' test. One Aussie actor was called in at 9am to work through the scene with the director and get notes on his audition. He left for a few hours then returned at 1pm for the actual test. Sometimes, you'll just attend your test appointment as though it were any other audition.

Once you're brought in, there are typically twenty to forty people in the room. It's very impersonal and there is rarely conversation at the start. You simply enter, and begin reading when asked. You go from one scene to the next, with no re-direction, they thank you and you leave.

The test is taped and sent to any network execs or producers who could not be present at the test, including the president of the network.

They don't always make it easy. At another test, for example, the actor didn't even know where the reader was until the scene began and a voice came out from amongst the executives with his cue line.

Chemistry Read

After this point, the selected group is usually reduced to two or three actors and a chemistry read is done with one or two of the other leads in the series to see how the actors play off each other. The chemistry read tends to be much more relaxed, with only the director, casting staff, and a few producers in the room. The actors are able to play and improvise and each scene is often done several times. The session is taped and sent either in addition to or instead of the tape from the network test (executives want you to look good so they will only send the best tape they have).

PROCRASTINATION

I have an audition tomorrow for a role opposite Jennifer Anniston. What am I doing? I'm writing this book. Why? After spending much of the week not writing the book, I decided that right now it is imperative to jot down a few paragraphs. Why now? Well, because I have an audition of course.

Why is it so hard for us actors to focus on our work? What is it about putting a hundred percent effort into a piece that scares us so much? I think many actors have a fear of doing their absolute best and still being rejected, so they cheat themselves by not doing the work.

When you catch yourself procrastinating, think of the hundred roles you submitted for and didn't get a shot at, the thousand actors who submitted for this role and didn't get the audition, and the thousands of actors around the world who are potentially right for this part but didn't even get submitted. When you have an audition for a film, you have something that literally millions of other people around the world would love to have, so don't take it lightly. Do the work. I'm going to do some myself right now.

SELF-TAPED AUDITIONS

Self-taped auditions have been used around the world for years but have only recently become a major tool in the casting process. Self-taping means you tape your own audition and the video file is sent to the CD. I have personally booked several TV and film roles from self-tapes, and these auditions should be considered as legitimate as any that you do in the room.

How to Create a Self-Taped Audition

If you are given specific taping instructions, follow them. If not, here are some basic guidelines for self-taping:

Use a Blank Background

The background should always be a blank wall (preferably light blue or grey, but any solid color is fine). For lack of a wall, hanging a clean, ironed bed sheet will suffice. You may use a plain chair if it is necessary for the scene. There should be NO furniture, books, props, etc. visible in the shot. An audition should never be shot or edited like a real scene.

Camera

Use a HD camera. Standard definition will record less detail, which will make the viewer feel less connected to your performance. There are many reasonably priced HD cameras. A cheap Flip HD™ camera, iPhone, iPad or any pro-sumer camera are all fine choices. Invest in a tripod; even a small one makes all the difference.

Lighting

The lighting should be neutral but strong. Watch the footage back to check this. Look out for shadows, especially under your eyes. Ensure your face is evenly lit and the light doesn't wash out your skin. I highly recommend purchasing a lighting kit with two fluorescent (cooler in summer) umbrella or softbox lights. Mine is an RPS Studio Dual Rectangle Folding Softbox kit (with 300 watt fluros), which cost around $160 from Sammy's camera.

Framing

Frame the shot from your chest to the top of your head. Ensure that the camera is at the same height as your face so that it doesn't have to angle down or up in order to shoot you.

Slate

Most casting offices prefer a quick verbal slate at the beginning of each self-tape. If the CD hasn't requested anything specific regarding the slate, state your name, role, and height: "I'm Kym Jackson, reading for [the role of] Hannah, and I'm five-seven". Any other relevant information is made fairly obvious from the file name and title of the video. Note: some offices like slates with a 'mid-shot' (from the waist to the top of the head), whereas others prefer a close up on your face. Generally, either is fine.

Reader

Ensure your reader is a strong actor without a thick accent. Using a bad actor or one who talks too loudly can distract from your performance and ruin the audition. Have the reader stand right next to the camera so your 'eye line' (where you're looking) is ten to twenty centimetres from the camera.

Tail Slate
The CD may ask you to do a full body shot after your audition. This means widening the frame to show from your feet to your head, then turning to the right and to the left to show your profiles.

Do I Use a Title Card?
A title card is not necessary unless requested.

File Format
The most commonly requested format is a QuickTime file, which has the extension '.mov'. Compress the file to under 100MB, otherwise it may take a while to download and might not be viewed. When exporting, 640×480 VGA is fine and be sure to check the box to preserve the aspect ratio.

How Should I Send My Video File?
If the file is small enough (under 25MB), send it via email. If the file is too large to email (most are), upload to Hightail.com, WeTransfer.com, or one of the other websites for sending large files. CDs often receive download links and it will rarely be an issue.

Another option is to upload the video to Vimeo.com. Give the file a password, and send the link with the file password in the email.

E-Cast
E-Cast is a service through ActorsAccess.com, where CD's request self-taped auditions to be uploaded to the site. This saves the CD from having to run a live audition session and allows actors in other cities to audition for roles. The site charges actors for each audition upload, but if you have a current Showfax.com membership uploads are free.

Services for Taping Auditions
There are companies with a room and camera set up to tape video auditions for actors who are unavailable to audition live for a role. You can find them online in the HSG resource guide.

CHAPTER 6

ACTING UNIONS

On March 30th 2012, SAG and AFTRA (the two main screen acting unions in the USA) merged to become SAG-AFTRA.

Prior to the merger, SAG (The Screen Actors Guild) represented actors in television, motion pictures, commercials, industrials, video games, and all new media formats. AFTRA (American Federation of Television and Radio Artists) represented performers in television, radio, sound recordings, industrials, internet and digital programming.

With the digital revolution, the two unions found themselves competing for projects, weakening the bargaining power of both. By merging, the one union can now negotiate with solidarity for all performers and ensure they lock in the best possible contract terms and pay.

Protecting and Supporting Actors

SAG-AFTRA's main priority is to protect and support members of the union. Artists in every medium are taken advantage of regularly. We love our work so much we are willing to put up with a great deal in exchange for an outlet and a chance to show people what we can do. Actors in non-union projects around the world regularly find themselves working in sub-par conditions, not paid by producers, having no residual payment structure in place, and myriad other negative situations spawned from the powerlessness of standing alone.

SAG-AFTRA is a vital governing body dedicated to fighting for actors pay rates, timely payments, residuals, treatment on set, and many other rights to which actors are entitled. By standing together in this strong union, actors are protected from those few filmmakers who may not be so forthcoming or willing to follow through on promises.

If Registering a Project with SAG-AFTRA Empowers Actors, Why do Filmmakers do it?

If a project is not registered with a union, a SAG-AFTRA actor is not allowed to perform in it. Hence, to use SAG-AFTRA actors (almost every celebrity and working actor in LA) a filmmaker must register their project with the union.

Joining SAG-AFTRA

Joining the union can be difficult but this degree of difficulty is what gives such great meaning to being a union member.

The 'Taft Hartley' paperwork a CD or producer must fill out to sponsor a non-union actor into SAG-AFTRA for a project has very specific requirements. While most are approved, if the situation doesn't qualify the submission may be denied by the union. This might garner a fine or force the CD to recast the role at the last minute.

Many CDs are therefore reluctant to audition non-union actors for SAG-AFTRA roles. Consequently most agents are reluctant to represent a non-union actor. Therefore, without SAG-AFTRA membership or eligibility, seeking quality representation and getting professional auditions in LA can be challenging.

The solution: Become 'SAG-AFTRA Eligible'. There are three main ways of becoming eligible to join the union:

• Vouchers
• Taft Hartley
• Union transfer

Definition: 'Principal Performer'

The term 'principal performer' refers to an actor being hired under a 'principal performer' contract, which is essentially any credited role in a film or TV production. An actor hired on any project is either a principal performer or an extra.

Principal performer roles are usually speaking roles. Sometimes, if a non-speaking role requires extreme emotion or specific talents, the actor will be credited and paid as a principal performer rather than an extra.

Principal Performer Taft Hartley

If you are lucky enough to be cast as a principle performer in a SAG-AFTRA film or TV project (other than 'ULB') as a non-union actor, the CD or the producers must fill out a 'Taft Hartley' form. This form essentially states that the production has fully explored the talent pool of union actors and none of them fits the role as perfectly as you, so it would hinder the project if the producers were unable to use you.

The Taft Hartley requests that your status become 'SAG-AFTRA Eligible' and permitted to work on the project. This seems to happen more often on commercials than in TV, and more often in TV than in film, but it does happen at all levels and in all types of SAG-AFTRA projects (except 'ULB').

Vouchers (Extra Work)

Many actors join SAG-AFTRA by doing extra work. The membership is the same whether you join as an extra or an actor.

When a feature film is being produced under a SAG-AFTRA contract, the producers are obligated to hire a certain number of SAG-AFTRA extras. Here's how it works: Say a film needs two hundred extras and according to their union agreement, fifty of those extras must be members of SAG-AFTRA. The other hundred and fifty extras hired will be much cheaper non-union talent.

Here's where your opportunity to join the union opens up: Out of the fifty SAG-AFTRA extras, let's say five don't show up. The film is legally bound to hire fifty SAG-AFTRA extras but they're on a tight schedule. Where are they going to find five union extras of the right type to come to set within minutes? They're not.

When a SAG-AFTRA extra doesn't show up for work, a non-union performer may take their place and their pay voucher. The name printed on the voucher is crossed out and your name is written in its place. Your pay is increased from the non-union rate (around $75 a day) to the union rate (around $148 a day), and you take that voucher.

The people who control the vouchers are 'third ADs' (third assistant directors, AKA 'second-second ADs' on some projects). The third ADs know every non-union extra on set wants a voucher, so be friendly and when a voucher comes up, they may offer it to you. This will be more likely on bookings lasting several days or weeks when you have time to develop a relationship with the ADs.

When the production submits the paperwork to SAG-AFTRA, they fill out a 'background performer Taft Hartley form'. You need THREE vouchers to become eligible. Once you are eligible, you can join the union at any time for an initiation fee of $3,000 . . . plus $198 per year in base union dues payments. SAG-AFTRA Federal Credit Union offers a 24 month 'Initiation Fee Loan' to aid actors in joining the union.

Sister Union Transfer

There are some unions that SAG-AFTRA considers 'sister unions'. Members of sister unions are automatically able to become SAG-AFTRA eligible if they have been members for a minimum of one year and have worked at least one day as a principal performer (speaking role) in a project under that union's jurisdiction. SAG-AFTRA sister unions are: AEA, ACTRA, AGMA and AGVA.

Upgrading Status from Non-Union to SAG-AFTRA Eligible

Once you work three days as a background performer or one day as a principal performer, the production company sends your payment information to the SAG-AFTRA offices and the Pension and Health Fund. It generally takes thirty to forty-five days for your eligibility to be automatically approved. You can check this either by calling SAG-AFTRA or visiting SAGAFTRA.org. This process can be rushed by mailing or dropping off your paystubs. Call SAG-AFTRA for details.

Staying SAG-AFTRA-E (SAG-AFTRA Eligible)

SAG-AFTRA guidelines prohibit members from working on non-union films anywhere in the world. Staying eligible without joining until you must allows you to continue working in non-union films until you become a 'must join' (an eligible actor who 'must join' a union prior to beginning work on their next project with that union).

Once eligible, your union status can be written on your resume as either 'SAG-AFTRA' or 'SAG-AFTRA E'. Tactically, it may be wise to only include the 'E' on your resume when attending non-union auditions. Some TV CDs avoid hiring actors whose status is 'eligible', because they have been burned by 'must join' actors not paying their joining fee prior to a shoot.

When this occurs, the production is fined and the casting office may be held responsible.

Upgrading from SAG-AFTRA Eligible to SAG-AFTRA

Please confirm this with SAG-AFTRA as details and rules may have changed, but here's how it was explained to me (by a union rep): Once you become eligible, you have thirty days in which you may work as many SAG-AFTRA jobs as you like. After that thirty-day period, when you book another SAG-AFTRA job, your status is updated to 'OK Thirty', which means you have *another* thirty days in which you are able to work on as many SAG-AFTRA jobs as you like.

After *that* thirty-day period, you can stay eligible until you book your next union job. At this stage, you become a 'must join', which means you must pay your joining fee and join the union **prior to** starting work. If you do not join SAG-AFTRA before your first shoot day, you and the film production become a 'Station Twelve' and the production is charged a fine. If you are eligible but not a must join, you are free to join the union whenever you like.

Rule One

Working on a non-union film as a union member is a violation of SAG-AFTRA 'Rule One'. If SAG-AFTRA finds you violating rule one you may be removed from the union permanently (though I've never heard of this actually happening). Being kicked out of the union would be detrimental to your acting career because most of the substantial film and television work in the USA is SAG-AFTRA.

Financial Core

Going 'Financial Core' or 'fi-core' in any union essentially means you are saying "I am part of the union because I have to be, but I don't believe in what the union stands for, so I'm going to work on non-union jobs too". When actors are fi-core they don't tend to publicize it as most industry folks and SAG-AFTRA members feel that it weakens the union. Fi-core actors (dues paying non-members) cannot write SAG-AFTRA on resumes, head-shots, electronic submissions, or websites.

Financial core actors can work on non-union and union films whilst re-maining members of SAG-AFTRA. You give up your physical SAG-AFTRA card and pay a reduced set of dues 'voluntarily' from that point onward. It is rumoredly difficult to get back into the union after going fi-core.

To avoid going fi-core, some SAG-AFTRA actors secretly work on non-union films under fake names. I strongly advise you to stick to the rules of the union. If SAG-AFTRA were to find out about you working on a non-union film, the union would be within its rights to permanently terminate your membership. This would completely impair your ability to have a successful film or TV career in the USA.

Honorary Withdrawal

If you are a SAG-AFTRA member not working on any SAG-AFTRA projects and can't afford your dues, avoid ending up in 'bad standing' with the union by applying for 'Honorary Withdrawal'. This means that if you're not working, you don't have to pay any dues until you get a job.

If you get a job within a year of going on honorary withdrawal, you will be asked to back-pay all dues that you would have had to pay since changing status. However, if you don't work on any SAG-AFTRA jobs for longer than a year after going on 'Honorary Withdrawal', you won't have to pay any 'back dues' when you finally reinstate your membership. If you get residual checks during your honorary withdrawal that would have raised your dues by more than $5, you will have to pay the difference (but not the base dues).

There is no stigma attached to honorary withdrawal and no judgment will be passed on you for doing it. It's likely that no one will even know. Just log in to the SAGAFTRA.org website and click on your user name in the top right hand corner. In the 'my info' page, click 'request inactive status' and a union rep will call you.

SAG-AFTRA Regional Joining Reduction

If you have a postal address in a State that is under the jurisdiction of a regional SAG-AFTRA office (e.g. Louisiana, Alabama, Mississippi) you can join the union for a reduced regional rate.

> **TIP:** If you are slack at paying your membership on time, make sure you at least pay it up to date from September to February each year. This is because free film 'screeners' (DVDs) are mailed out to all paid-up SAG members during awards season.

Even if the job from which you gain your eligibility is NOT in a regional location, you can still join through one of the regional offices, as long as you live in that region. Once you have joined regionally, if you book a job in a non-regional area like LA or NY, you'll be expected to then pay the rest of your joining fee.

Healthcare

One of the major benefits of being in SAG-AFTRA are the two healthcare plans that respectively kick in after earning a minimum dollar amount or (for SAGph only) working more than 76 days in the previous calendar year.

SAG-AFTRA is working on a system that will enable actors to select which P&H fund each paycheck is allocated to. This would help more actors to qualify for pension and health benefits because their earnings could contribute to a single fund (rather than being split). Details are at SAGph.org and SAGAFTRA.org.

AFTRA Minimum Yearly Earnings for Healthcare Coverage
Individual: $10,000
Family: $30,000

SAG Minimum Yearly Earnings for Healthcare Coverage
Plan 2: $15,100 or 76 days worked
Plan 1: $30,750

Global Rule One

Any production shot overseas with a SAG-AFTRA member in it must be covered by the 'Global Rule One' contract. This contract requires that the production pay actors the SAG-AFTRA codified basic agreement rates and has many stipulations regarding how union actors are treated and housed.

Under Global Rule One, non-union actors can be hired in principle performer roles without union memberships. The irony is that working in a principle role on a SAG-AFTRA Global Rule One project has no bearing whatsoever on a non-union actor's eligibility for union membership.

Projects produced internationally wanting to hire a SAG-AFTRA actor, must talk to a SAG-AFTRA signatory rep and sign a memorandum. The production must follow the rules and pay rates of the SAG Global Rule One agreement, but only for SAG-AFTRA members working on the project.

SAG-AFTRA FEATURE FILM CONTRACT CATEGORIES

Any project that utilizes actors in the USA is either 'union' or 'non-union'. SAG-AFTRA has several contract categories designed to govern feature films according to their budget.

Any film longer than eighty minutes is considered feature length. If a film tells a story by using actors in a narrative format (as opposed to documentary), it is a feature film.

On the next page are two terms used in most SAG-AFTRA contracts.

Diversity in Casting Incentive

The modified low budget and low budget SAG agreements include a clause that incorporates a 'diversity in casting' incentive. This incentive increases the maximum budget allowed for a project to qualify under each contract category.

The incentive applies if at least 50% of the cast *and* 50% of the total days of employment are made up of members of the following four protected groups (these are the official contractual terms): 1) women, 2) persons over sixty, 3) disabled people, 4) 'people of color'. In addition, at least 20% of the total days of employment must be cast with 'people of color'.

In English: if a film hires certain minorities, it can have a bigger budget but may still qualify to pay actors the lower pay rates usually only allowed for lower budget films.

Extras Daily Minimum

Many agreements require a minimum number of SAG extras to be hired before the film is allowed to employ non-union background talent.

Following are the SAG-AFTRA feature film contract categories (some figures increase annually; all are current at date of publishing). Please visit SAGAFTRA.org for current pay rates and contract terms.

Codified Basic Agreement

This agreement covers any studio funded feature film or independent feature with a budget too high to qualify for the theatrical low budget agreement.

Budget: Anything above $2.5 Million
Diversity In Casting Budget: Anything above $3.75 Million

'Scale' Daily (8hrs) Rate: $859
'Scale' Weekly Rate: $2979

Hire Non-Union Principal Performers? No. Must be 'Taft Hartleyed'
SAG-AFTRA Extras Daily Minimum: 50 performers

Theatrical Low Budget Agreement

This agreement is for productions filmed entirely within the USA (with an intended theatrical release) that fall within the following budget range:

Budget: $625,000–$2.5 Million
Diversity In Casting Budget: $937,500–$3.75 Million

Daily (8hrs) Rate: $504
Weekly Rate: $1752

Hire Non-Union Principal Performers? No. Must be 'Taft Hartleyed'
SAG-AFTRA Extras Daily Minimum: 30 performers

Modified Low Budget Agreement

This agreement is for productions filmed entirely within the USA (that may not have distribution secured) that fall within the following budgetary range:

Budget: $200,000–$625,000
Diversity In Casting Budget: $200,000–$937,500

Daily (8hrs) Rate: $268
Weekly Rate: $933

Hire Non-Union Principal Performers? No. Must be 'Taft Hartleyed'
SAG-AFTRA Extras Daily Minimum: 3 performers

Theatrical Ultra Low Budget Agreement

This agreement is for productions filmed entirely within the USA. Films of this size rarely have a theatrical release secured at time of filming, but (as with the other contracts) the payment to actors for projects under this contract DOES include theatrical distribution. Therefore, if the film hits theatres your pay does not automatically increase, however, if it is released in another medium you will receive residuals.

Budget: $50,000–$200,000 (excluding deferrals)
Budget: Up to $500,000 (including deferrals)
Daily (8hrs) Rate: $100

There is no weekly rate for work at this budget level. There is also no increase in payment for working a 6th or 7th day, or any pay bump for holidays. There is no diversity in casting incentive for films of this budget.

Hire Non-Union Principal Performers? Yes.
Non-Union Principal Talent Daily Rate: $100
SAG-AFTRA Extras Daily Minimum: None. All extras may be non-union.

Daily Pay Rate Note: *The 'Daily Rate' for each SAG-AFTRA project listed covers an eight-hour workday. Since most film sets work twelve-hour days, you usually end up being paid your day rate plus four hours of overtime (at time and a half), which works out to be another 75% of your daily rate. On a $100 per day film, for instance, a typical twelve-hour shoot day will gross you around $175.*

SAG-AFTRA Short Films

A short film must be under thirty-five minutes in full run time and have a budget less than $50,000 in order to qualify under the 'SAG-AFTRA Theatrical Short Film Agreement'.

If the film runs longer than thirty-five minutes, the budget exceeds $50,000, or principal photography lasts longer than thirty days, the film is automatically classified under the Theatrical Ultra Low Budget Agreement (for feature films).

Budget: Up to $50,000
Run Time: Up to 35 Min

Shoot Duration: Up to 30 Days
Daily Rate: $100 (this may be deferred)

There is no weekly rate for this budget level. There is also no increase in payment for working a 6th or 7th day or any pay bump for holidays.

Hire Non-Union Principal Performers? Yes
Non-Union Principal Talent Daily Rate: Not Specified
SAG-AFTRA Extras Daily Minimum: None, all extras may be non-union.

New Media Agreement
Projects of any length that are planning an initial release online may be produced under the new media agreement. There is no minimum pay requirement for new media projects so all actor fees are negotiable. If the project secures a TV or film release after that time, producers must pay residuals to the performers based on the applicable contracts for that medium.

What is 'Scale'?
'Scale', is the standard daily or weekly rate for a freelance performer working under a SAG-AFTRA contract. It is most often used in reference to the rates paid under the Codified Basic Agreement for films or the full rate for a SAG-AFTRA TV show. This rate increases by 2% each year.

Pay rates are often negotiated in multiples of scale. A working actor may have a minimum pay rate quote of 'double scale' or 'triple scale'.

Quote
Most working actors have a quote for film and a quote for TV. A 'quote' is the minimum amount of money an actor expects to be paid per day or week of work (or per job), rather than being willing to work for scale.

To get your first quote, your representation must push for you to be paid more than scale on a job. Once this happens, it is logged into 'Studio System' (a private industry database similar to IMDb) that you were paid a certain quote, which sets a precedent for what you should be paid on future jobs. Part of your reps job is to try to push each new project to pay your quote or a higher rate, which raises your official quote.

No Quote
If you have an official quote from previous jobs but you book a network or studio gig that refuses to pay your quote, MAKE SURE it goes into Studio System as a 'no quote'. Your agent and manager should know to do this, but

double check just to be safe. Your quote is based on what you were paid for your last job, so if you work for less your quote drops to the new pay figure. A 'no quote', ensures you keep your quote from the previous job.

UNDERSTANDING RESIDUALS

SAGAFTRA.org defines residuals as "compensation paid to performers for use of a theatrical motion picture or television program beyond the use covered by initial compensation".

Principal performers receive residuals; background actors do not. You will not receive residuals for an initial release; you are paid residuals when the project is sold in markets other than the initial intended market.

So, if a SAG-AFTRA film is made to be released in theaters, actors do not get residuals when the film comes out in theaters. This is because the initial paycheck already included a release in that 'media market'. The residuals are paid when that film sells in another media market, including DVD, VOD, cable, TV or new media. For TV episodes, your initial paycheck covers the first airing and residuals are paid on subsequent airings.

When Are Residuals Paid?

SAGAFTRA.org/content/residuals-faq states "For TV work, residuals begin once a show starts re-airing or is released to video/DVD, pay television, broadcast TV, basic cable, or new media. For film work, residuals begin once the movie appears on video/DVD, basic cable and free or pay television, or new media."

When Will the Check Arrive?

Residuals are sent to SAG-AFTRA and processed for up to sixty days before being sent to the actor. SAGAFTRA.org/content/residuals-faq states the following regarding when residuals are due to SAG-AFTRA from each production:

When are Residuals Sent to SAG by the Production

"For projects made for TV then released to:
• Network TV, non-network TV—30 days after air date.
• Syndication—4 months after air date

- Foreign free to air—up to 30 days after producer obtains knowledge of first foreign telecast and never later than 6 months after that first telecast
- Basic Cable—Quarterly when the producer receives revenue
- Supplemental Markets—4 months after initial exhibition, then quarterly

For projects made for theatrical then released to:
- Network Prime Time—30 days after initial broadcast, then quarterly when the producer receives revenue
- Free TV, Non-Network—4 months after initial broadcast, then quarterly when the producer receives revenue
- Supplemental Markets—4 months after initial exhibition, then quarterly when the producer receives revenue"

Commercial Residuals

Commercial pay cycles run for 13 weeks. Payments are sent directly to the actor or representation, NOT to SAG-AFTRA. If the commercial is not a 'buy out', residuals are owed for each airing.

Pay rates for each airing are on a sliding scale, ie: the 'cost per airing' is much higher for airings #1–#10 than for airings #50–#60. This continues until the cycle maximum (3000 airings). If the production company wishes to continue using the commercial after the 13 weeks, the pay rate scale resets and they must pay for each airing from the top of the pay rate sheet. This is known as a 'roll over' as the commercial 'rolls over' into the next payment cycle, and a nice shiny new check arrives in the mail.

Cable TV

Payment **for all intended airings within a cycle** is due 15 days after the date the commercial first airs. This first air date is considered the beginning of the first 13 week cycle. The next payment is due 15 days after the beginning of the 2nd cycle, and so on for every cycle.

Network TV

Network TV residuals are based on a 7 day payment period, running from Monday to Sunday. Whatever airs within those 7 days is due 15 days after the first Sunday following the initial airing of the commercial. The next payment is due 7 days after the following Sunday for all usage within that week, and so on. Although payments are being made every week, the payment rate sheet still resets (rolls over) after each 13 week cycle.

SAG-AFTRA SISTER UNIONS

ACTRA (Alliance of Canadian Cinema, Television and Radio Artists)
Website: ACTRA.org
ACTRA is the Canadian union for film, radio, and television performers.

AGMA (American Guild of Musical Artists)
Website: MusicalArtists.org.
AGMA is the union for workers in musical performance, including opera, dance, concerts, and even production staff in the musical field.

AGVA (American Guild of Variety Artists)
Website: AGVAUSA.com
Wikipedia.org gives this definition: *". . . an American entertainment union representing performers in variety entertainment, including circuses, Las Vegas showrooms and cabarets, comedy showcases, dance revues, magic shows, theme park shows, and arena and auditorium extravaganzas. It awards the 'Georgie Award' (after George Jessel) for variety performer of the year. There is some overlap between the jurisdictions of AGVA and Actors' Equity".*

OTHER UNIONS

AEA (Actors Equity Association National)
Website: ActorsEquity.org
Equity is the theatre union. Equity theatre productions must pay cast members, and are bound by the rules of the union with paid rehearsals and enforced break times, etc. Essentially, Equity does for theatre what SAG-AFTRA does for film and TV.

DGA (Directors Guild of America)
Website: DGA.org
The DGA represents over 14,000 directors in the USA.

WGA (Writers Guild of America)

Website: WGA.org

The WGA represents screenwriters in the USA.

I.A.T.S.E.

Website: iatse-intl.org

I.A.T.S.E. is the union for some crew departments, (including transport and casting) in the USA and Canada. I.A.T.S.E. has a 'Mutual Assistance Pact' with the Teamsters.

International Brotherhood of Teamsters

The teamsters is the union for drivers and other labor workers. Wikipedia states: ". . . this union now represents a diverse membership of blue-collar and professional workers in both the public and private sectors."

AMPTP (Alliance of Motion Picture and Television Producers)

Website: AMPTP.org

The AMPTP represents over three hundred and fifty producers, TV networks, and studios in the USA. Whenever unions like SAG-AFTRA, DGA, or WGA are renegotiating contracts it is with the AMPTP.

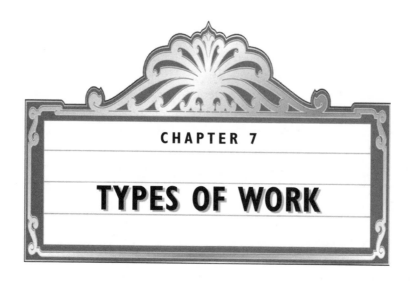

CHAPTER 7

TYPES OF WORK

There are many mediums and categories of projects in which your acting talent can be utilized. I'd like to briefly discuss each of the most common types of projects available for actors in LA:

- Studio feature films
- Independent feature films
- Short films
- Short features
- Television

- Local hire work
- Webisodes
- Commercials
- Extra work
- Theatre in LA

Note: The run time of a project is estimated at one minute for each scripted page. Many executives will not read feature film scripts shorter than 80 or longer than 125 pages because feature films require a run-time of between 80 and 120 minutes in order to more easily gain distribution.

UNION VS. NON-UNION PROJECTS

When a producer registers a project with SAG-AFTRA, it becomes a 'union' production. The project is assigned a contract type based on the size of the budget, and the production must follow all terms of that contract type.

There are union contracts for almost every type of salable project involving actors: features, TV, short films, webisodes, commercials, radio, etc.

Union productions almost always have bigger budgets, which improve the salability and quality. Actors prefer union jobs because most offer better pay than non-union gigs, plus guaranteed break times, warm meals on set, better facilities (e.g. trailers) and they must have production insurance.

If a project is non-union, producers don't have to pay, feed, house, or even give reasonable breaks to the actors. You are essentially on set of your own accord and there is no mediating authority to call if things go wrong.

Non-union films cannot hire celebrities except the few who are financial core. In order to sell a film to distributors, hiring recognizable actors is important. In addition to the lack of celebrities, the talent level of actors on many non-union films tends to be less than impressive. Solid acting is one of the most vital components of a great film, so if you are working opposite below-average actors, your scenes (and the project) will suffer.

Production Insurance

All union projects must have production insurance, and many non-union projects do not. If you trip and break your face on set the 'production company' should be liable, however, that entity (the LLC under which the film is being produced) may not actually have any money to pay your medical bills. When you are on a film shoot without production insurance, you are fully accountable for anything you agree to do because if you get hurt, you're probably going to be the one stuck with the bill. Avoid working on projects that don't have production insurance.

STUDIO FEATURE FILMS

As the name implies, **a studio film is partially or wholly financed and/or produced by a film studio.** This means that in addition to producers being involved in the decision making processes, studio executives also have a say on things like casting, script changes, and allocation of funds.

By definition, a 'film studio' is simply a large production company that has its own hard equity (actual money), and is capable of distributing and advertising its own projects worldwide.

The major studios are Disney, Warner Bros, Universal, Paramount, Dreamworks, Fox, and Sony. A 'mini-major' is a film studio that produces fewer projects, often works with smaller budgets, and functions on a smaller scale in most areas than the major studios. Mini-major studios include Summit, Revolution, Lakeshore, Lionsgate and the Weinstein Company.

A major studio won't usually produce or finance films with budgets under $20 million. Most studios have smaller independent arms that make projects with budgets from $6 million to $20 million. The mini majors will also work in the $6 million to $20 million range. You won't often find a film with a budget lower than $6 million being produced by a studio. A studio may come on board to *distribute* the film, but it would be rare for them to be involved in the financing or production of a project that small.

Not every film with a budget over $20 million is a studio film; there are some anomalies. For instance, Oliver Stone produced 'Alexander' for around $160 million dollars without the backing of a studio. This would therefore be considered an independent film regardless of the size of its budget.

Any time you can get a role (even a one liner) in a studio film, take it. It's big bucks, big residuals, big connections, great demo footage, and will look fantastic on your resume. The first studio film I did was in 2001. I had one line (it was cut), and I've since made over $20,000 in pay and residuals for four days of work. Even now, the residual checks keep arriving in the mail.

INDEPENDENT FEATURE FILMS

When a film is not studio financed, it is considered to be an independent film. Independent filmmakers raise their own money through friends, independent investors, crowd funding, financing companies, government funding, tax incentives, personal loans or even maxing out credit cards.

Knowing the budget and union status of an independent feature can give you insight into the quality the finished film. In the last chapter, the financial and contractual requirements of the various SAG-AFTRA contracts were listed. Following is a generalized description of a typical project from each budget category. Note that any film produced under any of the SAG-AFTRA low budget contracts is independent. All studio feature films must be produced under the SAG-AFTRA codified basic agreement.

Non-Union Feature Film (Budget is usually $5,000 to $150,000)
Daily Rate: $0 and up

Non-union feature films can be any budget, even millions of dollars, but this usually isn't the case. Non-union features are often unpaid and the majority don't even get a DVD or Direct TV release. Most are only watched by friends of the cast and crew, and audiences at a few obscure film festivals.

Rare anomalies like *Blair Witch*, *Paranormal Activity*, or the Asylum films are some of the few non-union movies actually securing a visible release. If I had a choice between a role in a non-union feature with an average script or a role in a well-written student thesis short film, I'd choose the thesis short in a heartbeat.

SAG-AFTRA Ultra Low Budget ($50,000–$200,000)

Daily Rate: $100 / 8hrs

The 'hundred dollar a day' jobs are the ones LA actors love to hate. SAG-AFTRA ULB projects are usually average scripts with maybe one 'familiar face' (actor who looks familiar but most people wouldn't know their name) attached. They are often genre films because the actors willing to attach on such low budgets are usually not bankable enough to garner even a DVD release without the niche market of a genre film audience to sell to.

Most of these projects are released straight to DVD, iTunes and Netflix. You should be treated well on the set of any SAG-AFTRA project, but in this budget range you may find yourself working with a first time director and a less experienced crew. This can be a challenge when trying to do your best acting work. While playing a lead role on any film, you may miss out on studio film or network TV auditions or gigs. Most ULB projects shoot an average of twelve hours a day for six days a week over three or four weeks, so many working actors avoid shooting them during pilot season.

When starting out it can be tempting to agree to any paid feature roles, but on such small budgets, it is even more important to be selective about which projects you attach to. Be wary of doing too many horror pieces as a mass of low budget genre films can devalue your 'brand' and make you appear to be only worth $100 a day. Consider the title of the film; playing the lead in *Vampire College Sluts 2* probably wont add value to your resume.

In saying all of this, NEVER reject a project based on the budget. Some amazing films are made under ULB contracts, and with today's digital cameras, many look as professional as any studio film. Make the quality of the cast, crew, script and character your deciding factors rather than the money.

SAG-AFTRA Modified Low Budget ($200,000–$625,000)

Daily Rate $268 / 8hrs

A $200,000 to $625,000 budget is nothing to scoff at . . . that's enough money to buy a house in the Valley. Usually at this budget the production has enough money to do decent rewrites on the script and attach a few DVD-worthy names. While it's not likely to get you famous, the film will almost definitely secure a DVD, VOD, Direct TV, iTunes and Netflix release, and may be screened on a cable network like Lifetime or Sci-Fi.

TV stars and up-and coming actors often attach as leads in films at this budget level. These films often only budget to pay for one or two known leads and can't pay overscale for supporting roles. This means new actors have a good chance of booking a solid support role earning reasonable money on a decent project with a professional cast and crew.

SAG-AFTRA Low Budget ($625,000–$2.5M)
Daily Rate: $504 / 8hrs

Most projects in this category will have pre-sold DVD rights to at least a few 'territories' (essentially countries) to secure finance. The film will almost definitely get a DVD, VOD, Direct TV, iTunes and Netflix release and maybe a limited theatrical or TV release. These films are generally well written and made, and most will have a recognizable name or two attached.

A note specific to dramas: It's hard to secure financing over $2.5M for a dramatic film even with celebrity attachments. Therefore, many of the best independent dramatic feature films are produced within this budget range. Many of these films have scripts impressive enough to convince crews, actors, and celebrities who usually work on bigger budget projects to take a pay cut in order to work on a passion project.

SAG-AFTRA Codified Basic Agreement ($2.5 million and up)
Daily Rate: $809 / 8hrs

The union status of these films is simply listed on the breakdowns as 'SAG-AFTRA', whereas films under other contract categories specify the full name of the SAG-AFTRA contract type. At this budget, a bankable top celebrity is almost always attached to secure finance. All studio feature films, and almost every American film that gains a wide theatrical release is produced under this contract.

SHORT FILMS

The definition of a 'short film' varies. According to SAG-AFTRA a short film is under thirty-five minutes, the Academy of Motion Picture Arts and Sciences caps short films at forty minutes, and IMDb defines them as shorter than forty-five minutes. Most run between three and fifteen minutes. Money is rarely made on short films, so for a filmmaker the purpose of making one is generally to:

- Tell a story that is too short to write into a feature
- Learn how to make a movie by actually doing it
- Use as a sample to secure interest and finance in a feature project
- Act as a reel or demonstration project for those working on the film
- Enter into a specific contest or festival
- Enter into festivals and gain industry familiarity for those working on the film
- Enter into festivals to win awards or money
- Sell to a short film compilation DVD
- Put online for free and gain public attention for those working on the film
- Post onto a website that pays per hit or per view
- Make a political or religious statement
- Create a film for class as a student short filmmaker

TIP: Marty's 'Never Work For Free' Policy

You're a professional, which means acting is your job, not your hobby. When my mate Marty was starting out, he created a foolproof system that will ensure you never work for free as an actor. For every project, make the producer give you a dollar. Simple. Sounds silly, but it's about switching your mindset to guarantee that you'll never act for free again.

Not all short films are created equal, so I'm going to highlight the fundamental differences that may save you from doing fifty unusable amateur short films rather than selecting two or three high quality festival winners. There is a huge difference between a short film being produced by a group of kids shooting their first film and one being produced by industry professionals working on a passion project.

As you read the VERY generalized short film definitions that follow, know that ANY type of short film can win an academy award, and ANY type of short film can be awful. It is important to assess each project based on its merits, not its type.

Actively find and participate in shorts that DO have the potential for success. These projects can lead to great exposure and further work as an actor. Research the director and watch their previous projects. Find out what camera the project is being shot on. A solid script is vital. If you can find the quality projects, performing in short films is a fantastic starting point for any actor.

Unpaid Non-Student Short Films

The percentage of unpaid short films that are successful on the festival or commercial circuit is tiny compared with the number left un-viewed on filmmakers bookshelves gathering dust.

The footage in many amateur short film projects is lit, shot, and scripted so poorly that it's unusable on your demo. The other actors may not be talented, and in many cases the filmmakers won't give you the footage at all. In saying that, some of these films come out amazing, so take the time to assess the project before making any decisions.

Student Short Films

Students receive thousands of dollars worth of free equipment from their university, so student films often have a higher production value than independently produced shorts. Some universities require that students pay the actors, but the majority of these films are unpaid.

Most of the students in film school want to be producers or directors, but must work in crew positions on each other's films, which means you're meeting between ten and twenty aspiring producers and directors on each shoot. These future filmmakers are paying good money to be at film school and are being marked on the piece, so most take it very seriously. Students are likely to spend weeks perfecting the script, editing the finished project, and entering film festivals around the world.

There's a category of student film called a 'thesis project', which is the final project shot by a film student before graduating. The quality of a student thesis project will generally reflect the fact that it's being made by a student who has just gone through several years of film school. Students involved in thesis projects are usually experienced enough to be proficient in each crew position on the set, which makes for smoother shoots and higher quality films than most non-thesis projects.

When selecting student projects in LA, make sure you target schools with strong track records and a high quality of previous work. I'd recommend submitting mainly for AFI, USC, UCLA, Chapman University, LA Film School and New York Film Academy. Many actors agree that projects produced by these schools have bigger budgets, more professionalism, and students with a higher likelihood of entering the workforce than the lesser-known schools. You can also contact the school if you're having trouble getting footage as students are obligated to provide you with a copy of your work.

Aim to work on student films that are registered with SAG-AFTRA. If they've registered with the union, it's more likely the students are planning to run a professional set and treat the actors well.

Professional Short Films

The production value on financed short films is often higher than that of low budget indie features. For example, a $100,000 feature may go for a hundred minutes, meaning production spends $1,000 to produce each minute of footage. A $20,000 short may only go for five minutes; meaning production spends $4,000 per minute of footage. In theory, this means that while the credit from the short may not look as good on your resume, the footage from the short should look four times better on your demo.

Check the section "Selecting Short and Independent Film Work" (see below) for tips on what to look for in film projects.

A Note on Short Films

Throughout your career, make time to work on high quality short films as often as you have the time . . . just hedge your bets by selecting projects with good scripts and experienced directors.

Short films are a great training ground and a way to get free footage for your demo. Short film sets are a valuable place for networking, doing what you love, staying on your game, and maintaining good on-set habits. Break your comfort zone in short films by trying characters you wouldn't usually play, or practice new voices and accents. Chances are very few people are going to see the project anyway, so why not learn from it and have fun?

Short films are the foundation projects for most filmmakers and actors, many of whom frequently revisit these mini-movies throughout their careers. Short films can be beautiful and touching pieces of art and cinema, which is why there is an academy award for 'best short film'.

Many actors gain representation and bigger roles based on a short film performance, and many filmmakers secure multimillion dollar studio deals based on the merits of a single short film. I would rather be in a great quality short film than an average quality feature any day.

SELECTING SHORT AND INDEPENDENT FILM WORK

Once you have performed lead roles in around five projects at a given 'level', it's wise to become more selective when considering future projects at that level. This is because you no longer need the credit and experience alone. Your focus will be on the quality of the project and role, how much fun it will be to work on, and the size of the paycheck.

Even when working on projects with higher budgets than you're used to, there are good reasons to refuse a role (like nudity or a morally questionable message in the film). Never accept a role that crosses the boundaries of what you're willing to do on camera.

Three Film Assessment Questions

Aim to walk away from each film project with good networking contacts, a strong credit, great footage, and the potential for success commercially or on the festival (or awards) circuit. Find answers to these three questions before doing any independent film:

• Who is attached to the project and what have they done before?
• What is the visual style of the film (eg. camera, lighting, shooting style)
• Is the script likely to turn into a good film?

When the cast or key crewmembers attached are talented, the shooting style sounds appealing and appropriate for the piece, or the script is well written, go for it.

Project Factors to Assess

Following is a more detailed look at the main factors to consider when deciding which projects to sign on for:

Script

Nothing matters more in any film or TV project than the script. If a film is brilliantly written, it could be shot on the director's cell phone and audiences will still respect it. I request a full script before every film audition regardless of the budget.

Occasionally a production is not willing to provide a script for the actors. This may happen if your role is just a few lines, the filmmaker is paranoid, or if it's legitimately a high security project (like a comic book adaptation or other studio financed project).

Assessing a script is as easy as reading and seeing whether you find the story engaging. If it is a comedy, ensure that it makes you laugh as you read it. If it is dramatic, ensure you are invested in the characters and consistently wanting to know 'what happens next' as you read. **If the script is hard to read, the film will likely be hard to watch.**

Role

A great actor in a great role is a great actor in a great role regardless of the rest of the script. If you love the character, your dialogue is great, and the actors you're opposite are talented, even a project with a below average script might be worth doing just to play that part. There are three main reasons for this: Firstly (duh), you get to play with and explore an amazing character. Secondly, if it's shot well you'll be able to use the footage for your demo. Thirdly, no matter how bad the film is, you just never know who might end up seeing it.

Union Status

If you're in SAG-AFTRA, you are only allowed to work on union films. If you're non-union, you should still aim to be involved in union projects because all actors on set are usually treated according to SAG-AFTRA guidelines regardless of their union status. Non-union actors can play 'principal roles' (speaking parts) in SAG-AFTRA Ultra Low Budget films.

Attachments

If name actors or experienced key crewmembers are attached, a project might be worth doing simply for the sake of networking and exposure. The bigger the celebrity attachment, the more likely the film is to get wider distribution. Plus, getting footage of yourself opposite a celebrity is a massive bonus for your reel.

Shooting Format / Camera

Films shot on film or HD (most films are) are more likely to produce high quality usable footage, which means they'll look much better on your reel, and be far more likely to gain distribution and critical acclaim.

Director / DP Previous Works

Watch previous work of the director and 'DP' (Director of Photography; see section: "Crew Definitions") to see whether they create the type of projects on which you want to work. It's unlikely (though it does happen) that a director or DP is going to get progressively worse with every film, so if you liked their last project, the next one will probably be even better.

Location

I would attach to just about any project if it were shooting in Hawaii, Brazil, or Australia (where my parents live). Remember, you are in this industry because you love it. If you are offered a job in an exotic location spending several weeks overseas getting to know a bunch of people who share your passion for film, you're probably going to have a blast. Unique life experiences are as important to your depth as an actor as any acting class could ever be.

Beggars Can't Be Choosers

Don't get too picky too soon with attaching yourself to projects, because it can be wise to gain a certain amount of experience working at each level before moving onto the next. I did around fifty short and independent films before coming to LA, and I learned, broadened my network, and improved my craft from working on every single one.

When you're starting out, do as many films as you can . . . for free if you need to. Each film is a free class in working on a film set, and will familiarize you with the terminology used and behavior that is required on set. Let's say that a film acting class would cost twenty dollars an hour. That means that every day you work for free on a film, you're saving two hundred dollars in 'on-set training' fees.

Unless you book a network or studio lead role straight out of the gate, building a film career is all about stepping-stones. Be prepared to work your way up from the bottom through the middle to the top (and hope you get to skip a few steps on the way!). The quality of a project is so much more important than the size of the budget so look for great concepts and always read the script before saying no (or yes!) to any project, no matter what size the paycheck is.

I still gladly work in very well-written low budget jobs because I absolutely LOVE being on set. I think it's like summer camp for grown-ups. You get to hang out with a bunch of cool (and often attractive) people who are being paid to do what they love. You eat for free every day, get your makeup and hair done, and every now and then (maybe three out of every twelve hours) you actually have to get up and do some work (which isn't really work because you love it).

SHORT FEATURES

Something about the math on all this isn't adding up . . . If a short is under forty-five minutes, and a feature is over eighty minutes, what is a film that runs between forty-five and eighty minutes? Well, the honest answer is: it's pretty much screwed.

It is really hard to do anything commercially or on the festival circuit with a film that is sixty minutes long. It's too long for short film festivals, too short for feature film festivals, and definitely too short to be released to the public on DVD or at the theatres. In short (ahem . . .), it doesn't really have a chance of doing anything . . . other than entering those few festivals with a 'short feature' category, or those willing to screen a short feature to fill gaps in the schedule.

Artsy filmmakers will say that a film should be "as long as it needs to be to tell the story". Good for them . . . that doesn't mean anyone is going to see it. The irony is that if the director is that passionate about 'the artistic integrity of their story', they are probably going to make a wonderful film.

For the sake of having great footage for your demo, you should probably jump at the chance to make a film with someone of that mindset. As far as anyone other than your family and friends seeing the film, however, I'd say the odds are not too good. In saying that though, there are no rules in Hollywood, so you never know . . . that short feature film you just shot might end up being the next big breakout success!

Ultimately, a great script is a great script and a great filmmaker is a great filmmaker regardless of the medium. If you truly care about your craft, nothing matters more than these two things. Not even a silly little thing like a short feature film.

How to Spot a Short Feature

Any film script that is between forty and seventy pages long (unless it's a TV pilot in disguise) is likely to end up being a short feature. Be aware of it and (if you're curious) ask about the intended run time for the project. At least then you'll know what you're getting yourself into.

TELEVISION

One television guest or co-star credit can have more impact on LA agents, managers and CDs than several (yes, even lead) credits from little-known independent feature films. Even if your goal is to work solely in film, gaining a few substantial television credits will give you access to better representation and consequently, better film auditions.

Film was once the most glamorous medium in which an actor could work. This was because shooting on actual film stock was expensive, so any feature film was automatically assumed to have a substantial budget. While studio feature films are still highly respected, digital cameras have now

Note: Once you work on a TV show you usually can't come back to play another role on that show. This is one reason some more experienced actors refuse to do co-star roles on TV. If you have a number of recent (in the past two years) guest star roles on your resume, your credit list is unlikely to be improved by adding a co-star credit.

enabled so many films to be made cheaply that an actor booking a feature length film is not considered the massive achievement that it once was. The credibility of a movie now depends on the budget, the director, who was in it, and what type of release it got. Some films with big budgets and A-list celebrities don't even get a wide theatrical release in the USA.

By contrast, network television now has production value on par with some studio films. TV offers actors consistent money and exposure with scripts that are meticulously developed and being brought to life by top level cast and crew. Existing TV shows also come with an inbuilt fan base who quickly attach to new regulars on the show.

Stepping Stones

People often believe an acting career is one in which there is no clear path to success, but this is not the case. Most working actors move up through the ranks step by step. Sometimes an actor may skip a few steps, (like when an actor with no credits books the lead in a series or feature film) but for most, there is a system and television credits allow this system to be very clear.

- Co-star
- Guest star
- Recurring
- Series regular

Once an actor has done four or five comedic co-star roles, CDs are more willing to audition her for a comedic guest star role. Once an actor has done four or five comedic guest star roles with one or two that have recurred on a show, networks are much more open to using her as a comedic series regular on a show. For drama, the same rules apply, but dramatic CDs take comedic credits into account also, whereas comedic CDs (while noting dramatic credits) much prefer to see comedy credits and training.

All of this comes back to building trust, and what could prove more conclusively that you are trustworthy than proficiently performing roles in high paid, high pressure, high profile projects? Keep in mind, having top rep can allow you to skip some of these steps because you have the reputation and connections of someone at the top of the industry behind you.

Network TV

The term 'network' is a reference to the major TV networks available 'free to air' (free to watch) in the USA. The major networks are CBS, ABC, NBC, Fox, Lifetime, Hallmark, Sy-Fy, and the CW. Shows on these networks are highly respected because a large audience is watching these few channels and timeslots. Also, most network shows have bigger budgets and better pay than cable shows because the larger audience brings more advertising dollars for the network.

Cable TV

Cable TV in the USA refers to any of the TV channels you pay a cable company to access. Shows on cable are generally given more freedom for nudity, violence, swearing, and other mischief than network TV shows. TBS, USA, Bravo, FX, HBO, Spike, Comedy Central, and Nickelodeon are some of the cable channels with the highest viewership, so shows on these channels tend to be more highly regarded than those on other cable TV channels.

Should I Work in Soaps?

There is a stigma attached to soap actors that they are not talented. This is not usually the case, and I believe it stems from the stylised storylines, dialogue, music, and editing rather than the acting itself. These actors are shooting almost every day of the week, are often given multiple pages of rewrites on the spot, and have copious lines of dialogue to memorize.

Given the time constraints, lack of prep time, and high-pressure work environment, it's safe to say that soap acting is probably some of the hardest work on TV. Many industry members who actually know what soap acting requires say that if you can handle acting in a daytime soap, you can handle acting in anything.

If you are still developing your career, working on a daytime soap for a year or two is an excellent starting point, networking ground, and a great platform from which you can move on to bigger projects.

I don't see why anyone who doesn't have substantial credits on network TV or in studio films would refuse a role on a soap, because it gets you into the Hollywood system. Professionals want to work with people who are already in the system. After all, it worked for Colin Egglesfield, Eva Longoria, and Megan Fox, so who is to say it won't work for you?

LOCAL HIRE WORK

Some foreign federal and state governments provide financial incentives to qualifying productions in the form of equity (money) contributions and/or tax rebates. This motivates many filmmakers to shoot in states or countries outside California.

When a film shoots outside LA, the smaller roles are almost always cast with actors hired locally in the area. This is partly because it is expensive to fly and house a bunch of actors from Los Angeles to play smaller roles.

Government incentives are often contingent on the production hiring a certain percentage of their workforce from within the region. The rebate amount often increases in ratio to how much of the production budget is spent on local labor. This means the more local cast and crew the production hires, the more money the production receives from the government.

Who Casts Local Hire Roles?

If a project is being filmed away from Southern California, the Los Angeles CD is usually only responsible for casting the larger roles. The size and number of roles allocated to Los Angeles talent versus 'local hire' talent varies greatly between projects depending on the talent budget. The smaller roles are usually outsourced to a CD who is local to the region in which the project is being filmed. On big US films shot overseas, the same system usually applies, with the 'region' being within the foreign country.

The regional CD sends the character breakdowns to the agents in her local region. Regional CDs in the USA almost always accept video auditions in addition to holding live sessions, so you can simply tape your audition at home and your agent will send it to the CD.

Working as a Local Hire

A 'local hire' lives in the area in which a project is being shot. In the USA, this means you need a street address within 500 miles of the shooting location or within the state from which the production is claiming tax incentives (depending on the production). Many actors list their friend or agent's address, however, some productions expect actors to provide legal identification or official mail (like utility bills) specific to the state or region.

You're considered a 'local', so if you're travelling to set from another city you must pay for your own flight, accommodation, transportation to and from set, and all other expenses. As a local hire you are not paid a 'per diem' (daily cash payment to cover day to day expenses during a shoot on location). While it is not contractually acknowledged that you have incurred any travel expenses, most are claimable on tax.

It sounds expensive, but when you factor it in that a full scale SAG-AFTRA speaking role pays almost $900 per day (plus residuals), that $100 a night hotel and $400(ish) return flight to New Orleans doesn't seem all that costly. Even if you're just travelling for one day's work you'll generally break even financially and walk away with a credit, the enjoyment of being on set, money towards your union pension and health, footage for your reel, new contacts, new friends, and a free working holiday.

Over sixty feature films were shot in Louisiana in 2013. Other areas booming with local hire work due to impressive tax incentives are Atlanta, New Mexico, Toronto or Vancouver.

Modified Local Hire

Local hire contracts can be negotiated. Sometimes the production will pay for you to stay in a hotel in the area, pay gas money for the drive from your address (up to 500 miles from the shoot), or give you a per-diem, which can make up for the cost of your travel. Production usually knows if you're not a 'real' local, so if you've booked a good role see if your agent can get them to make things a little more comfortable for you. The least the producers can do is arrange for the hotel that's housing the cast and crew to give you the production's corporate discount on a room.

WEB SERIES

Made for the internet episodic shows and films are a multi-billion dollar industry. The top Hollywood agencies have staff in their 'New Media' departments dedicated to scouting talent from online videos. Some of these self-made celebrities have larger and more loyal followers than the mainstream celebs we know and love.

The power of the 'Tween' market (proven by the success of such franchises as *The Hunger Games* and *Harry Potter*) is something to which Hollywood execs pay a great deal of attention. Tweens are a major paying audience, so if you can get into a web series that catches on, you may be able to skip all this Hollywood jazz and create your own fan base.

While there are many successful web series, there are also thousands that sit out there un-watched. As an actor, selecting a web series requires a different list of criteria than selecting independent film work.

Web series are designed to be viewed at a low resolution for faster buffering, and are competing with home videos and gag reels, so audience members are much more forgiving of low production quality.

When selecting a web project in the hope that it will 'go viral', remember most people online will forward a link to something short and funny more often than something long and serious, so the more popular web series are comedic ones with shorter episodes. Make sure comedic scripts make you laugh out loud on every page and you'll have a much better chance of your webisode being successful. FunnyOrDie.com has some great examples and is a wonderful place to post any skits you produce.

Avoid lewd, derogatory, political, or racist webisodes. Remember, webisodes are footage of you that will permanently circulate the internet. Before saying yes to something extreme, think of the five people you respect the most in the world and decide whether you'd be happy for them to see you saying or doing what's being asked of you in the web series.

Professional Web Series

Netflix.com, Hulu.com, Vimeo.com, Amazon.com, YouTube.com and numerous other online networks are launching their own content for millions of subscribers worldwide. Many of these (eg. *House of Cards*) have celebrity cast, a huge following and massive marketing budget. Booking a role on any of the top rated internet TV shows is now considered as legitimate as any network or cable TV series with similar ratings.

Some existing TV shows have web spin offs produced by the same networks or EP's who write or produce the actual shows. High profile producers and directors put together web series (eg. *Electric City*) to release content that may be too extreme for or simply not suited to network or cable TV. Auditioning for one of these shows is a fantastic way to meet CDs, directors and producers for whom you may otherwise struggle to gain an audition.

Internet Sketches and Skits

Just be laughing. The entire time you read the script you should be thinking this is the funniest thing you've ever heard and it absolutely HAS to be made. OR know that the actors you are working with will create characters who bring the script to life.

Production value doesn't have to be life-changing, but should be of a reasonable level. Look at previous projects of the director, editor and other actors. Editing can make or break a comedic project, so find out what they have worked on before and see if it makes you laugh.

COMMERCIALS

Thousands of actors audition for commercials every business day in Los Angeles. There is a great deal of money to be earned from both the initial paycheck and the residuals that come with long running commercials, so it is definitely worth doing the many auditions it usually takes to book each job. Most actors think of commercials as an easy way to cover living expenses while pursuing film and television work.

There are ways to improve your commercial booking rates. Small things such as 'talking as though the viewer is your best friend' (when it's a delivery to camera), and 'truly believing in the product' can make all the difference in getting the job. Any actor looking to get into commercials should take a commercial audition technique class to learn and perfect these basics.

Casting Frontier

Casting Frontier (CastingFrontier.com) provides a system in which each actor is given an ID number and a membership card with a personal barcode on it. That barcode contains all of your information, including height and weight, special skills, and any other information that you have entered into your casting frontier online profile.

This system made it possible to phase out the hardcopy forms actors used to have to fill out at commercial auditions, though you still need to fill out a sign in sheet. When you attend an audition for almost any union commercial in LA, you swipe your barcode before heading into the audition room and all of your information is uploaded. Your agent is then notified that you have attended the audition and whether you were there on time.

EXTRA WORK

Non-union extra work usually pays minimum wage ($64/8hrs), which is less than half the current SAG-AFTRA extra work rate ($142/8hrs). SAG-AFTRA actors booked under a 'model rate', are paid $175/8hrs) and commercials pay $328/8hrs, so extra work can be very profitable.

When booked for a day of SAG-AFTRA extra work (regardless of your union status), you are guaranteed a minimum eight hours of pay, which means sometimes just a few hours of work can earn you a paycheck for a full day.

Extra work gigs on TV shows tend to get out around the six to eight hour mark, while film extra work gigs regularly run into overtime, meaning it's not uncommon for an extra on a film to work regular twelve-hour days.

Overtime

Extra work overtime pays time-and-a-half for the period from eight to twelve hours, and double-time for hours twelve to sixteen. **Golden time kicks in after sixteen hours, which means you are paid your full eight-hour day rate for every hour of work.**

Central Casting

'Central' (Central Casting) is the main casting company for extras in LA. There are many smaller extra work agencies, but Central is definitely the biggest and the best.

To sign up (as detailed at CentralCasting.com), go to Central during the bi-weekly two-hour registration time with your passport, license, and original social security card and fill in the forms. Dress well and have your makeup and hair done, because when you register a photographer will take the photo to be used in Central's files.

Once you join Central, you may call a 'work line' every day for your type according to sex and union status. The various Central Casting CDs leave messages on a voice mailbox that detail the roles currently casting. When a role suits your type you have to take down the info, then call the CD and leave a message saying you're interested in the job. The CD listens to the submissions and decides which background actors to hire.

I would suggest avoiding all this time consuming legwork by using a 'booking service' (explained below) instead. Other extra work companies are listed in the resource guide.

ExtrasAccess.com

ExtrasAccess.com is part of ActorsAccess.com. It works in the same way as most of the online casting sites . . . simply sign up for an account, set up your profile, and start submitting.

Booking / Call In Services

A 'booking service' (or 'call in service') is essentially a management company for extras. Most charge a substantial membership fee (around $60/month) and require you to be in the database at Central Casting.

Note: Central no longer accepts O1 visas, but most of the other extra work casting companies around town will accept your O1.

Central casts most roles through booking services because they keep track of exactly which days each extra is available to work. For example, Joey's List keeps your availability information current by requiring that you log in every day and select which of the following seven days you are available to work. At midnight each night, your availability is reset and the next day you must confirm your availability for each of the *next* seven days.

The CDs at Central go to the online database of their chosen booking service and enter the date/s they need extras and the basic physical requirements. The CD can then select from the list of extras (all of whom are definitely available to work that day), and book the chosen talent immediately.

Most booking services have a 'no cancellation' policy. This means that if you mark yourself as available on a certain day and the CD books you to work, you must work. If you are booked to work and you cancel or don't show up, you are immediately kicked out of the booking service. It's harsh, but with the unreliable nature of many actors in LA, it's a rare thing for a CD to know that if she books thirty extras, all of them will show up.

There are many pay-per-month booking and call in services in LA. If you rely solely on the CDs at Central Casting finding you in the database, you might get one or two phone calls a year. If you call into Central on the 'work lines' every day and submit for work, you might get a job once a month. With a booking or call in service, you can often work several times a week, especially if you're attractive or can play a popular type (like 18 to 30 year olds).

Here is a list of the better-known booking services around LA:

- Joey's List
- Jessica's A-List
- Extras Unlimited

Featured Extra Work Warning

One warning for any professional actors out there who are choosing to do extra work: avoid having your face seen on camera. It's not as much of a big deal in films as it is on TV. There are two reasons for this: firstly, you don't want the CDs you've met to see you as an extra as it may taint their view of you as a professional actor. Secondly, if you are a heavily featured extra in a TV show, you can sometimes take yourself out of the running for playing a principal role in that series for several years.

In most cases, the casting department and producers of a show will have no idea that you did featured extra work on a show, so it will not hinder you at all.

VOICE-OVER

Voice-over artists can be heard in animation, film, TV, commercials, radio and any medium in which voices are heard. You don't have to do a variety of 'voices' or accents to work in voice-over . . . in fact much of the work simply calls for an actor's natural voice. There's plenty of voice work in LA, and a great deal of competition, so while you will probably get a number of voice auditions, it's likely that you will also have to do more auditions to secure each booking.

For networking, it can be good to record voice auditions in the sound booth at your agency; however, it's easier to record them at home. The microphone I have is an Audio Technica AT2020 USB. There are many software programs you can use but a great freeware one is called 'Audacity', which works on both Windows and Mac. If you have an iPhone, your 'Voice Memos' app records at a quality level that should suffice for most voice-over auditions. Just put the file through to iTunes to convert it to an MP3 and email it to your rep.

When you do book voice-over work, you will be well compensated for your time. SAG-AFTRA has voice-over contracts that cover most types of projects and have rates comparable to on-camera talent. Voice work through the union also often pays residuals much like on-camera work.

David Lawrence, one of LA's top voice-over artists has put together an introduction to voice-over work in LA. Details are in the resource guide, and I recommend you check it out and learn how to get started in this lucrative side of the acting world.

Loop Group / Looping

Crowd scenes in film and TV require varying levels of ambient conversation and chatter in the background, specific to each individual scene. To save paying actors to talk in the background of each scene, the production uses extras on screen, then brings in a 'loop group' in post-production to fill the room with voices.

Since their faces aren't on screen, the loop group is able to voice several crowd scenes by modifying their pitch, accents, energy, tone of voice, etc. This means a single loop group may be able to provide ambient voices for every scene in a film.

Looping artists are paid very well (the same rates as on-screen actors) and receive residuals on those rates. Most TV series use the same loop group of five to ten actors for all thirteen or twenty-four episodes of each season.

THEATRE IN LA

There is a myth that there is no decent theatre in LA. While the theatre scene here may pale in comparison to that of New York or London, great theatre productions can be found most nights in Los Angeles. Hundreds of theatre companies are scattered throughout the city, so it's hard for audiences to find the good plays simply due to the sheer quantity of options. It tends to be difficult to get locals to attend live shows because most have been burned by having to sit through many bad productions. The flip side of this is that when a great show comes up, people usually talk about it, so every theatre buff in town will want to see it!

In LA there are several very different types of theatre you could be working in, and these are detailed on the next page.

Equity Theatre

Any show performed in a theatre with more than 99 seats in it must be registered with Actors Equity (AEA) and hire union actors. 'Equity' theatre is often quality theatre with professional actors. Actors are paid full union rates and the productions are usually financed and marketed with a reasonable budget.

Equity Waiver

When a theatre in Los Angeles has 99-seats or less but is using union actors and following union guidelines, equity will often waive some of the contract provisions (e.g. actor paychecks). Now officially called 'Showcase Code', the term 'Equity Waiver' is still used informally.

99 Seat Theatre / Non-Equity

Most theatres in LA have 99 seats or less in the house. Producers of these shows do not have to register the production with Actors Equity. Non-equity theatre is generally unpaid. Occasionally the theatre company will split the profits amongst the cast and crew, but most of the time the love of the craft and small amount of exposure is your only reward.

Co-Op Theatre

Called a co-op or theatre troupe, there are a number of theatre companies around LA that charge a monthly membership fee to cover overheads due to the small crowds and low ticket costs. It usually costs between twenty and sixty dollars a month to secure a spot as a member of a co-op theatre company.

Members audition for roles in the various plays throughout each year. Co-op theatre groups sometimes run a class type structure alongside the theatre.

If you plan to join a group like this, attend one of their plays first to assess the quality. Ensure that entry to the group requires an audition, and that there are not too many active members of your type with whom you may have to compete for roles. In some co-op theatres, the best parts go to the founders and long term members, so new members may end up paying dues to be in a theatre group with which they rarely get to play lead roles.

Theatre Audition Listings

Most theatre companies list auditions for new company members on their website. Most auditions for theatre productions and theatre companies are also listed on the standard film and TV audition websites:

- NowCasting.com
- BackStage.com
- ActorsAccess.com
- LACasting.com

CHAPTER 8

NETWORKING

WHAT IS NETWORKING?

Networking, also known as 'schmoosing', or in Hollywood: 'setting foot outside your apartment', is often misconstrued as a dirty word. There are many slimy, dishonest people who will make friends with anyone they think can help them in their quest to be whoever they are trying to be. These people are usually easy to see through and avoid.

Networking doesn't mean meeting people who are in a position of power and sucking up to them. There are thousands of friendly, interesting, likeminded people who just happen to also be very well positioned in this industry. Networking does mean meeting and working with *these* people and establishing organic personal and business relationships with them over time. It is as simple as being good to your friends and co-workers, and staying in touch.

Avoid successful egomaniacs, regardless of what you think they can do for you. They're no fun to be around, and realistically people like this are not likely to get you a job or help you out because they are too busy thinking about themselves.

Networking continues at every level of your career. Most celebrities still procure a large portion of their work through relationships they have built over the years with filmmakers, CDs and other actors.

There's an old adage in Hollywood: "People don't do favors for acquaintances, they do favors for friends", which essentially means people are not likely to help out some person they met for five minutes and swapped cards with at a party. However, if someone spends some time with, connects with, and respects you they might be willing to make a referral. Once you've gone for beers with someone a few times, they might be motivated to pull a favor for you.

This doesn't mean the only way you should gain contacts is by making friends with every cool person you meet and ignoring those you might not get along with. If someone is in a position to give you a job make sure they know who you are, what you do, and that they have your information. Make sure you get contact information from them . . . and follow up on it. You can tell when someone isn't the type of person you'd hang out with socially, so don't be fake about it, just keep it as a clear business relationship.

When I started attending festivals, I thought I had to meet 'everyone at the party' . . . but that's not necessarily true. It's about finding a few people of value and passing time at that event getting to know them. It's about finding real long-term friends and future co-workers who are passionate about directing, producing, or any other aspect of the industry in the same way that you are passionate about acting.

NETWORKING TIPS

Just Say "Yes"

The first rule of networking is that you almost always have to go somewhere to do it. You cannot network while alone in your apartment watching TV, or cleaning, or reading a book. It is oh-so-easy to stay inside with a DVD and a blanket (especially if you have someone to snuggle under it with!), but you have to leave the house if you want to meet people. So, say "Yes" to seeing your friend's play, band, or film screening. Say "Yes" to that day of volleyball at the beach or the house party you were going to ditch. Get off your comfort-zone-loving butt and go somewhere social, and you'll find yourself meeting all sorts of people you couldn't have dreamed you'd get to know.

Please Have Fun

In the pages that follow, I'm going to explore the different approaches to building your network in LA. As you read this please remember that most of these events, screenings, festivals, and parties are FUN! You're an actor in Hollywood hanging out with a bunch of cool and successful industry folks . . . people dream about this stuff! So while it is good to be aware of the business side of why you are there, please enjoy yourself.

Some actors are so intense about meeting the right people and not 'wasting time' at networking functions. Over time, you'll find most of the best 'contacts' in this industry are the ones who are your real, true friends . . . the people you can call when you do a bad audition or who hike with you (yes, we hike a lot in LA) when you're going through a breakup.

Don't ever forget that this is your life, now. When you 'make it', it simply means that you have bigger paychecks, invitations to more exclusive parties, and a few strangers asking for your autograph on the street . . . other than that, not a whole lot changes. You still have to network and fight for your next role, and you will still be going to events, parties, and film festivals. This world in LA is your life, so remember to relax, take a breath, and enjoy being out in Hollywood 'living the dream'.

Maintaining Your Network

While it's very nice to hand out your little actor business card with your face all over it, people are unlikely to be proactive enough to follow up and stay in touch with you, so make sure you **get a business card from every person you meet**. If a person doesn't have a card, ask for their contact info.

After each event, write on the back of each card (or next to their information in your phone) the date, location, and how you met. Add something to jog your memory like a physical description, something personal about them, or something topical that you discussed. This way you will have a reference for them when you go to contact them at a later date. You may think this is a little too much effort, but trust me, when you're sorting through your pile of 200 business cards (or scrolling through your list of contacts) at the end of each year, you'll be glad you've made notes.

Most actors are pretty terrible at maintaining contact, so if you can master this you'll have us all beat. Keep in touch with the people you've met. Follow up with them a few days later saying "Nice to meet you", and (if you have the cash) invite them to a casual lunch or coffee. Touch base with your contacts every six months or so. Keep in loose social contact with all of the people you've ever met, and over the years they will remember, respect, and (hopefully one day) hire you.

The best way to stay in touch with your 'business only' contacts is to email them when you drastically update your demo reel or have a new project coming out. Don't make it an overly formal sounding communication. Don't try to pack in every little thing you've done in the past year. Just write a simple email mentioning where you met (if you think it is necessary) then get straight to the point in under a hundred words. Avoid sending updates more often than every three months and ONLY when you have a project coming out, otherwise people may feel harassed.

Networking with Future Friends
If you meet someone at a party or function that you enjoy the company of socially, who also happens to be a great contact, become friends with them! Don't be afraid to invite a filmmaker to go for a hike on a Sunday, or for a lunch, or to drinks when you're heading out with friends. Don't imagine that they wouldn't want to hang out with you just because you're an actor. That's so silly! Every producer, director, and CD I know has actor friends and when they meet someone they get along with they are often more than happy to make a new friend. One exception: For safety's sake, if you're under the age of 25, avoid inviting older filmmakers out at night as it may give the wrong impression.

Filmmakers are busy people, so if they can't join you don't get offended, and definitely don't decide not to invite them out again . . . just change the type of invitation. If they didn't want to see a play or go to a party, wait until you're doing something a little more high profile (maybe a charity or a red carpet event) and invite them as your plus one.

Event Plus-One's
When you're invited to a high profile event with the option of bringing a guest, invite your high profile friends rather than your friends who desperately want to come. This way you're not only attending something of quality, you're contributing to the mix by bringing someone of value. Most will appreciate the invitation, respect you for being in a position to offer it, and know people at the event to introduce you to. It also may inspire them to return the favor and invite you to something fun!

Facebook and Social Networking
Facebook is a fantastic networking tool. If you got along well with someone at a party, Facebook them! Conversely, if you meet a CD at a workshop or

audition, DO NOT Facebook them because in this instance you have met them as a work contact rather than socially as a potential friend.

Facebook contains details of your private life. You're giving a thousand strangers access to your pictures and information on what parties you'll be attending and who your friends are. It's scary. It's even scarier for industry professionals like CDs who have hundreds of actors requesting them every month.

If you have industry members as Facebook friends, be very careful about posting photos of yourself drunk or posting status updates that imply anything involving too much debauchery. There's a certain understanding that everyone in Hollywood parties, but the people who are considering putting their reputation in your hands by hiring you really don't want to see proof of you doing it. Be a little discreet and be careful what you post.

NETWORKING WITH YOUR REPRESENTATION

An agent and manager work very hard for just 10% of your wages. In most cases, that 10% in no way covers the hours of work they put into your career. When you are just starting out with a small job or two per year, you may only be earning five or ten grand a year. This means your representation is only getting $1000 for a full year of working for you. All the time spent on phone calls, contract negotiations, submissions, dealing with your other rep, answering your emails and phone calls, meeting with you, and consulting on your headshots is worth a lot more than a thousand bucks.

In order to make your agent or manager feel like working for you was worthwhile (and to help you stay on their roster if they're ever dropping clients!), here are a few things you can do each year to make them feel loved:

Gifts

If your rep hosts a party, make an effort to show up. If they have gotten you a decent number of auditions, get them a simple birthday and Christmas present. Each present should cost between $20 and $100. Something like a bottle of booze or a voucher for a back massage would be perfect. Doing this is simply a sign of appreciation and good business. If the gift costs more than $100 it's excessive UNLESS you've booked a substantial job.

If you've booked more than $30,000 of work through your agent or manager in a given year, it's important to get them something substantial to show that you appreciate their hard work. A Mont Blanc™ pen, a day at a spa, or a weekend getaway would be remembered. A gift valued between

1% and 2% of the amount you've grossed through jobs secured by them in the past year is appropriate.

Lunch

Invite your representation to lunch once a year. It is a nice way to get some face time with them and lets them see you in a social setting. Just make sure you're nice to the wait staff and that you tip a solid 20%. If you're with one of the top agencies or management companies, they have an expense account so lunches and dinners are on them!

Premieres

If you have a film that is premiering, try to get your representation a ticket (and a plus one) for the screening and the after party. This will show that you bring something exciting to the table rather than being just another actor. Also, when you are in a GOOD play, get them two tickets for opening night. If the play is bad, don't be afraid to tell them it's bad and advise them not to come. On a side note, please don't waste your time doing a bad play.

Going Drinking with Your Representation

This is a tricky line to walk and your approach will vary according to how well you get along with your rep on a personal level. If you feel like you're on the same social wavelength as your rep and they invite you out at night it's fine to socialize with them. Be aware, however, that any time you form a personal relationship (yes, even a platonic one) with a colleague there is a risk that the personal side of things may damage the working relationship.

Going out with your rep to events or industry parties every few months is good business and they'll hopefully introduce you to industry contacts. Avoid drinking too much and make sure you don't involve your rep in too many dramatic details of your private life. You want your representation to see you as a fun person and a serious actor, not the drunk they had to carry into a taxi two nights ago.

If your rep dates people of your sex, be careful of spending time out drinking with them. There's always something that attracts an agent or manager to a client, and very occasionally it's that they are physically attracted to you. There's nothing wrong with this and it will almost always lie dormant as long as it's never spoken about or acted upon, so avoid circumstances in which this could occur.

If there is any friendly flirting between the two of you, avoid doing anything more than lunches and their birthday party outside of the office.

It comes back to the old "Don't poop where you eat" rule because if one of you makes a move and is rejected, it could be a very awkward situation. I think this comes down to an age thing again for young people . . . as a general rule, if you're in your early twenties, you probably shouldn't be out partying with your rep.

Networking with Your Representation at the Office

There are many agencies that represent close to a hundred clients per agent. If this is the case, your agent is likely to have several clients who look like you, which can make it hard to stand out amongst the crowd. Take any legitimate opportunity to drop by the office (no more than monthly).

If your rep requests updated headshots or if you have to deliver a check, drive in and drop it off instead of mailing. Don't have long conversations, just say hi and know that this quick interaction is keeping you fresh in their mind.

Workshop Updates

As mentioned, if you haven't heard from your agent or manager in four weeks, make contact via email. I think the smartest way for a development actor to do this is to send "workshop updates" every two weeks.

Make it a simple email to both your agent and manager (to remind them of your 'team') that opens with "I hope you're both/all well! Here are the CDs and associates I've met in the past two weeks:" then simply list the names and what show the TV CDs are on. Do NOT go into details; just make it a simple list of names that can be scanned in ten seconds. Make a short note if a CD specifically pulled you aside and chatted with you.

EARNING PEOPLES TRUST

It is vital in Hollywood is to EARN PEOPLE'S TRUST so they will refer you to the right people or hire you for work. To earn trust in Hollywood (and in life) you must be consistently:

Reliable

Be careful about what you commit to, people will remember and expect you to follow through.
- Always be where you say you will be when you say you will be there.
- Always do what you say you will do when you say you will do it.

Punctual

It is often said in Hollywood that you can get away with just about anything as long as you show up to set on time. In the same vein, you can be one of the nicest, most talented actors and if you're fifteen minutes late to set, the crew will not be happy.

Discreet

Discretion is vital in an industry riddled with rumors and hearsay. As *Person A* divulges *Person B's* secret to me, prefacing it with "I'm not even supposed to tell you this so please don't tell anyone", all I can think of is the fact that *Person A* can't keep a secret. I'd be silly to then include that person in any circle of trust. Be trustworthy and people will trust you.

Consistently Talented

Make sure that your talent level stays consistent. Whatever level of talent you represented yourself as having on your demo or in the audition, you must be at least that good on set. Clearly the hope is that you will exceed expectations, but to at least match the skill level you showed at the audition is vital. This means that if you coached privately for your audition, you should also coach privately to craft every scene in the movie.

Professional

• Know all your lines when you show up on set or to an audition.
• Treat all members of the cast and crew with respect.
• Follow the recommendations in the 'On-Set Protocol' section of this book.

Never Be Demanding or Lazy

Think of those times when you're on set during your downtime and you can't be bothered making your own coffee, and those PA's are just so eager to do it for you. If you are not in makeup or otherwise engaged, please muster up the energy and do it your self. PAs have many jobs on set and are there to help you when you're NOT ALLOWED OR ABLE to help yourself, not to be your personal slaves.

Be Honest

Never tell a lie about anyone or anything. In a town that probably only has around twenty thousand true 'industry players' (professional producers, investors, directors, distributors, executives, key crew, agents, managers, CDs, and top working actors), everything will come back to bite you. Don't exaggerate your credits. Some people may tell you it is okay to say you have a much larger role in a project than you actually did . . . but it really isn't. People will find out and will not be impressed.

Be Honest on Your Resume

If you can't surf, you probably won't be able to learn how in three weeks before a shoot. My currently aching arms and bruised hips and lower ribs are a testament to that. The same goes for other special skills: if you can't do it, don't say that you can.

Don't Exaggerate Your Relationships

When I first came to town, for the sake of brevity I once said: "A mate of mine did *xyz*" and went on to tell a story. The other person replied: "How is he? He's a good friend of mine" and I had to backtrack with: "Well, actually I only met him a couple of times". Exaggerating undermines the accuracy of any future statements you make.

Look Like Your Picture

If you audition for a CD and you don't look like your picture, you are wasting her time and yours. She's brought you in because she needs an actor who looks like that picture, and if the producer or director is in the room it wastes their time also. Build trust by making sure your headshot looks like you, wrinkles, moles, scars and all.

Remember and Repay Favors

Give credit where credit's due. LA is a town built on favors, and a bit of a 'pay it forward' attitude. People are generally willing to help you as long as you are the type of person who would do the same for them if the positions were reversed. Appreciate and respect what other people do for you, be sincerely thankful, and always repay people when you are able to. When you are given an opportunity to help someone who needs and deserves it, rack up some karma points and do it.

Make Quality Introductions

By introducing a talented director to a great producer, you are validating yourself to each of them by showing your association with the other. You are also giving them both an opportunity, which means they may be moved to share an opportunity with you one day in return. Keep in mind also that if they end up working together, you're likely to be top of the list of actors invited to audition for their projects.

If you spend enough time displaying the qualities and taking the actions listed above, people will be happy to put their name behind you.

Warning: Beware of Time Vampires
There are a number of 'time vampires' in LA who have no limit to what they will take if someone is willing to share resources, time, or anything else with them. Be conscious of this, and know when to say no.

THE FOOD CHAIN

It's just as hard out there for a director or producer as it is for an actor . . . often harder.

For every film there may be thirty actors, but there is usually only one director, one writer, and maybe three producers. Directors have to 'network' with producers to get their next job. Producers have to 'network' with finance people. There's a food chain, and the best part about actors being on the 'bottom' of the food chain is that we get to make friends with everyone!

Below is the Hollywood food chain AS IT PERTAINS TO ACTORS. There are many other job titles that could justifiably be on this list but aren't as directly linked to the acting side of things. People often hold two job titles and may be much higher up the food chain than you think. Industry members with more success and longevity have more contacts and power, which means they may be much higher up the chain than their job description implies.

1. Financier / Investor
The financier provides all or part of the money needed to complete and market a film. There are generally several financiers on each film who will receive an 'executive producer' credit.

2. Studio and Network Executives
Executives can provide or remove the finance and distribution from a film. The attachment of a studio or network can be hard to acquire without existing equity, and executives are able to have celebrities, producers, directors, and almost anyone else removed from a project.

3. Bankable Celebrities

A bankable celebrity brings an anticipated 'ROI' (return on investment) to a project. This goes for any 'celebrity', not just actors. Some bankable celebrity directors and producers (like Steven Spielberg or James Cameron) carry more weight than an A-List actor.

4. Celebrity Representation

Top agents and managers are gateways to celebrities. Their access to the name talent secures them a spot just beneath the celebs at the top of the food chain.

5. Executive Producer

There are many roles on a film or TV show that are credited with the title of 'executive producer', including:
- The person providing the money (the investor or financier).
- The person who brought the person with the money to the project.
- A person who oversees and supports a project by attaching their name to it and/or assisting with any major issues that arise.
- The writer who wrote the pilot episode of a TV show.

6. Producer

The producer negotiates the purchase of the script, hires the director, sits in on casting, puts the project together, allocates ownership percentages of the project, allocates credits, and runs the entire show. The producer hires everyone and can also fire anyone, often including the director. A producer may even have the authority to have an executive producer removed from a film set.

7. Director

The director is hired by the producer to interpret a script and turn it into a finished work by utilizing actors, locations, crew, equipment, and anything else needed to tell the story.

8. Writer

The writer writes the script.

9. Casting Department

The casting director(s) and casting staff create lists, put out offers, run audition sessions, negotiate deals, and help decide which actors are cast in the film or TV show.

10. Agents and Managers

Agents and managers submit actors to the CD for consideration.

11. Actor

An actor acts.

Actors often mistakenly believe that everyone else in this industry has a secure job and plenty of money and that we are the only ones struggling to get work. This isn't true. Actors may be at the bottom, but every single person on that food chain is fighting to meet the people above them.

Look how close the agents, managers and CDs are to actors in the food chain. **I promise you, they are on our side and they constantly fight for us.**

There are people at every level who are driven by their egos . . . never let them make you feel 'less than' (yes, now I'm talking in 'bumper sticker').

If your agent says something that doesn't sound logical to you, don't assume he's right just because of his job title. Agents, managers and CDs are not 'all-knowing' creatures. While it is important to listen to those guiding you in the industry, never follow anyone blindly. Always consider your own intuition and take anything anyone says with a grain of salt, a lot of afterthought, and preferably a second opinion.

Don't be afraid to approach an industry member you'd like to meet. The best thing that can happen is that they become a friend and may help you move forward in your career one day. The worst thing that can happen is they don't want to connect and you're back where you started anyway.

NETWORKING AT EVENTS

One of the most enjoyable (and probably most productive) ways to expand your network is to attend events at which most attendees will be 'industry types', and then be open to meeting anyone around you. Eventually you'll come across someone interesting and inspiring, with whom you get along and would probably be friends regardless of their job. This is the person you 'network' with. Remember, networking is not about 'fishing for contacts'; it's about finding people with a similar mindset and similar goals who also happen to be working in the industry of which you are a part.

Conversation Tips

Be Interested

At any social event, be sure to truly engage in the conversation when you speak with each person. There is no clearer indication that someone is looking to 'make contacts' than when they are scanning the room as you talk to see who else they could be meeting.

Don't waste a person's time by pretending to listen. This aggravates most of the people I know and if I notice someone zoning out while I talk, I'll just end the conversation. If someone is legitimately annoying and you can't find an opportunity to politely get away, think of it as a character study . . . sometimes the strangest people can be the most fascinating if you really pay attention.

Be Interesting

Before you choose to be insulted by someone scanning the crowd behind you, assess whether it might be your fault. Be aware of people's body language. If you've been talking for more than a minute without the other person saying anything, they may have stopped listening. You can tell you've lost a person's interest by any sign of disengagement: loss of eye contact, body turned away, checking their phone, changing the subject, giving short functional responses that don't further the conversation, or not asking you questions.

The person you're talking to may be politely waiting for a break in your story so they can excuse themselves. Heck, it might just be that they need to use the bathroom. Please don't be that person who chews someone's ear off with no regard for whether they are interested in what you're saying.

When you do tell a story, think which details would be interesting to you if someone else were telling it, and only include the interesting bits when you relay the tale. If you realize you're rambling, cut yourself off with an ". . . anyway, what do you think?" Listening is golden and you will learn so much just by asking people about themselves and their opinions.

Small Talk

Use SMALL TALK! As an actor, it's so easy to fall into the trap of talking for five minutes about auditions and work you've done lately and the projects you 'might have' on the horizon, and it's your job, your passion, why shouldn't you talk about it? Well, because after about sixty seconds of highlights, it is really not that interesting.

The more an actor talks about the jobs they've done and how some guy said he might get them into his next film, the more desperate they sound. So when someone asks how your career is going, give a brief overview. If the person doesn't probe for more information, ask them something about themselves or bring up something topical or fun.

172 • THE HOLLYWOOD SURVIVAL GUIDE

Industry small talk is great because it makes you sound more informed than the 'average actor'. Make sure you read the 'trades' (film and TV industry publications) like The Hollywood Reporter and Variety or even sites like DeadlineHollywood.com. Also stay aware of non-industry current affairs. It's interesting when someone says: "Did you hear about *x*?" and gives an opinion on recent news that could spark up a conversation or debate. Discuss a movie you've seen recently, sporting news, or chat about a new restaurant or a bar that you loved.

Non-industry small talk humanizes you and breaks down barriers. It brings you and someone higher up the food chain onto the same level and temporarily removes the employee/employer dynamic. Whatever you talk about, please, **please** be interesting, because after nine years in LA, conversations with many actors sound exactly the same.

Invite Other People

When you invite someone to an event they will be more likely to invite you to an event in the future. If you have an invitation to a party, think of which of your friends would fit in with that crowd. Don't be afraid to invite a few well-groomed folks who are fun but not likely to get too drunk and push the host in the pool.

I used to show up to everything alone or with someone who was already going because I didn't want to have to babysit my friends all night. Over the years I began to realize something: Most people in LA are outgoing and independent. If you put three of your friends who've never met before in a car together on the way to a party, they'll probably get to know each other. If you bring a few people to a party, they'll meet new people there. It's unlikely that you'll have to babysit a friend at an event, and if you do, just don't invite them next time. The great thing about Hollywood is there is always another party!

Separate from Your Friends

Yes, I know I just suggested that you invite other people, but the flip side of that coin is that I've met many new friends at events by separating from the people with whom I arrived. When you're with your friends, you tend to spend your time with them. When you're alone, you have an excuse to meet new people. You find new drinking buddies and go on random adventures together.

If you are with a group of people, try 'losing' your friends. Go to the bathroom furthest away from the people you're with and when you come out, head to the food table or find some way to stay solo for a few minutes. You'll be surprised at who you end up chatting with. Safety-wise, this isn't a good idea for girls who are drinking so please use discretion.

Personal Hygiene / Presentation

People form a subconscious impression of others within seconds of a first interaction. We take in a person's sense of style, quality of clothing, behaviors, posture and cleanliness. Most of us analyze these details (often subconsciously) to decide whether a person is worth spending our time and energy on.

You may think people should like you for you, and that it shouldn't matter what you wear. Look, I'm sure you're beautiful on the inside but your presentation is the only thing those who don't know you have to go by to assess who you are and where you are at in your life. If your clothes are stained or damaged, people may assume you can't afford to clean or replace them. This means you're not working, so you're desperate for a job, so your acting must not be very good. If your hygiene is poor, people may subconsciously assume you're dirty, hence covered in bacteria and may avoid you physically as an instinctual self-preservation method.

This isn't just a personal issue; it's business. Part of your job is to be well presented. People don't want to be around other people who smell bad, look dirty, or seem un-healthy. If you are sweaty, fix it. If you are sick, don't go out. If you meet someone when you're obviously ill and they get sick, they may assume they caught it from you. When a person is ill at a public event it's inconsiderate, selfish, and nobody wants them around.

Maintain Good Posture

Standing up straight shows confidence and success. No matter how well you dress, if your posture is bad you will look unsuccessful. Likewise, even a poorly dressed person walking with confidence appears to have more going on than meets the eye.

For men, being 'grounded' is a very clear sign of strength. If you know anyone who grew up surfing or doing martial arts, look at how they stand. Usually it's with their weight evenly balanced, back straight, and shoulders back, down, and relaxed. Martial artists seem generally relaxed but alert and somehow more connected to the ground than most, as though it would be very hard to push them off balance.

When someone has strong posture it is due to (and hence a sign of) strong core muscles. This gives the impression of overall strength, which applies to both the inside and out. If you want to look confident, strong, and successful, strengthen your core with core muscle exercises or yoga and get used to standing tall.

Stay in Shape

People who eat well and exercise are generally more effective and healthy than those who don't. I want my friends and colleagues to be people who treat me well and are a good influence. If a person appears to take care of and respect his body, I believe he will also be more likely to take care of and respect me as a friend or colleague, and will take more care and respect in his work.

Most people are more likely to invite a healthy, energetic, mentally sharp person to social events than someone who is consistently out of shape and exhausted. You are also far more marketable as a lead actor if you fit a more 'Hollywood' body type simply because a healthy and toned body is more aesthetically pleasing to the majority of viewers.

Don't Drink Too Much Alcohol

If you want to survive running the gamut of nightly networking events in LA, don't drink too much. If you go out drinking every night, you're not going to be as productive the next day. You'll start getting more lines on your face as the free radicals from drinking begin to inhibit your cells ability to reproduce. Your memory will be impaired and you won't be able to learn your lines as well. Not to mention, after a few weeks of nightly drinking you may burn out and stop going out . . . but then you don't get the benefits of the networking events or the fun of the parties.

It's not a frat party, it's Hollywood, and you're here to do business. It's one thing to be stumbling around a club in Hollywood with a few mates; it's another to do so at an event filled with industry players. I go out three or four nights a week, but I also wake up around 7AM daily to start working out. I can do this because I only drink alcohol maybe once a month.

If you go out a couple of nights a week for a few hours and have just one or two drinks then head home at a reasonable hour, you can get up early the next day to work and you'll have the best of both worlds!

COMMON NETWORKING LOCATIONS

Red Carpets and Premieres

When you're at a red carpet event, the people to meet are the suits and those who don't look like they got to be there because of their looks. Any starlet can dress up and get herself onto a red carpet, but the suits invited to these things are the producers, directors, and writers of the films. They are the ones more likely to be able to hire you for their next project.

Parties / House Parties

Parties are fantastic places to meet people. Whether at a bar or a house, almost everyone is present because they were invited (read: referred). Most people tend not to bring an idiot friend to a party. Generally, the friends you bring to parties are friendly, attractive, smart, and generally cool people who probably aren't going to embarrass you. For this reason, house parties are filled with pre-screened people with whom you already have an icebreaker "So, how do you know [the host of the party]?" Attend LA house parties whenever you can, and unless it is fully catered always bring food or drink to give to the host upon your arrival.

Dog Parks and Doggie Hikes

It's awful to imply that your poor pooch should be used as a networking tool, but many friendships have been formed on this, the most neutral of all networking grounds. Most LA locals frequent the same hiking trails and dog parks regularly and the casual surroundings are a great equalizer. Take your time getting to know people, avoid pushing to get contact info as it may seem insincere and you will probably run into them again.

Bars / Clubs / Celebrity Hot Spots

Some young actresses go out to bars and clubs in LA hoping to meet a producer or director. This is NOT a good strategy for networking. I know filmmakers with legitimate production companies who have met many actresses in bars, and I've yet to hear a story that ended in any of those girls getting an acting role.

There are a few exclusive hotels and restaurants that do cater for many legitimate industry types. If you are invited to Soho House, Chateau Marmont, or any similar membership-entry locations it may be wise to attend.

FILM FESTIVALS

A film festival is an event (most lasting anywhere from a few days to a couple of weeks) at which many films are screened. There are short film festivals, feature film festivals, and festivals that screen both. Prizes are awarded to films in various categories. You'll generally meet more legitimate filmmakers in five days at a major film festival than in a full year in LA.

I truly believe the best places to 'network' are film festivals. It's the perfect combination of a relaxed atmosphere and a professional environment in which filmmakers who are usually unapproachable become extremely accessible. Many attendees have just finished working sixteen hours a day for several months to get their films finished, and are there to drink, have fun, and meet people.

If you're going to a festival, call the organizer or publicist and try to add your name to the lists for any parties affiliated with the festival. If you are in one of the films they may waive the festival attendance fee, or at least ensure you are invited to the red carpets and press events.

CDs and smaller agents don't tend to be at film festivals as often as directors, producers, and reps from the top agencies and management firms. Filmmakers at festivals hold many of their meetings casually over drinks in nearby restaurants, bars, and hotel lobbies. If you want to actively make connections, find out where the meetings are happening. Instead of going to another bar, grab a drink or a bite at the bar where the right people are. If you're going to make arbitrary conversation with a stranger it might as well be a filmmaker!

When I was twenty-two, I went to Cannes in a pair of baggy jeans and a t-shirt, no makeup, and no idea of what I was doing. I left that festival with over eighty business cards from producers and directors I had met, many of who are still friends of mine now.

I also met a woman who hired me to work for her production company in Hollywood (never mind the fact that the company shut down six months later and I wound up subsisting for three months in a Hollywood basement storage room on Ramen noodles and the thirty cases of Arizona Green Tea that were stacked next to my futon). The important thing is that a chance meeting at a film festival turned into a tangible, paying job and a life changing experience.

Major Film Festivals

At the major film festivals, the world's top independent films are screened and often sold to distributors. For networking purposes, these are the best to attend. Top directors and producers screen their films and party with the rest of the crowd. You'll meet true industry professionals in a relaxed and comfortable setting.

There is no right way to approach going to a major film festival. You could go there, not attend a single screening, spend the entire time in a local bar, and still meet as many filmmakers as someone who is hitting every film in the place. You meet people on the beach at Cannes, on the ski slopes at Sundance, in line for movie tickets, in the local restaurants and bars, in the lounges, at the parties, on the street, in your hotel, everywhere! Attending a major film festival is a fantastic way to make a bunch of new friends in a 'summer camp for grownups' type environment.

The major film festivals are:
• Berlin
• Cannes
• Sundance
• Toronto
• Venice

Notable American festivals include:
• AFI Fest
• Cinevegas
• LA Film Festival
• Palm Springs
• Slamdance
• South By South West (SXSW)
• Telluride
• Tribeca

In Competition vs Out of Competition

When a film is accepted 'in competition' at a festival like Cannes, Sundance, Berlin, or Toronto it is one of a few films selected out of thousands to screen and compete for awards at the festival. The acceptance process is rigorous, so films in competition are well respected by the filmmaking community. Distributors attend the screenings, sales become much more likely, the filmmakers get to put those little 'Official Selection' wreaths on the front of the DVD box . . . it's kindof a big deal.

A lesser-known fact among non-festival goers is that almost any film can be screened at some of the major film festivals without actually being selected to be at the festival. Production companies and sales agents looking to gain exposure for their films will 'four-wall' (rent out) a screening room or theatre, often one that is being used by the festival but has spare time slots available. Movie stars contracts often stipulate that a film must have a theatrical release, so some film companies will have to 'four-wall' a theatre in order to honor that contract.

Four-walling a theatre at a festival is a very valid and respectable way for a film to be seen by distributors in various countries, and to market a film within the industry. However, it also means filmmakers sometimes tout the film as having been 'at Cannes' or another festival in order to amplify the perceived quality of the film by implying that it was accepted into the festival. If you are curious as to whether a film was invited to be there or if the producer paid a fee for it to be there, simply ask whether the film was screening in competition.

When a film you are in is screened at one of the big festivals, the film-maker may either ask you to come out to the festival to market the film, or to tell people about it. It is important for you to know in what capacity the film is being screened before you start telling people things that may or may not be true.

If a film you are in is playing at Sundance or Cannes, I recommend going to the festival regardless of the film's competition status as it is a wonderful networking opportunity. See if the filmmakers are willing to arrange flights, accommodation, and/or publicity for you.

Cannes Short Film Corner

A fact that is well known within the industry but little known to the public is that the Cannes Short Film Corner is actually a paid screening space for filmmakers. Rather than a fee to enter a 'competition', the money paid is simply a registration fee. There is no competition and no 'judging' of the short films. If you pay the fee, you can screen almost any watchable short film there. Details are at ShortFilmCorner.com.

Registration of a film with the Short Film Corner has nothing to do with the Cannes short film competition, which is a highly regarded short film competition.

When you register a film with the short film corner you are granted two Festival De Cannes accreditation badges for cast and crew. This allows you access to the stands in both the Marché Du Film and Village International, which are two major parts of the festival. This is cheaper than paying the ticket fee to attend, and being there with a short film allows you to attend the festival as a filmmaker rather than simply as a spectator. As a bonus, you are able to attend some Cannes screenings, and may have meetings set up with legitimate sales agents and distributors.

Academy Award Short Film Qualifying Festivals

The Academy Awards™ short film nominees are selected from the winners of pre-designated categories in around seventy five Academy selected film festivals worldwide. A list of these festivals can be found at Oscars.org under the Academy Awards Rules and Eligibility tab.

CHAPTER 9

ON-SET PROTOCOL

H ere's what happened before you arrived on the set of your latest feature film: A writer spent many months (possibly years) hammering out a fantastic script. A producer (who either hired the writer or read the writer's script and loved it) spent at least a year collaborating on script rewrites, putting together financing, and hiring a director and other key crew.

The director spent weeks creating a 'shot-list' and 'storyboard' (a comic strip of the film). The line producer, director, and other key crew members found locations, arranged filming permits, hired actors, hired more crew, rented equipment, and drew up the schedule. Since the writer began working on the script, it has taken anything from twelve months up to ten or more years to put all of this together. Let's say on average it takes around four years to get from the conception of the story to the first day of shooting a film.

So, at last it is the first day of shooting and there are a thousand things going on. The filmmakers have spent a lot of time on this project and you rock up on day one and think the whole thing is going to collapse if you're not happy with your trailer? I don't think so. You're one tiny little itsy bitsy piece of a HUGE puzzle, and get this: you are also REPLACEABLE.

I got a phone call from an indie producer a few years ago "You auditioned for us and were our second choice. Our actress turned up on set three hours ago and she's already being a diva. Would you happen to be available for the next three weeks to play her role in the film?" The actress was removed from set within three hours of behaving badly.

The producers have no obligation to you. These people have a film to make, and filmmaking is a collaborative process, so every person on set must do his or her job like a consummate professional. After years of working on a project, an experienced producer will not put up with inflated egos on set.

No Ego

Operate with an absence of ego. Nobody is above or below you. An actor is no more or less important than anyone. Every series regular and executive on NCIS: LA introduces themself and shakes the hand of every co-star and guest star at the table read for each new episode. This ego-free, welcoming gesture helps nervous guest actors to relax and feel part of the team, which ultimately helps all talent to feel included and perform at their best.

Almost every producer and network executive I know started out as a PA or runner. Brad Pitt, Cuba Gooding Jr., Harrison Ford, and many other celebrities started out as background actors or PAs.

It's amazing how fast people move up (and down) in this industry, so the best approach is to treat everyone around you as an equal regardless of their current status. Everyone from the producer to the PA deserves your full respect because they are all doing exactly what you're doing: following their passion for working in the film and TV industry.

No Bragging

There is no need to tell everyone on set about all the impressive people you know and projects you've done. Most adults are aware enough to recognize that anyone who speaks too highly of themselves is usually masking insecurity. If you have to tell us how good you are and what you've done, it is probably either because you're not that good and haven't done that much or you fear that your talent and credit list are your only desirable attributes.

Bragging does not impress anyone. In fact, if you stop talking for long enough to let other people tell you a little about themselves, you'll often be shocked to discover how much those quiet folk actually have to offer.

Don't Be Late

One of the best compliments an actor can receive is "She's always on time". Be on time! Be early! Plan to get to set fifteen minutes before your call time so if there is a delay, you may still be on time. Check the call sheet the night before for location changes so you know how long it will take to get to set.

Let the Makeup Artist do your Makeup

Unless you are an extra or have been asked to do your own makeup, avoid wearing makeup to set in the morning as the makeup artist will simply need to remove it. NEVER sneak into your trailer to alter your makeup after it has been done. These artists are paid good money to apply the appropriate makeup for the role. They don't tell you how to act, so let them do their job.

Communicate

You're on your way to set but you're running ten minutes late. Do you need to tell anyone? "Ah, it's only ten minutes". WRONG. The Second AD's phone number is on the call sheet, so call and say you're running ten minutes late to allow him to plan accordingly.

Always Read the Revised Sides

Revised sides arrive daily leading up to a shoot. Even if you have no lines in a scene, always scan these for changes. I didn't do this on a TV gig once and they had given me two extra lines. I didn't find out until I got to set!

Always Be Locatable

It is imperative that one of the AD's always knows exactly where you are. If you've been in your trailer for a while and you feel like going for a walk, it's usually fine as long as you tell someone where you're going. On bigger budget films the production's time can cost upwards of two thousand dollars a minute. If you go missing for fifteen minutes, you may not think it's a big deal but that's thirty thousand dollars, and a very unhappy cast and crew who are going home fifteen minutes later because of you.

You're an Actor, not a Director

If the director and the DP are discussing which angle or camera movement would look the best or how to fix a problem, that's their business. Do not interfere. Do not offer suggestions. You are there to say the lines and play your part, not to do someone else's job. The director will listen to you, smile politely, and never tell you how much it may have aggravated him. Imagine if one of the grips piped up to give you acting tips . . . it would not be cool.

Don't Direct the Other Actors

I'm going to repeat myself: you are an actor, not a director. If you direct other actors, tell them what they are doing wrong, or change their blocking, you're going to peeve everyone off. The director will be aggravated that you're undermining his job and the actors will be irked because it will appear you think you know better than they do. If a fellow actor asks you for advice on her performance, give it quietly and preferably off set, but be careful as you may contradict the direction already given.

"Um . . . Your Lav Was on That Whole Time"

Oh, how easy it is to forget that you have a microphone attached to yourself that records your voice, and allows the director and selected crew to hear everything you're saying. Don't say anything bad about anyone on set . . . ever. I know actors who have forgotten they have a lapel mic attached to them and have insulted the director or other cast and crew members, only to come back to 'video village' (the place where the director watches the monitors) and find that everyone could hear them. If you MUST say something private, flick the switch on the lav box to 'mute' . . . just don't forget to turn it back on for the sound check. It is also wise to flick the switch to mute when you leave set to use the bathroom.

Don't Touch a Hot Set

A 'hot set' is a set on which the props and furniture have been positioned for the shoot. DO NOT MOVE ANYTHING unless you are using it while rehearsing or shooting your scene. The set dresser, props department, and grips have painstakingly positioned everything exactly as it needs to be for the shot and oftentimes to match previous takes. Moving items on a hot set can cause massive continuity issues in post.

Safety First

On set (particularly low-budget sets), actors can get hurt or permanently injured. You're probably going to get bruised or grazed on some shoots; this is part of the job and often unavoidable in chase or fight scenes.

Be wary, however, of stunts or blocking with the potential to cause more substantial or permanent injuries. Independent filmmakers occasionally ask actors to do dangerous stunts. Novice directors may rush you into stunts when they are 'losing the light' (the sun is going down) or under time constraints. If a director is asking you to do blocking or a stunt that may seriously injure you, never be afraid to say no.

Be reasonable: it's silly to say no to a necessary piece of blocking for fear of tripping and bruising a knee, but if there's real danger in a stunt that you aren't comfortable with, don't do it. If you're happy to do a simple stunt, but concerned that you don't fully understand what the director wants from you, ask the stunt coordinator or one of the stunt guys to show you how it's done. Never be afraid to ask when your safety is concerned.

Guns

When you are on a film set and someone is pointing a gun at you in a scene, you must check at the beginning of every set up that the gun is not loaded with real bullets. Anytime the gun gets packed away and brought back out, take out the magazine and open the slide or cylinder to check (or ask the armorer to). It is hard to distinguish some prop guns from real ones even when you're holding them. Some armorers use real guns with blanks, the barrels filled in, or the firing pins removed. Check the gun for live rounds every time, no exceptions.

Film Sets are Not Always Glamorous

If you've done big budget studio films or TV shows, things probably ran more smoothly and were run more professionally than the average low budget indie film set. However, that doesn't mean you need to tell everyone about the pampering you're 'used to'.

Some actors on their way up feel a need to tell everyone they have "had it better than this" to make it clear they are slumming on an indie film shoot. These actors complain about the schedule, the director's incompetence, the flaws in the script, and how it "should be done". Well guess what? The indie film producers don't have as much money as the bigger budget producers. The indie filmmakers are probably trying their hardest, learning from their mistakes as they go along and putting all of their money, time, and energy into making this film, so cut them some slack. If you've signed on for the project you're choosing to be there, so respect the process.

Here are some things I saw on several occasions when I used to work on non-union or ultra low budget (under $200,000) indie film sets:

- Call time at 6AM when your first scene is shot at 2PM (applicable to films of any budget)
- Poor quality toilet / bathroom / change room areas
- No trailers (non-union), or perhaps one shared trailer for the entire cast
- Script with cool concept but bad story structure and weak dialogue (you knew this when you signed on)
- Makeup artists not following appropriate hygiene procedures (look out for this and remedy any issues immediately, because as an actor the health of your skin is vital)

- Actors sharing hotel rooms or a house, rather than private hotel rooms
- Remote locations requiring tents, sleeping in a van, or camping
- Freezing weather with poor heaters (always bring a ski-jacket to night shoots) or hot weather with no air conditioning
- Hot meals (required by SAG) consisting of pizza, pasta, or fast food
- Lighting issues or poor lighting
- Crew trying to do too many jobs, hence not doing each job efficiently
- Too much deliberation by director between takes meaning less time for actual takes to be done
- Ego battle between DP and first time director.
- Very frustrated 1st AD who is trying to stick to the schedule but noone else appears concerned
- Investor becoming involved with the creative side of things
- Producers or directors reprimanding cast or crew in front of others

When you're going through all of this, remember: most other actors have been through it too. I'm not saying these occurrences are okay . . . I'm saying don't be surprised when they happen. They are just part of being involved in projects on which people in most of the key positions are inexperienced and finding their feet in their respective careers.

A film set at any budget is like a melting pot of personalities thrown together for a few months in a high stress situation where money, time, and enthusiasm are always running out. These issues are magnified ten-fold on a low budget indie production. Be pleasantly surprised if there are no arguments or personality clashes on set. Be amazed if you are comfortable, well fed, and sufficiently looked after.

In saying all of this, be assertive. When issues arise, consider the time and budgetary restrictions of the project and **if a problem is** *fixable*, don't be afraid to pull the second AD aside and voice your concern. Be sure to make any suggestions or complaints out of earshot of cast and crew, and definitely don't make them on set between takes.

Complaining about unfixable issues won't improve the situation; it will simply create tension on set. Accept that although you can see a better way of doing something, it isn't your job (or your place) to fix it.

It is often said 'every finished film is a miracle' and trust me . . . it's true.

CHAPTER 10

PRESS AND PUBLICITY

If you are already working professionally as an actor and are interested in generating press to establish a more substantial public profile, this section is for you. If the majority of your acting work is in commercials or unpaid films, you are limited in your ability to gain quality publicity for yourself. **Once you are working as an actor** in film and TV, publicity is a necessary and important facet of your job and vital for achieving and maintaining power in this industry.

Celebrities are commodities . . . products. When people know your face, they are more likely to hand over their hard earned dollars to rent your movies. The question is: How many people would rent a film because your face is on the cover? Also, how many of those same people would spend fifteen dollars to watch you at the movies?

Using figures from prior projects in each genre and the celebrity's current level of public visibility, movie studios are able to estimate the probable audience size and financial return each celeb brings to a project.

It's also genre specific. For example, an A-List actor might be more bankable in an action film than he is in a drama because his previous action films have earned a much greater profit ratio (the ratio of total gross return to production and marketing budget plus all other costs) than his dramatic projects.

Celebrities use press and publicity to become a brand name. Like Coca Cola's huge advertising campaigns or McDonalds sponsoring a charity, you need to create the brand name of 'You', which is a saleable commodity in the eyes of the film community.

Magazine articles and interviews don't just happen. Unless you're a well known actor or a 'celebrity of the moment', *Vanity Fair Magazine* isn't likely to hear about your latest low budget indie film and invite you in for an interview.

Most articles come from information submitted to media publications as a 'press release', or a personal message from a publicist to a writer. A press release is an announcement to the press that describes a current event by focusing on the 'angle' (viewpoint) most likely to appeal to readers.

When I was in my teens, I used to call the local newspaper and say "I just did '*x*', is it story-worthy?" I'm sure the editors thought it was 'cute', but this approach resulted in two articles being written about me in the paper, and taught me a valuable lesson about press. I learned that most publicity for actors is centered around a specific event, like when you have a feature film being released or a role airing on a current TV show. Therefore, **the best time to seek publicity is when you have a current film or TV release to promote**.

If you'd like to test this theory but can't justify the cost of a publicist, here's one option: Next time you have a role in a feature film or TV series, write a short article about it and have a friend send it to a few online publications (that run stories about actors) and newspapers on your behalf. Sure, one article isn't going to make you famous, but it will get you used to understanding how the press works and what does or doesn't interest them. Any resulting articles will also get your press kit started and give you a little something to show agents or managers when you're trying to sign with them.

When you book a series regular role on any network TV show, or a lead or strong support in a bigger budget film, don't just rely on the publicity department hired by the network or production company to get press for you. Hire the best publicist you can afford and utilize the attention in any way you can by doing charity events, red carpets, film festivals, etc. If you're on a TV show, find out whether the network will let you do independent films on your hiatus. Don't get lazy just because you're on TV. When the job ends you'll eventually need another one, and that will be a lot easier if you're famous.

Some actors say press is just ego stroking and that red carpets are just for insecure starlets. This is a naïve viewpoint. Every celebrity in the world has walked a red carpet, endorsed a product, or done an interview.

It's a business. A company cannot sell its product without marketing. If people don't know about a product, how can they buy it? If people do not know about you, why would they buy your DVDs? Do as much publicity as possible while you are able to, and consider it a part of your job.

A girl I know was a series regular on a TV show in the USA for several years. There were millions of viewers tuning in around the world each week, but she didn't do any press beyond what the show set up for her. She had very few articles written about her, didn't do many red carpets, and she didn't get 'seen' out at events. No one knew who she was except for the show's audience, and when the show ended she had trouble getting her next job. Her top agent dropped her and she had to go out on commercial auditions to pay the rent. How did this happen? She didn't utilize the opportunity for publicity while it was there.

Look at the show you're on and find out the demographic of the main audience. Are the fans in another country? If so, why not hire a publicist and agent in that country and head out there for a few weeks in your hiatus each year. Do some red carpets, magazine articles, and interviews. Meet filmmakers and executives in that country and establish relationships while you are still on the show.

Take every tiny opportunity and exploit it in every possible way. Don't let your ego convince you that your notoriety will stick around. I know many ex-TV stars that are now working in commercials or normal jobs. Simply being the star of a TV show is not always enough to secure your next acting gig.

Get the Public to Know YOU

When actors are on TV shows with high exposure, it can be very difficult for them to move on to their next job because their fans see them as their character from the show. By getting the press that came with marrying Brad Pitt, *Friends* character 'Rachel' became known as public figure 'Jennifer Aniston', which definitely aided her subsequent speedy foray onto the Hollywood A-list. It is important to note that it was Jennifer's talent and selection of quality projects that kept her there.

If you look at the IMDb profile of leading cast members of old TV shows, you'll find that while many find work on another TV show, very few end up successfully playing leads in studio feature films. There are so many actors on TV and so few parts available in studio projects. You need to give yourself a better shot at it by getting the public to know you as YOU, not just as the character.

Not everyone can date Brad Pitt, but any press you can get while you're on a show can make all the difference. Eva Longoria didn't sit around doing the minimum press allocated for the series regulars on *Desperate Housewives*. Eva hired a top publicity company that made sure she hit carpets, events, and openings around town from the minute she got on that show. Her publicist had magazines writing about her, endorsement deals, everything possible to get her name out there . . . and it worked. Eva Longoria will be known as 'Eva Longoria' for as long as she chooses to stay in the public eye.

There are publications and TV shows across a broad range of topics. If you are already in the public eye, think of an angle to get yourself respectable press. What are your hobbies or affiliations? Use anything you do that's unique to get your face out there more often. If you love cooking, be a guest on a cooking show. If you love cars, drive in a celebrity race before one of the big rallies. Think outside the box and expand your fan base. This is part of the reason (altruism hopefully being the main motivating factor) so many celebs support various charities: because it's newsworthy.

PUBLICISTS

If you are a working actor, your publicist should work in conjunction with you and your manager to decide on the image you are trying to create, then obtain the following for you:

- Referral to a stylist
- Entry to red carpet events
- Magazine and newspaper articles and interviews
- Online articles and interviews
- Invitations to gifting suites (these rock because you get a bunch of free stuff!)

Once you are a celebrity, a publicist should also provide the following:

- Magazine covers
- Product and brand endorsement deals
- Awards shows and ceremonies
- Charity luncheons
- Speaking panels
- Relevant conventions (comic, horror, and sci-fi conventions or other locations where autographs are sold)

A decent publicist in Hollywood will cost anywhere from one to ten thousand dollars a month.

Publicists Hired by a Film or TV Show

A production company may hire a publicity company to promote a film or TV show and its cast. As part of the film's marketing team, the publicist should attain the following for the lead actors in the project:

- Red carpet events (not necessarily affiliated with the project)
- Online, magazine, newspaper, radio, and TV interviews discussing the project
- Charity appearances, other public events and general press

Top Publicity Companies in LA

- Anderson Group Public Relations
- BWR (Baker, Winokur, Ryder)
- PMK / BNC
- Miller PR
- True Public Relations
- WKT PR

Event Planners

An event planner does just what the name implies: plans and organizes events. Although a publicity company may work in conjunction with an event planner or have an event-planning department, the two perform different functions when it comes to events.

In addition to planning and organizing the event, an event planning company employs a 'talent coordinator'. The talent coordinator decides which guests are invited to attend. Your publicist submits or pitches you to the talent coordinator for consideration to be added to the guest list, much like your agent submitting you to a CD for a role.

PRESS KIT

A 'Press Kit' was once a hardcopy folder in which an actor would display press items like magazine and newspaper articles, lists of TV and radio interviews, photos on red carpets, and film or theatre reviews. These days, a press kit is sent via email, so any hardcopy articles are scanned and assembled into a .pdf document or webpage. The kit also includes links to a selection of the online media and interviews an actor has.

A press kit is especially important if you are famous in a country other than the USA. Filmmakers in America may not have heard of you, regardless of the exposure you have in your own country. Having a solid press kit will ensure that you are not just another headshot in the pile. It is also very important to have a strong press kit if you are applying for an O1 acting visa.

When I was working in casting, I cannot even begin to tell you how many times the top foreign celebs were submitted by their agents, only to be overlooked by American CDs. Many times I would tell a CD "this actor just starred in a HUGE film (or TV show) in Australia . . . they have thousands of fans" and the CD would have no idea who the person was. Not only that, but they sometimes still chose not to audition the actor.

In Los Angeles, foreign celebrities are just another photo in a pile (or on a computer screen) unless your agent makes your fame clear when submitting you for a role. Your agent is able to make your celebrity known more easily with a substantial press kit that can be emailed to the casting office. This is why obtaining press over the years is vital.

Keep anything written about you, but (as with your resume credits) remove the less impressive or outdated articles from your press kit when new ones are written. This will ensure the more substantial items are not overlooked.

Press Kit Material

The desirability of each type of press item is generally based on syndication figures (for hardcopy) and number of subscribers or hits online. For hardcopy, the frequency of publication is important. For example, a monthly magazine has more impact than a weekly magazine in the same way as a weekly paper has more impact than a daily paper.

The value of any press obviously varies according to the brand awareness and target demographic of the publication. Any online publication that automatically links its articles with IMDB is always great because the story will be listed on the press section of your IMDB page. In addition, IMDb lists press in two categories: 'Industry News' and 'News'. While 'News' is fantastic, 'Industry News' carries much more weight.

The level of impact interviews on TV, video interviews online, radio interviews, and appearances at live events have on your press portfolio varies.

It depends on which network or station the interview appeared, and the size of the audience that regularly watches the show. Links to footage of video interviews should be listed on a dedicated page in your online press kit.

Each of these press items has little impact on it's own . . . it's when you put them all together as a package that they add to your perceived notoriety and marketability.

Benefits of Red Carpets and Gifting Suites

The fun of attending red carpets dissipates quickly, and they rarely have any immediate effect on your career. So, other than getting to see free movies, consume free booze and food, and take home awesome gift bags, what is the point of being photographed on a red carpet?

For celebrities, public appearances are imperative in order to maintain their 'brand'. While Paris Hilton and Liz Hurley can attribute much of their fame to attending red carpets, the average actor or actress is unlikely to be 'discovered' by doing red carpet press. If you are an unknown actor, there are many indirect and less tangible benefits to be gained from being photographed at premieres and events:

Material for Your Press Kit

Red carpet photos make you appear to be part of Hollywood. In reality, almost anyone can get onto a Hollywood red carpet; all you need is the money to pay a publicity company. Regardless, indie filmmakers still consider these photos valuable because they can be used to promote a film.

Material to Market a Film

When a filmmaker (or sales agent) tries to sell an indie film, a press packet is created for the project. A bio about each lead actor is included, along with the most high profile pieces of press the actor has done. Red carpet photos help the film look as though it has cast who are famous or up and coming talent on the verge of breaking out. This alone is unlikely to garner a sale, but when combined with the many other pieces of information in the press kit, it helps give the overall impression the film is a saleable commodity.

Establishing a Celebrity and Media Presence Online

Recent red carpet photos are some of the first images to show up when a name is entered into Google. Filmmakers often research actors online when deciding between the final few choices for a role.

There are also many sites that pull 'celebrity' information from IMDb then cross-reference it with the actor's red carpet photos to create a 'celebrity page' for that actor. IMDb has a deal with WireImage.com, so photos on red carpets are occasionally added to the relevant actor's IMDb page, which gives a nice professional tone to your IMDb profile.

Marketing in Another Country
If you are from another country, you can use your American press to promote yourself in your home country, and your foreign press to promote yourself in America. This may cause indie filmmakers in each country to perceive that you are a more saleable commodity in the other.

Networking
At most red carpet events you are in a room, cinema lounge, or bar with a few hundred people who are important enough in the film industry to be invited there or savvy enough to get on the list. This is a nice opportunity to make a few new friends.

Establishing Familiarity with the Press
Magazine editors look at press photo websites on a daily basis, so consistently attending events will give them a familiarity with your face and name.

Appearance in the Fashion Pages
Press photo sites are where the pictures are sourced for those fabulous best and worst dressed lists. When a magazine is marketing a certain trend, like saying how 'purple' is the new 'orange', a writer might search the term 'purple necklace'. If you happened to wear a purple necklace that week, the writer may pull your pictures and add your photo to the magazine alongside celebs.

These lists offer actors free exposure. Some actresses even go so far as to wear something hideous, or find out what the colors and accessories of next season are to increase their chances of being added into these pages.

Establishing Familiarity with Photographers
Red carpet photographers often delete unknown actor's pictures without uploading them. If you're heading out to a carpet every few months, the photographers will get to know you and will be more likely to upload your shots. If you don't have a publicist, ask the event staff member running

the carpet to announce (and spell your name) to the photographers on the carpet.

Websites That Publish Red Carpet Photos

There are many websites that publish red carpet photos, but the major press publications only buy photos from the top few. Shots from one photographer may end up on several websites. Usually the top photographers are given the best position at the start of the carpet, so make sure the first twenty or so photographers all get clean shots of you.

Here's a list of the five websites that have photographers in the lineup on most notable red carpets:

- **GettyImages.com**
- **WireImage.com**
- REX.com
- FilmMagic.com
- DailyCeleb.com

TIP: Girls Shouldn't Wear Black on Red Carpets

Black clothing lacks definition in photos, so magazines tend to avoid printing red carpet shots of non-celebrities wearing black unless the cut is really unique. Red carpet photographers usually take more photos of non-celeb girls when they are in colored outfits because these pictures are more likely to sell to magazines.

Google Alerts

If you set up a Google alert for your name, you will be notified by email any time it is added to or mentioned on a website. This will help you to find press that you weren't aware of (like if your red carpet photos ended up on obscure websites). Enter your name within double quotation marks so that it alerts you only when the two words are found together, rather than separately.

Paparazzi vs Red Carpet and Event Photographers

Red carpet photographers are often freelancers, who may earn a small fee per event but mostly work for a commission on photo sales. The photographers each work for, own, or sell shots to red carpet websites or press publications. Each photographer registers for a spot in the carpet lineup and waits their turn to take photos when the celebs are at work (i.e. organized press events) and ready to have pictures taken in public.

There's a big difference between the photographers taking legitimate shots on the red carpet and the paparazzi hiding in the bushes. Some paparazzi simply take photos of celebs in public places. This ultimately helps keep the celeb in the media and is widely considered an occupational hazard that comes with being a celebrity. The more aggressive paparazzi, on the other hand, turn up uninvited to the houses of celebrities, stalking them on their private holidays or chasing them in cars. Desirable shots sell for big commissions and these paparazzi go to many unconscionable lengths to get the highest grossing shot.

Red carpet photographers are not paparazzi, so help them get clean shots of you. It will be hard with all the flashes going off and voices calling for you to look in every direction, but be nice and try to do as the various photographers ask.

A photographer friend once told me about an A-list actress who was rude to the red carpet photographers at several events, then showed up to a film festival on the carpet ready to pose for her photos. Apparently, in a rare act of solidarity, every photographer immediately put their camera down and refused to take her photo. She stood, confused, as not a single flash went off, her ego fast replaced by red-faced embarrassment. Suddenly aware of her folly and of just how important a service these press members provide, this celebrity had to issue an official apology. Remember, you need the photographers way more than they need you.

Radio Interviews

There are radio press companies in LA that run interviews for several radio stations. Celebs sit in a sound booth with a microphone, and every six minutes a different radio station patches through and tapes an interview. The talent doesn't have to travel to individual stations, and can do ten interviews in the space of an hour. Phone interviews are also an option if you can't make it into a studio, though the quality is rarely as good.

Q Score

According to Wikipedia.org "The *Q Score* is a metric developed by Marketing Evaluations, Inc. that determines a "quotient" ("Q") factor or score through mail and online panelists who make up representative samples of the United States. The Q score identifies the familiarity of an athlete, celebrity, licensed property, TV show, or brand and measures the appeal of each among those persons familiar with each. Other popular synonyms include **Q rating, Q factor**, or simply **Q**."

A Q Score is an assessment of how recognizable and appealing a celebrity is. This rating is utilized by CDs, studios and network executives when assessing which celebrity will bring the largest audience to a project.

The ultimate purpose of doing publicity as a working actor is to increase and improve your Q Score so that you are more likable and recognizable to your fan demographic.

AWARDS EVENTS

Here are the top Hollywood-related awards events held in LA each year.

- Academy Awards™ (Oscars)
- AFI Awards™
- American Music Awards™ (AMAs)
- BAFTA Film Awards™
- Billboard Awards™
- Black Music Awards™
- Country Music Association Awards™
- Critics' Choice Awards™
- Daytime Emmys™
- DGA Awards™
- Emmy Awards™
- Golden Globes™
- Grammy Awards™
- MTV Video Music Awards™
- Producers Guild of America Awards Ceremony™
- SAG Awards™
- Spirit Awards™
- Teen Choice Awards™ (TCAs)
- Television Critics Association Awards™ (TCAs)
- WGA Awards™

CHAPTER 11

THE 2007 TO 2009 EFFECT

From 2007 to 2009, myriad events drastically altered the film and TV industry. The WGA (writers union) went on strike, SAG spent almost nine months threatening to strike, and the global economy tanked. Additionally, affordable digital cameras evolved to make filmmaking a less exclusive endeavor, and audiences turned to the internet for much of their viewing entertainment.

Every three years, the contracts negotiated by each of the Hollywood unions come up for renewal. At this time, negotiations are entered into between the AMPTP (representing the producers, studios, and networks) and the writers, directors, and actors unions (respectively the WGA, DGA, and SAG-AFTRA).

In 2007, the WGA went on strike to force the studios to give better terms to writers particularly in the previously uncharted new media realm. This strike was necessary to give writers the leverage needed to successfully renegotiate their contracts. Unfortunately, the strike almost completely shut down Hollywood for three months. Very few studio or network projects were in production, rewrites on film scripts were not being done, and most TV series had to stop shooting mid-season because they had run out of completed scripts. This put a strain on the wallets of the studios, but to a much greater degree, it put a strain on the wallet of every person in LA who relied on the film industry for their income.

The SAG contracts expired on June 30th of 2008 and the AMPTP would not agree to many of the contract terms proposed by SAG. Because the Hollywood economy was so badly impaired by the writers strike, SAG was gun shy on actually striking. This 'almost-strike' created a limbo; TV projects were still going ahead, but many feature films weren't able to secure completion bonds (insurance) due to concern that in the event of a strike, the union would pull actors from work in the middle of the shoot. Eventually SAG started giving guarantees to projects that if a strike occurred, all actors on the project would be permitted to continue working until close of production.

While SAG was debating whether to strike and negotiating new media agreements with the studios, AFTRA (the radio and television union) made a deal with the AMPTP. The fact that the AFTRA contracts were finalized while SAG was still deliberating pushed many of the new TV pilots in 2009 to register with AFTRA. This weakened SAG's bargaining power and eventually, after almost nine months with very few films going into production, SAG signed new contracts.

After the almost strike, many new TV shows were produced under AFTRA contracts. This further weakened SAG's ability to negotiate on behalf of its members, and **prompted the March 2012 merger of the two acting unions, now known as SAG-AFTRA.**

The US stock market crashes of October 2008 and early 2009 occurred while SAG was deciding whether to strike. These crashes, together with the global recession that followed, removed a great deal of the equity that was previously used to finance films. Films as an investment are generally considered either a high-risk venture or a tax write-off. Most investors and investment funds took losses during this period, which meant they no longer needed the tax deductions. Many had their money tied up in stocks or real estate (or gone from selling at a loss), so the money usually used to finance films was almost completely removed from the global economy.

This shortage of hard equity investors caused the number of films made after October 2008 to drop dramatically. Many films that were due to go into production lost their financing and others that had not yet found financing simply had nowhere to turn for money. This forced the budgets of most films being developed to be substantially reduced in order to secure what little financing remained in the market.

On top of all this, advances in digital filmmaking have made it easier to create great looking films for less money. Thus among the thousands of films for sale at any market, there are now hundreds of low budget features with professional quality footage. To get the attention of buyers at markets these days, even a great film needs celebrity cast members, press, and awards at the major festivals.

These events, together with an unprecedented global shift to online media for entertainment, have created a divide in the film industry. Independent films with mid-level budgets have all but disappeared. A few years ago, an actor at the beginning of their career could aim for strong supporting roles in films with budgets ranging from $2 million to $6 million. Filmmakers on these projects would lock in one or two B-list celebrities and the remaining parts would go to unknown or up and coming actors.

Films in this budget range are the highest risk projects for investors. With a budget under two million dollars, an investor has a chance of making his money back through Netflix, iTunes, and international DVD and VOD sales. With a budget over $6 million, a producer has enough money to attach bankable celebrities to interest a mini-major studio and/or guarantee distribution. From $2 million to $6 million the filmmaker is in limbo, with no studio attached but a lot of money to recoup.

The current lack of available equity means investors are more likely to avoid this high-risk budget range than they were before 2007. Producers of the few films made for between two and six million dollars these days must secure their investment by attaching bankable talent in several of the larger roles.

When the economy was at the peak of its financial boom, the price of everything was inflated. Housing prices, stock prices, film budgets, and actors quotes were all much higher than they are today. Now, just as housing prices are lower, actor paychecks (quotes not base rates) are lower because the reduced number of mid-budget features has created more competition for the few available roles.

The public shift to online viewing and illegal downloads drastically reduced the size of residual checks that used to support actors between jobs. **The reduction in actor quotes and residual checks mean actors at all levels are now willing to work for less, in smaller roles, and on projects that they would have previously refused.** Celebrities and working actors are taking roles that used to be cast with up-and-coming actors. Many up-and-coming actors are consequently relegated to playing walk-on roles in substantial projects and strong supporting roles in much lower budget projects.

Another major industry entry point for new actors has always been guest star roles on TV. In recent years there has been a substantial improvement in the production value, delivery technology, and quality of the writing on television series. This, paired with the reduction in the pay rates and consistency of work in the film industry and has lead many actors who used to only do film, to work in television. Likewise, those who used to work in larger television roles are now willing to play smaller parts. So, when you audition for a guest star role, it's likely that you are competing with actors who have previous series regular or studio film credits. That doesn't mean you won't get the part, but it does mean you need to do an exceptional audition in order to have a shot at it.

The middle group of actors has thinned out in the same way as the middle group of projects has. Think of it like an hour glass with a group of already working actors on the top, a group of up and coming actors on the bottom, and a small middle section through which up and coming actors must climb to get to the top.

The events from 2007 to 2009 have made it more difficult for an up-and-coming actor to get started in what was already one of the toughest industries in the world . . . but the effects are not permanent. As the bank accounts of potential investors worldwide slowly recover, the entertainment industry does the same. LA is still the hub of the film and television world and when it is difficult here, it is downright impossible everywhere else. Many careers have been made during these lean years and the entertainment industry is definitely well on the road to recovery.

CHAPTER 12

OTHER LA RESOURCES

The Pilot Report

Compiled annually by James J. Jones, President of The Premiere Talent Group, this invaluable report contains fascinating statistics on the usage of actors in American TV pilots each pilot season. The report reveals the number of pilots shot in each city (including US productions shot internationally), the number of roles allocated to actors of each sex and age demographic, and the percentage of roles allocated to development clients vs 'named and known' (working) actors (those with a substantial Q score or recent series regular credits).

The Pilot Report can be found under the 'media' tab at: ThePremierTalentGroup.com

American Film Institute (AFI)

As mentioned in the 'Student Film' section, the American Film Institute is a prestigious film school at which the students produce high quality short films with a professional level of cast and crew. AFI students are often existing industry professionals looking for further training, and most have a thorough understanding of what is required to make a good film. Proven by the frequent attachment of high profile working actors, AFI shorts are (in my opinion) the best student short films you can work on in LA.

SAG-AFTRA Conservatory

The Conservatory offers SAG-AFTRA actors free classes on a variety of subjects including accents, cold reading, voice-overs, and improvisation. The conservatory also casts most of the AFI student projects.

Joining information is at: SAG.org/HollywoodConservatory

SAG-AFTRA Orientation

To join the conservatory, you must go to a SAG-AFTRA orientation, which is a surprisingly informative two-hour presentation about the union. Call SAG-AFTRA or check SAGAFTRA.org for more information.

SAG Foundation

The SAG Foundation is independent from the union and runs free casting director workshops, seminars, and classes for actors. From the SAGFoundation.org website: *"Founded in 1985, the Screen Actors Guild Foundation is an educational, humanitarian, and philanthropic non-profit organization."* That's cool and everything (seriously, it sounds amazing), but the main reason most of the actors I know join the foundation? Free movie screenings at the DGA throughout the year.

ArtistFootprint.com

Artist Footprint is a fantastic resource that gives actors the ability to track auditions and jobs, while storing useful information such as booking and callback rates, average monthly income earned, and employer history. The site is free and a brilliant way to track your career.

iActor

SAG-AFTRA has a database called iActor. The idea is that each SAG-AFTRA actor creates a profile and casting professionals can scroll through the database when they are looking for talent. If you are a SAG-AFTRA member it only takes a few minutes to set up a profile here.

iActor can be found under the 'Union Info' tab at: SAGAFTRA.org.

ActorsConnection.com

Actors Connection runs seminars, classes, and special events every month on all acting related topics. They cover seeking representation, the business of acting, auditioning skills, networking, and much more.

The HSG Resource Guide

A comprehensive resource listing classes, photographers, headshot printing locations, taping services, representation, CDs and many other actor-related resources. The site and app offer a user-voted star rating system and review section that will help you select the best resource for your needs at every stage of your career. Check TheHollywoodSurvivalGuide.com for more details.

Samuel French

This entertainment industry-focused bookstore on Sunset Blvd. is a well known and reliable source of plays, books, mailing labels, and other industry-related materials.

IndieGoGo.com and Kickstarter.com

If you are interested in creating your own projects, IndieGoGo.com and Kickstarter.com are great new ways to source finance. The idea behind each site is that you post a project you'd like to create and invite both friends and independent investors to donate money in exchange for various incentives.

iPhone Apps

Actor Genie

The *ActorGenie* iPhone app has updated information on what's casting, who's casting it, where to find representation, plus valuable tips from top actors, directors, writers, and casting directors.

Rehearsal

The *Rehearsal* app is a brilliant creation that allows you to save, highlight, and rehearse sides on your iPhone. It has a function with which you can hide your lines while you're running them, and another to record only the other character's lines so you can create your own 'virtual scene partner'.

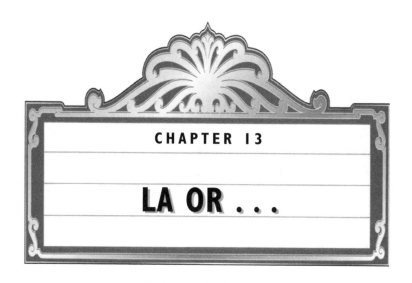

CHAPTER 13

LA OR . . .

Should I Try to Get Famous in My Hometown First?

Oh boy, this question opens a massive can of worms, and a huge debate that carries many strong opinions. The answer is completely dependent on where you are from, your connections, and where you are at in your career.

Firstly, if your hometown or country does not have a substantial quantity of film or TV production taking place, there's no point in staying around to fight over the scraps. If the place you are hesitant to leave has a strong film and TV industry, staying to build credits may be a viable option.

If you want to stay in your home country or state and are able to get into one of the top acting schools, do it. It doesn't guarantee you success, but it does give you the most important thing in acting: solid training, which is the foundation for all of your work.

Here's where problems arise for actors who are not regularly auditioning for the top jobs in their area: All CDs have a pool of actors they already trust large enough to give the director several solid options for most roles. In LA, actors are often busy on other jobs and TV shows are unable to reuse actors, so CDs are forced to find new talent. In smaller markets, the top tier of the acting talent pool vastly outnumbers the quantity of roles available, which means CDs often give most of the available audition spots to actors with whom they already have relationships.

Think about it from the CD's perspective. A CD might know forty talented actors who are right for each part. If she only has time to audition thirty per role, she is hardly going to use that time to see thirty actors she has never met before and exclude the people she already knows. A CD will always try to see a few new actors for each role, but that still doesn't leave a whole lot of opportunities for new talent. The new talent they do see will most likely be actors they have met through referrals or seen performing around town.

Think of it also from the perspective of those forty talented actors. If you know a CD well and she is casting a role you're perfect for, you would hope she would bring you in to audition, right? It's not fair on those talented actors (who have spent years building the relationship by doing great work for a CD) if they are excluded simply so the CD can take a risk and try out new talent.

Unfortunately, this means there are not a huge number of audition spots left for newcomers. It is not the CD or the agent's fault; in smaller markets there is just not enough work to go around.

If you are able to procure strong local representation and are auditioning monthly for film and TV roles, staying in your home town or country until you have a few jobs under your belt may be a good move. You'll get some networking contacts, footage for your demo, and credits to help validate your O1 visa.

If your agent isn't getting you out, the projects you're working on are not the types of jobs you want to do, or you generally don't feel close to becoming a working actor in your local industry, go where the work is: get to LA.

Age Matters

If you are an aspiring lead actress, remember that once your playing age is over twenty-five it is hard to break into the industry in Hollywood. If your goal is to play lead roles in major films, you have a very small window of time in which you are likely to be considered for these projects without substantial credits. This is partly because so many American actresses move to Hollywood straight after high school, so by the time they turn twenty five, they've got seven years of auditions, networking, and booking jobs under their belt.

If you can safely get to Hollywood as soon as possible, I recommend that you do it. Note that the age issue doesn't apply to character actors in the same way that it does to leads. Leading men have a little more time and a lot less pressure than ladies regarding their age but are still expected to have substantial credits by the time they hit around thirty-five.

TIP: If you live overseas and get into one of the top schools in your country, I recommend spending the eleven months after graduation giving the local industry your best shot. If you aren't making solid progress, move to LA for a year on a J visa, which is a working visa for people who graduated from formal study **within** the past twelve months. Research whether this visa applies to citizens of your country.

Am I Ready for LA?

Los Angeles isn't some mystical, magical fantasyland. It's a city, like any other city, whose principal industry happens to be the exact industry in which you want to work. Starting at the bottom in LA is easier than in other markets because there is more acting work available at every level. What if you were born in LA? Would you leave and go to a smaller town because you're "not ready for LA?" Heck no!

If you have **solid acting chops, a perfect standard American accent, a quality demo reel, enough money to support yourself, and the means to obtain working papers**, you are ready for LA. If not, it may be wise to wait until you have all of these tools in place.

Be prepared for the fact that it is likely to take several years before your career begins to gain momentum in LA. In the meantime, however, the acting classes here are some of the best in the world. Getting to know your classmates as you grow together is an outstanding way to build a network, because actors refer each other to the right people far more often than agents, producers, and directors do.

What if you want to stay in your home town? What's the point of establishing all these great connections and getting work in LA when your home town is ultimately where you want to live? Returning to any city or country with American credits and footage will open a substantial number of doors for you. In fact, if your sole goal is to succeed as an actor in another country, my advice would be to head to LA for a while.

If you spend a few years acting in Los Angeles, you will almost definitely improve your talent, accumulate several new credits, and gain some impressive contacts. You will likely encounter a substantial paradigm shift that will endow you with a greater understanding of the entertainment industry than you could ever imagine. This will give both your performances and your professional relationships a maturity and depth that will help you find longevity and success in the film and TV industry in any city.

But I Already Am Famous Back Home . . .

If you are already a celebrity in your home country or State, it will not guarantee you success in LA. Many small town and foreign celebs who head to LA struggle to find work, and those who leave top TV shows in other countries should be commended because they are taking a big chance with their career. Regardless, there are many benefits in heading to LA straight off the back of an award winning foreign film or regular role on a foreign TV show:

• If you have a top agent, they can probably refer you to a top manager or agent in the USA.
• Having a 'series regular' credit means your LA rep can pitch you to CDs in America as a series regular, which means during pilot season you will be much more likely to get series regular auditions.
• You will have recent press in your press kit.
• If you have a tangible fan base and online presence, it will help when your representation pitches you for jobs.
• Your celebrity will probably qualify you for an E or O visa.
• Hopefully you'll have some cash saved, which will give you a nice head start. LA isn't easy, so please live frugally out here regardless of the kind of lifestyle to which you are accustomed.

Head to LA immediately after you leave a TV show or wrap your latest film. A delay of even a year is like centuries in LA and can be detrimental to your chances of getting strong representation. If you're fresh off the back of a show or film when you move to LA you are seen as 'up-and-coming talent', on your way to the top and a much more desirable asset. It's all about perception.

Should I go to LA or New York?

To answer this question is actually very easy.

While the film and TV industry in New York is much bigger than it is in most other places, the big apple is predominantly a theatre town. Broadway and Off-Broadway plays and musicals dominate the performing arts world there. It houses the financial epicenter of America (Wall Street), so the cost of living in New York is higher than in LA. New York feels cultured, alive, beautiful, and you'll probably live a wonderful life there (just as you would in say, London) but it will be difficult to embark on a successful film career.

LA has a theatre scene that, while vast in quantity, is not reputed to be high in quality (although there are some amazing shows). LA is the home of Hollywood, and clearly the place to be for film and TV.

If you are interested in a career in theatre, move to New York. If you are pursuing a career in film and television, head to LA.

The exception is if you are strongly connected to well-positioned people who are willing to help you in either city. If you are close with a top film and TV CD in New York, chat with her about whether she can refer you to the right people in town or audition you for roles. Likewise, if you are pursuing a theatre career and have solid connections at the big theatre companies in LA, head there.

Move where the solid referrals are regardless of the main artistic focus of the city. Once you've built up your American resume, you can decide whether to move where the work is or stay where your connections are.

What About Canada?

If you can't gain working papers for the USA, I strongly recommend heading to Canada. Citizens of some countries (eg. England, Australia, New Zealand) who are under 31 years old are eligible for the IEC-WHP (International Experience Canada—Working Holiday Program). This gives you a visa for up to two years to live and work in Canada.

Toronto and Vancouver have substantial film incentives, which draw many productions from LA. The talent pool is slim, so actors in the main cities often gain access to auditions that would be reserved for those with substantial credit lists if they were in LA.

Hopefully, after a year or two of working in Canada you will have enough credits to qualify you for the 01 visa and entry into the USA. Credits on American shows shot in Canada would assist you in gaining LA representation and give you professional footage for your reel.

RESOURCES IN YOUR HOME TOWN

If you are unable to get to LA tomorrow, work hard every day to gain as much experience and training as possible. I missed many opportunities in my home town because I didn't know where to find acting work.

Search online for the best acting classes and theatre companies near you. Ask where other local actors source their work from. Target the top representation in your area or in major cities nearby in which regular auditions are held. Be proactive and you will find opportunities presenting themselves to you in ways you never thought possible.

Actor Networking Sites

One of my favorite things is the camaraderie that exists between actors of all ages, backgrounds, and financial means. Online networking sites allow actors with varying levels of experience to guide each other through problems, questions, decisions, and to share when projects are casting. No matter what career issue you're dealing with, these sites are filled with people who can empathize with and advise you. Look for acting groups online through Facebook (eg. 'Casting Directors For Actors'), Yahoo, and Google to start a dialogue with likeminded people.

Breakdown Sites

Find out which casting websites are used in your country, set up a profile and submit for roles.

University Acting Degrees

Studying acting for two or three years full time is how many of the top actors began their careers. These schools provide you with the theatre training and experience so important to an actors tool kit, and give you a starting point for your resume. Formal training shows industry professionals that you intend to take this career seriously and understand the importance of studying your craft. It should also provide you with fundamental skills that will serve you in crafting characters and scenes for the rest of your career.

Find the most highly regarded schools in your country or State and apply for them first. While it is not imperative that you go to a top school, if you have to go somewhere for three years, it might aswell be the best.

Local Agents

When selecting a local agent, aim for one who has strong relationships with each of the local casting offices. Go to IMDBpro and see if the agent has clients with recent guest or regular spots on recognizable TV shows. See if the clients have credits on films that were **cast by actual CDs**. If a film didn't hire a CD, the actor may have sourced the job themselves without the help of their agent.

If you aren't able to get into the top agencies, look for smaller agents with clients who have played roles on shows or films in the past year. This implies the agent is at least on the radar of the casting offices.

CHAPTER 14

PREPARING FOR LA

If you can't get to LA for a while, there are things you should be doing right now to prepare.

- SAVE AS MUCH MONEY AS POSSIBLE. Think of every fifty dollars you don't spend as one more day you can survive in LA.
- **STUDY YOUR CRAFT.** Take the best acting classes you can find as often as you're able.
- Learn a PERFECT standard American accent.
- GET ON STAGE. I can tell whether an actor has a substantial theatre background within moments of watching them perform. It will add tangible depth and layers to your work. Do community theatre, school plays, whatever you can get your hands on.
- Learn how to do as many accents as you can. This skill will aid you for the rest of your career.
- Girls should learn how to do hair and makeup to suit different roles.
- Fix your teeth. Make sure they're straight and white, unless your type is 'creepy homeless guy'. This is more important than you'd think for lead roles in LA.
- Fix your skin. Eat less sugar, drink more water, eat well, exercise, cleanse, tone, and moisturize your face twice a day . . . and if that doesn't work, see a specialist. Clear skin is a must for American TV and film.

- EXERCISE! You need high energy and great stamina to stay alert on a film or TV set for twelve hours a day. If you want to play lead roles, get your body looking healthy and toned for your body type. **Do not simply try to 'get skinny'.**
- Find two great two-person scenes from films. One comedic and one dramatic. Memorize and prepare. These will be your showcase scenes.
- Find two great monologues: one comedic and one dramatic. Memorize and prepare. You will use these in the rare instances a director asks you to audition with a "monologue of your choice".
- Film yourself performing scenes as often as possible.
- Go to AS MANY AUDITIONS AS YOU CAN. Think of every audition as a free class on audition techniques.
- Do LOTS of short films and indie features to gain on-set experience.
- Read scripts of great films online at Scriptapolooza.com or InkTip.com to become familiar with what a good script looks like.
- Watch every single one of the 'top 250 movies' listed on IMDBpro and observe who cast and directed them.
- Select a top director and watch a selection of their films. Become familiar with the top directors in the industry.
- Watch every movie that has ever won best picture, actor or actress at the academy awards.
- Watch American hit TV shows and learn the CD and actor's names.
- Join every casting website in your area.
- Improve your cold reading skills by reading dialogue into a mirror for fifteen minutes a day.
- Get some friends together and shoot a web series for FunnyOrDie.com or YouTube.com.
- Get your resume, headshot and demo up to a professional standard.
- Practice memorization. Memorize one page of a character's dialogue from a two-person scene every day. Aim to be off-book in ten minutes.
- Go to every film festival close enough for you to get to.
- Try writing a film or scene. Writing helps you understand more about what goes into creating characters and stories.
- 'Follow the top filmmakers and actors on Twitter and Facebook. Watch how they market themselves and interact with their fan base.
- Write a business plan for your acting career. Write one for the next 1 year, 2 years and 5 years.

Recommended Reading

Read the following recommended books and others like them. Become an expert on the industry and on acting.

Acting-specific texts:

- 'The Artists Way' by Julia Cameron
- 'Acting In Film' by Michael Caine
- 'An Actor Prepares' by Constantin Stanislavski
- "On Acting' by Sanford Meisner
- "Respect For Acting' by Uta Hagen
- 'The Art of Acting' by Stella Adler
- ''The Actor and The Target' by Declan Donnellan
- 'Acting Class: Take a Seat' by Milton Katselas
- 'The Hero's Journey' by Joseph Campbell

Industry-related literature:

- 'Save the Cat' by Blake Snyder
- 'From Reel To Deal' by Dove S-S Simons

These other books are wonderful for taking on a successful mindset and managing your life and career. Find other literature that covers core traits artists often need the most help with: emotional intelligence, money management, manifesting, social skills, fashion sense, and maintaining a healthy body and mind:

- 'The 7 Habits of Highly Effective People' by Stephen R Covey
- 'Blink: The Power of Thinking Without Thinking' by Malcolm Gladwell
- 'Rich Dad, Poor Dad' by Robert Kiyosaki
- 'Think and Grow Rich' by Napoleon Hill
- 'How to Win Friends and Influence People' by Dale Carnegie
- 'The Art of War' by Sun Tzu
- 'The Law Of Attraction' by Jerry and Esther Hicks
- 'The Power of Receiving' by Amanda Owen

CHAPTER 15

HOW TO GET TO LA

Before uprooting your whole life to 'make it' in Hollywood, why not come to LA for a few months to see how the town works and whether it's right for you? The more money you have when you get to LA, the more freedom you will have to focus on your acting work, so save every cent you can from this second until the moment you arrive. There is a full budget in 'Part 3' of this book, but for now, estimate that it will probably cost around $12,000 to survive comfortably for ninety days in LA.

Giving LA a test run is simple . . . don't build it up in your mind to be bigger and scarier than it really is. Just get your marketing tools ready, buy a plane ticket, and go.

For those only staying 90 days: if you are unrepresented and hoping to take meetings, avoid arriving in LA between January and April. Managers and agents are very busy during pilot season and it will be hard to schedule a time. If you are staying longer than 90 days, come any time.

Here's a little checklist so you can see how straight forward this is:

1. Start saving money NOW.
2. Get great (color) headshots taken and formatted into 8×10s at 300dpi with name banner.
3. Put a great resume together.

4. Put a 1–2 minute reel together with a perfect 'standard American' accent scene first.
5. Buy a plane/train/bus ticket (or service your car).
6. If you are not a US citizen, apply for the visa waiver online.
7. Find a place to stay on AirBNB.com or CraigsList.org.
8. If you are from another country, join your local LA group, ie: Brits in LA, Australians in LA, Canadians in LA. Use these to find accomodation, car rentals, advice, and social events.
9. Join ActorsAccess.com, NowCasting.com, Backstage.com, and LACasting.com then start submitting online a week before you get here.
10. Travel to LA.
11. If needed, rent a car with insurance.
12. Spend the next three months doing workshops, classes, and auditioning for anything you can (to make contacts and get used to LA auditions and film sets), going to industry events and meeting representation.
13. During your ninety days, decide whether you want to stay.
14. If you want to move to LA officially, look into visas or contact Next Stop LAX and they will guide you through the visa process.

It really is that simple. After ninety days, if you really integrate, you'll know whether LA is the type of town in which you want to spend more time. There's no point applying for official documentation until you have a feel for what LA is like and whether living here is right for you.

LA BUSINESS TOOL CHECKLIST

Here is a very basic checklist of the business tools an actor starting out in LA needs. Now that you have learned about each of these items, go out and get them!

✓ MONEY TO SURVIVE
✓ Confidence that you can act well . . . backed up by the actual ability.
✓ Headshot
✓ Resume
✓ Great Demo Reel Online
✓ Perfect standard American Accent
✓ Online Profiles: ActorsAccess.com, NowCasting.com, LACasting.com
✓ USA Work Papers (see part 3)

✓ SAG-AFTRA Membership
✓ Manager
✓ Agent
✓ Networked connections to CDs, producers, and directors

That's pretty much all it takes to get started!

PART 2

The Filmmakers World

A Sneak Peek on the Other Side of the Camera

INTRODUCTION

Film and TV is your industry. You must educate yourself on the business of filmmaking. As a working actor, everything in this section will affect you directly or indirectly.

Actors often quote the line "It's show **business** not show **art**" because they have heard it from a teacher somewhere. Few of these actors really understand the inner workings of the business side of the industry. Most actors are like the blind leading the blind, giving each other advice on how to approach and attack an industry they do not fully understand.

You have two choices. You can be an actor who turns up on set with no idea what is going on around you, or you can learn a tiny bit about the fundamentals of how these films and TV shows actually work. The former option allows you to be a meat puppet, following directions blindly and holding out your begging dish (read: headshot and resume) hoping someone will give you a chance. The latter will help you hold and follow intelligent conversations with the various filmmakers with whom you plan on working over the next fifty years. It will also give you an understanding of what is happening on set, so you can behave appropriately.

When you understand the basics of film sales and distribution you can assess a project based on its salability, and know going into each film its probable market potential. Combine this with strong screenplay assessment skills, and you can confidently choose to work on strong projects rather than those that aren't likely to turn out well.

In this section you will learn how films and TV pilots are made and sold, who the people are on each project, and some of the jargon and language that is thrown around on set.

It is possible to become a successful actor without knowing any of the information that follows, but really, what sense does it make to try to strategize your way through an industry when you don't understand how it works? Besides, if you truly care about this career, this dream of yours . . . don't you want to know what happens behind the curtain?

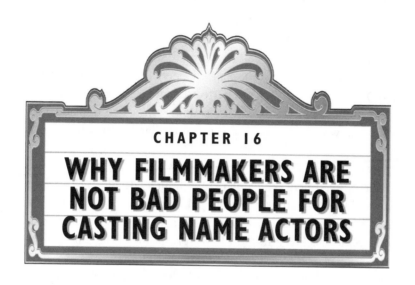

CHAPTER 16

WHY FILMMAKERS ARE NOT BAD PEOPLE FOR CASTING NAME ACTORS

Actors often come across to other industry members as narcissistic, naive 'artists' with no real understanding of how the industry works. These actors complain when they don't get an audition, or say "Once again, they are casting a name in the lead." Well, guess what? The 'name' brings a probable return on a percentage of the film's budget due to the fan base and pre-existing branding that the name actor most likely spent many years working to establish.

Some actors see producers, directors, and CDs as powerful oppressors, unwilling to give an unknown actor a chance and only interested in money and celebrities. These actors are blind to the fact that producers, directors, and CDs are just doing their job, which is to make the best movie possible (given the time constraints and budgets) that is also able to MAKE MONEY. This is not because they are greedy.

Many of the producers (and almost all of the CDs and directors) I know are primarily interested in making great films. They must also recoup the money for their investors on each film in order to secure financing to make the next one. Once a producer releases a film that doesn't make its money back, he doesn't just lose the backing of the current film's financiers, he also has a much more difficult time procuring finance for the next project. This means less work for the producers, directors, CDs, crew, and actors.

The amount of fighting, begging, and borrowing a producer does to get a film financed and developed is unfathomable. By the time a film is casting, years have usually been spent. In a perfect world, filmmakers would audition every actor to find the perfect talent for every role regardless of notoriety . . . but how can they justify doing this when they know that by casting unknown talent, there is no guarantee that anyone will buy or watch the film?

How can a producer go to an investor, look them in the eye, and ask for a $3 million investment, knowing that without a saleable celebrity attached, they are unlikely to recoup that money? He can't.

To be perceived by financiers and sales agents as having the potential to make its money back, a film must have at least one of the following things:

- A very low budget to recoup teamed with an original concept, exceptional script, and an incredibly talented cast and crew (plus a lot of luck!)
- A low budget combined with the ability to be marketed as a genre film like a horror, thriller, action, or teen comedy
- Ground breaking special effects (like *300* or *District 9*)
- A pre-existing fan base and franchise (like book or comic adaptations)
- Bankable name talent in at least one of the lead roles

As audiences it's our fault, not the filmmaker's. When you're in the DVD store and a friend asks "How about this one about a guy who kidnaps the girl he likes so he can pretend to rescue her", the first thing you probably say is "Cool, who is in it?" If your friend says "Some guy called [insert talented unknown actor name here]", you're likely to be indifferent towards watching it. But what if he says "Ryan Reynolds and Robert Downey Jr"? Then it becomes a whole different film. You can picture Robert Downey Jr rambling maniacally, and Ryan Reynolds being sarcastically amused and annoyed by each challenge they encounter. Your decision to spend money renting the film is mostly based on WHO is in the film.

When people use films like *Napoleon Dynamite*, *The Blair Witch Project*, and *Paranormal Activities* as examples of how low budget films with no celebrities attached can make money, it makes me want to scream. The odds of this are so slim. For every film with a tiny budget that has miraculously made millions of dollars, there are probably ten thousand indie features that were made worldwide and didn't make a single sale, let alone make their money back. Many of these films probably had better stories, characters, AND filmmaking than the ten 'miracle' projects of the past decade.

Filmmaking is a business. In business there are business models, and when a producer is dealing with millions of dollars of someone else's money, he must respect that investment, follow the proven business model, and make choices that assure some level of guaranteed return.

If the budget is over $200,000, if the producer knows the script is good but not amazing, if there are no groundbreaking special effects, pre-existing franchises, or uniquely marketable concepts, the producer has an obligation to cast an actor with a 'name value' substantial enough to get a large portion of that investment money back.

CHAPTER 17

THE FOUR STAGES OF PRODUCTION

Development

The term 'development' is very broad. It refers mostly to creating and re-fining a screenplay and putting the key pieces (cast, director, etc.) of a project into place to secure financing. The financing stage itself is also part of the development process.

The cost of development stays with the budget of a project and is repaid like any other money invested in a film. This can often be detrimental to a project going ahead as the film's budget might be bulked up by development costs to a figure that is no longer likely to be recouped.

An example of the financial baggage that can come from development costs is the 2006 movie *Superman Returns*. The film had a reported production budget of around $200 million, but with that came an additional $40 million (give or take) in costs that had accumulated over the seventeen or so years that the project had been in development.

Script Development

Development of a screenplay can either involve a writer developing a story 'on spec' (for free), or being hired to develop a story for a production company or studio. Before a script is written, most professional projects go through the following stages:

- **Concept**

A concept is simply an idea for a project . . . preferably an idea that can easily be summarized into a logline.

- **Logline**

A logline consists of one or two sentences that summarize a film. An example of a logline would be: "A bumbling scientist must rescue his family and the world when an army of aliens tries to wipe out the human race."

- **Synopsis**

A synopsis is a general outline of the main plot points in a film in under a page (around 300-450 words) in prose (like the blurb on the back of a book).

- **Treatment**

A treatment is like writing your script out as a novella or short story. A treatment can be anything from two to thirty pages. Sometimes longer. It should cover the entire story from start to finish and include every scene in the film.

Note: *A project can be at the concept, outline, and even at the treatment stages with a producer before a writer is hired.*

- **Outline**

An outline lists every scene of a film in order. It establishes each location and summarizes what happens in each scene. Outlines can be several paragraphs per scene (complete with characters, what happens in the scene, and even some dialogue), or as simple as one sentence per scene (e.g. "EXT: STREET scene where Chris, Lee, and Gemma save the cat"). There are no rules governing how long or short an outline needs to be as long as it includes all of the intended scenes in the film, creating a modifiable skeleton for the screenplay.

- **Script**

Once the treatment is done, a script or 'screenplay' is written. Optimally, a producer hires a writer and pays them to write a screenplay based on a

TIP: The most respected script writing competition in Hollywood is the Nicholl Fellowships in Screenwriting. If you have any interest in being a writer, enter this before entering any other screenwriting competition. Details are at Oscars.org.

concept. Writers will also often write a screenplay on 'spec' (for free) without a producer attached, hoping that a producer will later 'option' (lease) the already written screenplay and produce the film.

An acceptable length for a feature film script in Hollywood is between 90 and 120 correctly formatted pages. Any script shorter than 80 pages or longer than 125 pages is unlikely to be read. A screenplay in LA should be laid out in the format that is used in the screenwriting program Final Draft™.

Pitch

'Pitch' is a very broad term used when a writer, agent, manager or producer is either seeking finance or looking to sell a concept or script by 'pitching' it to production companies and/or studios. A writer will also pitch film ideas to agents and managers while seeking representation. A pitch can be anything from one sentence (a logline) to a meeting lasting several hours with substantial supporting documentation and visual aids. Pitch meetings are usually arranged through an agent or manager but can be as simple as running into the right person at a party and pitching them a concept by the bar.

Note: A professional writer will pitch outlines or treatments for unwritten scripts in the hope that someone will pay him to write the screenplay, rather than having to write the script on spec and try to sell the finished product. Often, a story alone will be purchased from a writer and another writer will be brought in by a studio to write the screenplay. For this, the original writer should receive a 'story by' credit.

Optioned Property / Under Option

A producer or film studio can option a script by paying a negotiated fee of at least one US dollar. When a project is 'under option', it means the producer owns exclusive rights to make the film during the term of the option using the optioned material. An option contract usually allows the producer or studio to modify the script, possibly bringing in new writers to work with the existing material. As soon as the film goes into production, the producer typically agrees to pay an additional fee to the writer in order to purchase the screenplay in perpetuity.

Attaching Finance and Talent

A producer pitches a project around town seeking finance, pre-sales, name cast attachments, and/or distribution. It's a vicious catch twenty-two because often the name talent won't attach until the money is in place and the money won't commit until the name talent is locked in.

Note: *Very rarely, a project at the concept stage can be financed prior to the writing of the screenplay. This would tend to only be the case if the concept is based on a current event or subject matter with a pre-existing fan base, like a film version of a comic book or popular TV series, a sequel, or a biopic on a public figure.*

The finance on many projects is therefore 'cast contingent', which means the financiers have said "We will fund your film if you can attach any of the following celebrities: [insert celebrity list here]".

Celebrity cast may attach to a project on a 'pay or play' deal, which means if the film doesn't go ahead, the celeb is paid an agreed amount of money for setting aside time and giving their name to the project.

Turnaround

Turnaround is not a regular part of development, but something that filmmakers encounter from time to time. When an option held by a studio expires and becomes available for purchase, the project that was under option is now 'in turnaround'. When the rights to a project developed by one studio are sold to another studio (usually in exchange for the cost of that project's development), it is referred to as a 'turnaround deal'.

Pre-Production

After finance is secured and the script is production ready, a film may go into pre-production. This is generally a one to six month period immediately prior to the shoot during which the producer(s), line producer, director, and other key crew work full time preparing for the shoot.

Among other things: locations and permits are secured, casting sessions are run, talent is locked in, crew are hired, schedules are put together, vehicles are rented, props are purchased, prosthetics and costumes are crafted, sets are constructed, and storyboards are drawn.

Production

From the first day of principal photography (shooting) to the final day (wrap) of the shoot, a project is considered to be 'in production'. 'Pick-ups' (shots that the director wasn't able to film and must shoot days, weeks, or even months later) and 're-shoots' (shots that need to be filmed again) are part of production also, but often take place during the post-production period.

Post Production

Post-production literally means 'after production'. It refers to the editing, sound design, and paperwork finalization of a film project. Some post-production work begins during production. The footage shot each day is taken to an editing facility (AKA 'post house'), digitized, cloned for safety, and pieced together. Here are some of the footage-related stages of post-production, many of which occur simultaneously:

Rough Assembly / Rough Cut

The footage is placed into a basic order without too much focus on timing or transitions between scenes. This can be done by an assistant editor or by the editor without the director present. The takes marked by the script supervisor as the directors 'pick' are usually used for this initial assembly.

Edit

The editor works with the director to put the footage together to tell the story. Scenes are added, deleted, trimmed, manipulated, or even placed in a different part of the movie. Once the visual edit is finished, the filmmakers have 'picture lock'.

Visual—SFX / Color Correction

The post VFX (Visual Effects) or post SFX (Special Effects) team creates any 'CG' (Computer Generated) effects needed. 'Color Correction' ensures that lighting and color tones are relatively even from scene to scene (and from shot to shot within a scene), and that they make the films 'look' match the tone of the story and the director's vision.

Sound—Composition / Foley / Sound Edit / Sound Design

After the picture is 'locked' the composer will 'score' (compose) the soundtrack and original songs specifically written to play throughout the film. Famous examples of scoring would be the music of impending doom in *Jaws* or *Halloween*.

The music supervisor clears the rights to the additional songs selected by the writer, editor, or director to use in the film. The 'foley' artist creates ambient sound, which includes things like footsteps and wind rustling through trees. The composer and music supervisor deliver these sound components. The music editor, sound editor, and editor tweak the levels, edit points, and volume as they integrate each piece into the film.

ADR (Additional Dialogue Recording)
ADR is often required when dialogue isn't recorded at production quality on set and must be recorded in a studio afterwards. Almost every film and TV show requires some ADR work. In ADR an actor must watch the taped footage of their character talking, and at the same time read the dialogue aloud (as the character) into a microphone. The actor must try to match words to the mouth movements, energy, and tone of voice in the footage.

Distribution
Distribution refers to a completed film being sold to various territories (countries) around the world. See Chapter 19—'Independent Film Distribution' for a detailed look at the process.

CHAPTER 18

TV PILOTS
AND STUDIO FILMS

TV PILOTS

What is a TV Pilot?

A TV 'pilot' is a single episode of a TV show that is shot as a demonstration of how a TV concept and script would be executed. Chronologically, a pilot is almost always the first episode of a TV series in which the regular characters are introduced, the setting is established, and the viewer is shown the intended dynamic, pacing and format of the show.

What is Pilot Season?

The term 'pilot season' refers to the period from mid-January to March each year, when makers of many TV pilots seek cast for series regular, guest, and co-star roles. A much smaller pilot season also runs from mid-July to September.

Since the writer's strike of 2007 and the 'almost SAG strike' of 2008 and 2009, new pilots can be announced anytime throughout the year. Most pilots, however, are still cast during the traditional pilot season periods.

Actors come to LA from all around the world during pilot season (mostly during the January to March period) in the hope of booking a series regular role on a new US TV show. One positive attribute of the condensed nature of this 'season' is that there is competition between the networks to cast each celebrity in the series lead roles. This competition leaves smaller series regular roles open to less familiar faces.

One major shift in Hollywood since 2008 has been the increase in the number of top film actors now willing to work on TV pilots. This has created much more competition for available roles and meant that many series lead roles are now cast through offers to A and B list celebrities.

Types of TV Shows

There are many styles of television show, but the main narrative styles are:

- 1 hour drama (1 episode per week)
- 1 hour comedy / dramedy (1 episode per week)
- ½ hour comedy / sitcom (1 episode per week)
- Mockumentary (1 episode per week)
- Children's show (may be 1 or 5 episodes per week)
- Soap (5 episodes per week)

Where Do TV Series Come From?

When a writer comes up with an amazing idea for a TV show and wants to pitch it to a network, a 'Show Bible' is created, which includes the following materials:

- Overview of the show
- Target demographic
- Style of show
- Intended network
- Intended timeslot
- Intended number of episodes per season
- Intended budget per episode
- Series lead character breakdown
- Series regular character breakdown
- Intended cast attachments or character prototypes using existing celebrities
- Full 'treatment' for each of the episodes in the first season
- Pilot script for the show
- Marketing plan
- Financial figures from comparative shows in the genre or style
- Full scripts for additional episodes are occasionally added

These items are combined with a few additions that may be specific to the project. The writer's agent, manager, or producer (or anyone who knows the right people) sets up a 'pitch session' with executives from each of the TV networks for which the show may be appropriate. The writer and/ or producer attend each meeting, show bible in hand, and pitch their concept.

Each major network only has enough time slots for a certain number of new shows each season, but will finance several times that number of pilots. For example, a network might finance fifteen TV pilots for a given season. Those fifteen pilots are cast, filmed, edited and viewed by network executives and test audiences. Of the fifteen, the network may only select three or four shows to 'pick up'.

A TV show being picked up means the network agrees to finance additional episodes of the show (usually in blocks of 12 for network TV and 13 for cable), and allocates a time slot for it to be aired. The creator(s) of the concept and the writer(s) who wrote the pilot episode almost always become executive producers or consulting producers of the series. Modifications are made to the show according to the results of test audience screenings and network input. Storylines are changed (if necessary), and some characters may be removed, added, or re-cast.

Unfortunately, pilots that don't get picked up are rarely 'saved' for another season. This is partly because the cast and crew move on to their next projects. With a different cast and crew, the existing pilot episode would no longer be an accurate 'sample' of what the show could be like. Sometimes, however, a show will sell a TV series to another network after not picking the show up themselves.

When a TV show airs, the 'ratings' (number of viewers) it gets on American TV determine whether it stays on the air. The ratings are called 'Nielsen Ratings' (named after Arthur Nielsen). Shows can be taken off the air after as few as one episode, or after many seasons, depending on how the show is rating at the time.

The pilots that are 'picked up' are announced in May each year. A week later, the 'upfronts' (meetings where many TV commercial time slots are pre-sold) take place. ABC and NBC each shoot an average of 20–25 pilots and pick up around ten. CBS and CW each shoot between ten and twenty, and usually pick up around five.

TIP: A good place to see weekly ratings for many American TV shows is TVByTheNumbers.com, under the 'Renew / Cancel Index' link.

Fox Switches to Cable Development Model

Fox Studios made an unprecedented change in January 2014 when they announced they would no longer participate in pilot season. The network would typically shoot between ten and twenty pilots each season and pick up around five. Since the change, Fox still shoots pilots, but fewer, behaving more like a cable network in that they aim to pick up the majority of the pilots they shoot and order some shows to go straight to series.

How Do Test Audiences Work?

Test audiences are groups of non-industry people from selected demographics who are paid to attend screenings at independent testing centers. In many testing centers, each viewer is given a gauge that ranges from 'not interested' to 'very interested' and can chart tiny increments between the two. Each test audience member must hold the dial on the gage while watching and keep it at the appropriate point to reflect the degree of enjoyment at each moment.

If at any point an audience member feels they would have 'changed the channel' or 'walked out of the movie', there is a red button that can be pressed only once throughout the test. This way the network knows when people in each demographic lost interest in the show or film.

Afterwards, a questionnaire about the show is filled out, asking participants to list their favorite characters, memorable moments, etc. Some people are taken aside for filmed discussion sessions so the network and studio execs can hear what 'normal' (non-entertainment industry) people within the target demographic say about the show.

Through all of this, the testing center is able to give approximations to the network of how many viewers from each demographic are likely to watch the show on a regular basis. This process helps networks figure out which pilots to pick up, and within each pilot, which cast members or storylines to keep or remove. It also gives an insight for the writers into which jokes or conversation topics are well received by the target demographic.

Feature film test audience screenings work in a similar way, but usually rely on a hardcopy questionnaire and verbal Q&A at the end of the screening rather than the electronic gauge.

What is Syndication?

TV syndication is when the right to broadcast a television show is sold to multiple individual TV stations, instead of going solely through a broadcast network. This means a show is sold to local TV networks in various regions of the US rather than just screening on the national networks. The term 'syndication' also refers to selling those broadcast rights internationally, though broadcast rights can still be sold internationally for shows that have not been syndicated domestically.

Syndication affects actors because when the show is sold to the various networks around the world, union contracts state that talent from each episode must be paid residuals. A show's syndication can last for decades, which is awesome because it means residual cheques can keep coming long after the show has finished shooting.

HOW IS A STUDIO FILM FINANCED?

Well now, isn't that the two hundred million dollar question? I'm going to give you the most simplistic explanation of studio film finance that you may ever see, but at least you will have a vague idea of what happens along the way.

A writer, producer, or director attends a pitch meeting with the development department of a studio. They give studio execs the pitch: what the intended (or existent) script is about, why audiences will see the film, who might star in it, what attachments the project already has, and what existing films it is like.

If the studio's development executives like the project, it is sent to the marketing department with potential cast and directing attachments. The marketing department assesses how the film would be advertised to the public and what the anticipated P&A (Print and Advertising) cost would be for the budget and genre.

The studio may test various 'markets' (essentially countries) as they draft a 'cost / benefit analysis', to compare the total anticipated cost (production budget plus P&A budget) with the probable return for the project. If the investment looks likely to turn a sufficient profit, the studio will commit to a production and P&A budget for the film.

The studio may option the idea from the writer and hire that writer and/or another writer to write the story. If the concept comes with a script, the studio may option the script and employ that writer and/or other writers to re-write it.

Note: 'P&A' includes posters, billboards, online marketing, and advertisements on TV or in magazines. The P&A budget for studio films is typically 80% to 100% of the budget of the film.

If the project was brought to the studio by a director or producer the studio will evaluate the filmmaker and either keep them attached to the project, or buy them out of the project so the position can be filled with a more suitable candidate.

While the script is being written and rewritten, 'name' cast, producers, and directors are attached. Additional non-studio production companies, financiers, or studios may come on board with partial finance, and presales are made to mitigate the financial risk. Once financing for the full budget has been acquired, or allotted by the studio, the film is 'green-lit', which means producers are given a budget to begin spending money on production costs other than script development and talent attachment.

What is a 'Tentpole' Movie?

Each year studios take risks with the movies they finance. It is becoming increasingly difficult to anticipate which film projects will be profitable. This is proven by the success of films devoid of A-List actors like *Bridesmaids* and *Chronicle*, and the financial losses taken on celebrity-laden [tentpole] movies like *The Lone Ranger* and *R.I.P.D.*

Note: *While the cost of production is financed by the studio's production 'arm' (department), the marketing arm pays for the P&A. When a film earns money, the P&A is paid back before production costs. On independent projects and some studio films, a P&A fund may finance the Print and Advertising.*

For this reason, every studio tries to release at least one 'tentpole' film per year. A tentpole is a big budget movie that covers all 'four quadrants' of viewership: male, female, young, and old. They are usually expensive action-adventure films a family can attend together, which means both parents and children are likely to enjoy them. Examples of tentpole movies would include *Harry Potter, Iron Man*, and *Avengers*. You may see a trend here . . . these days most tentpole movies are based on pre-existing franchises that have an inbuilt fan base.

When most of the guys I know heard that a movie version of *Transformers* was being made, they wanted to see it. Why? They'd grown up playing with Transformers toys and watching the cartoons. Millions of dollars had already been spent marketing the brand to people around the world, so the name already had a fan base. This meant much of the branding normally required to promote a film of its type had already been done, so the studio could save money by spending less on marketing.

This is why Michael Bay was able to hire largely unknown actors to play the lead roles. What if the film was called *Robot Battle* instead, and was still made with a mostly unknown cast? That may sound pretty cool but it wouldn't have the same nostalgic attachment and pre-existing fan base that *Transformers* has. This would reduce the number of people who would pay to see it without celebrities in the leading roles.

Tentpole movies are films that studio executives expect to make enough money to subsidize potential losses on every other movie the studio has done that year. Tentpole movies keep studios in business and give them the freedom to finance riskier projects (like *The Butler*, or *Zombieland*).

State and Country Film Incentives

When a film production comes to an area, it can bring millions of dollars into that community. This money comes from expenses like location and hotel rentals, the cast and crew shopping and going out on their days off, and the local community being hired for work on the project. Countries like Romania and New Zealand, and US states like Louisiana and New Mexico have had their economies positively affected by becoming frequently used locations for film productions.

As state and federal governments worldwide became aware of the money to be made by hosting a film production, many started creating incentives to persuade producers and studios to shoot in their region. The governments reduced or removed taxes for the production, and began offering tax credits or refunds for investors financing films shot locally. Many regions now offer a cash incentive which simply writes the production a check for a pre-designated percentage of all money that was spent in that region on the shoot.

Runaway Production

When a Los Angeles production company produces a project that shoots outside LA, the project is considered a 'runaway production'. Runaway production is a huge issue for the Los Angeles economy and local work force as money is spent and workers are hired in other cities rather than in LA.

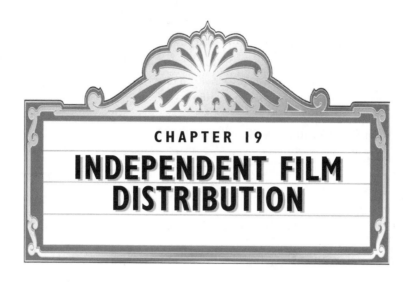

CHAPTER 19

INDEPENDENT FILM DISTRIBUTION

This is a quick and basic run down of how an independent film (without distribution locked in during production) is sold. There are three terms you'll need to understand this process:

Territories

There are almost two hundred separate 'territories' (essentially countries) in the world to which a film can be sold. Of these, only thirty-five are considered 'meaningful' for film sales.

Sales Agent

A producer takes a completed film to a 'sales agent', who acts as a salesperson for the film. The sales agent meets with 'distributors' (see next page) often at 'film markets' (see next chapter) to sell the film in as many territories as possible. A sales agent will usually represent several films at any given time. Sales agents often specialize in a particular budget range and genre, which helps create and nurture strong relationships with buyers in that realm. Prolific indie producers sometimes act as their own sales agents.

> **Note:** The phrase "sell the film" means the sales agent is selling a distributor the rights to reproduce, screen, and distribute copies of the film within a specific territory for a contracted term (usually 7 years).

Distributor / Distribution Company

'Distribution companies' ('distributors') purchase the rights to distribute films throughout a specific territory. Films are distributed through many channels within each territory, including:

• DVD rental (eg. RedBox, Blockbuster)
• Video On Demand (eg. Direct TV, Dish Network)
• Online VOD (eg. Netflix, iTunes, Hulu)
• DVD sales in stores (eg. Walmart, Target, Best Buy)
• Television
• Theatrically via movie theaters (eg. Birch Carol & Coyle, Arclight)

When a distribution company buys the rights to sell a film in a specific territory, they can only sell the film within that territory. For example, if a distributor in France buys the rights to distribute *Toy Story 3* solely throughout France, that distributor cannot then sell the film to theaters in England. Likewise, the distributor may only distribute the project in the format for which they have purchased the rights: as a 'theatrical release' (in theaters), a DVD release, VOD release, or otherwise.

Here's where it gets a little tricky: **many distributors also act as sales agents to sell films to other distributors worldwide.**

HOW AN INDEPENDENT FILM GETS SOLD

Here is an example using microbudget figures to simplify the math: *Film A* cost $50,000 to make. If the film appears to be highly marketable, several sales agents may want to represent it and the producer may find a bidding war developing between sales agents willing to pay for the rights to sell the film. This is rare with micro and low budget projects, which are usually taken by a sales agent with no upfront payment and the negotiation of a substantial sales commission.

The producer gives *Film A* to a sales agent to sell. The sales agent meets with distributors from many countries regarding *Film A*. Distributors from England, Germany, and France love *Film A* and want to buy rights to a full theatrical and DVD release. The English distributor pays $45,000, the French distributor pays $35,000, and the German distributor pays $40,000. The distributor from the USA offers $30,000 for DVD only.

In total, the sales agent has just made $150,000 for the film. He takes his percentage (usually 15%–35% of all sales, plus 'costs'), which (at 20%) is

$30k. Let's assume modest costs of $10k to cover flights to film markets and $5k for meager marketing costs, leaving around $105,000 for the producer.

The producer made the film for $50,000 in hard equity, but has 'deferments' (money owed for labor provided by cast and crew, aka 'sweat equity') of $45,000. The deferments are paid back and the investors are reimbursed their $50,000, plus $10,000 to cover a pre-negotiated 20% interest on the money they contributed. Once the deferments and investors are reimbursed, the producer, investors, and anyone else who owns a share in the film can start making a profit. Fees, interests, and costs vary as they are all negotiated on a per film basis.

FILM A—PROFIT AND LOSS

REVENUES	
England	$45,000.00
France	$35,000.00
Germany	$40,000.00
USA	$30,000.00
Total Revenue	$150,000.00

EXPENSES	
Sales Agent 20%	$(30,000.00)
Sales Agent Expenses	$(10,000.00)
Marketing Costs	$(5,000.00)
Receipts to Production	$105,000.00

PRODUCTION PROFIT & LOSS	
Deferments	$(45,000.00)
Investor Equity Receipts	$(50,000.00)
Investor Equity 20% interest	$(10,000.00)
Net Revenue to Production	NIL

It is important to note that even though $150,000 has been paid for a film that only cost $50,000 to make, the project has still only just broken even financially. No profit has been made other than the interest for the investors. This is a pretty common scenario for independent film. If the sales agent made a solid deal with the distributors, the producer will get a percentage of movie ticket and DVD sales in each country. However, due to the small budget and lack of star names, the distribution rights were probably sold for a one-time fee with a tiny share of further profits from each territory sold.

Pre-Sales

Another option for selling a film is to acquire 'pre-sales'. Pre-selling is when distribution rights are sold to various territories before a film has been made. It can also apply to a sales agent agreeing (prior to completion) to pay for the rights to sell the film. The pre-sale is based on the cast attachments, genre, script, and concept. Although the distributors and sales agents do not actually 'prepay', they do sign documentation stating that they will buy the film when it is complete or 'delivered'. This allows the filmmaker to acquire loans from banks based on the amount that each distributor has agreed to pay to distribute the film.

Letter of Intent / Interest

The purpose of these letters is to show potential investors and attachments that others are interested in the project, much like a reference letter when applying for a job.

A **letter of interest** is simply a letter (that should not be phrased to be legally binding) stating that a member of the cast or crew, a production company, financier, distributor, or sales agent is 'interested' in the film.

A **letter of intent** is very similar to a letter of interest but should be a more committed document that states that if certain components are in place, the writer of the letter intends to contribute x to the project.

WHY SOME MOVIES DON'T GET DISTRIBUTION

Most of the actors I know have been in at least one independent feature film that was completed and never released. Cast and crew receive screeners (if they are lucky) and the film sits gathering dust on the director's bookshelf. I've been in around ten of them and it's heartbreaking. You spend a month or two on set, the energy is high and everyone is excited about the collective creativity going into the project. Perhaps there are a few familiar names in the film, so it's assumed that it will get a release and then it just . . . doesn't.

Why Do Some Films Never Get Released?

With the advent of digital cameras, just about anyone can shoot a film these days. The image quality on a $2,000(ish) Canon 5D or 7D camera is arguably better than that of most cameras that cost $20,000 five years ago, and those that cost $200,000 fifteen years ago. Hence, quality filmmaking equipment has become much more accessible.

In the past, for an independent feature film to get made, an agent or manager had to like the script enough to give it to a producer. The producer had to like it enough to pitch it to financiers, and the financiers had to like it enough to invest a lot of money into it. This meant the script (or at least the idea) had to be pretty darned good. In this same scenario, the director and cinematographer each had to be selected from hundreds of talented directors and cinematographers as the best person for the job. The producer and director then sat through hundreds of auditions to find the most talented actor for each part.

This is still the case with studio and bigger budget indies, but in the micro (under $50k) and ultra low (under $200k) budget indie world, something entirely different is going on. Cameras like the RED and the Canon 7D have revolutionized digital filmmaking. Anyone with a spare few thousand dollars can grab a camera and shoot a feature film with professional quality equipment.

Let's say your buddy Lee is managing the local DVD store, and he saves $25,000 to buy a camera and rent some equipment so he can direct and edit a feature film that he has written. Lee asks his friend Nick (who takes photos for the local newspaper) to be the cinematographer, and posts on the breakdowns that he's casting an unpaid feature film.

Is a film made with this script, director, cinematographer, and actors likely to be as good as a film made with a professional cast and crew, and a script that has been approved by all those agents, studios, and producers? Probably not.

Each year, there are thousands of "Lees" around the world spending their free time making bad micro and ultra low budget feature films. Sales agents are not going to represent most of these films. This means that if you attach as an actor to a micro or ultra low budget indie with no names in it, that has a below average script, director, editor, DP, and cast, the film probably won't be good enough to secure legitimate distribution.

But what if a low budget indie you were in is actually really good and still didn't get released? When good indies don't get a sale, it's often because films like "Lee's" have diluted the low budget marketplace. Out of every ten thousand low budget indie films, only a hundred might actually be good films, and maybe ten might be great . . . but how does a filmmaker convince a film distributor to watch his film and see that it's not one of the bad ones? Especially when the good films are shot on the same cameras as the bad ones, with similar budgets and storylines. Even if the distributor does watch and like it, how does he then convince the public to pay money to watch the film?

In order to sell, a film needs to be something the public will pay to watch. Usually this requires name talent, a great hook or concept, or the ability to fit into a niche market with a pre-existing (preferably cult) fan base like a horror or thriller. Major selling points (other than celebrity cast) that can help movies gain distribution are nudity, gore, and extreme violence. Many low budget movies incorporate these factors to aid with foreign sales, and market to niche audiences who enjoy these elements.

The ultimate reasons most low budget indie films don't get sold are simply because they are not marketable, don't look professional, are not very good, and are simply not enjoyable to watch. The reason some of the better low-budget indies don't make a sale is because with so many bad ones around, it's hard to get buyers to watch your film and see that it isn't like the rest.

One solution to the "no-one will watch my great film" issue is to enter festivals where judges are forced to watch it. Once a project starts to win awards at well-reputed film festivals, distributors are more likely to give it a chance. It also enables the distributor to market the film as a 'festival winning indie'. Films like *Primer* (made for $35k) and *El Mariachi* (shot for $7k) are micro budget indies that found success after being seen by the right people at film festivals. This isn't a guarantee, but at least it gives the film a fighting chance of being seen by the right people, and a little bit of industry credibility.

Why do most Indie Films take so Long to be Released?

Literally thousands of tiny things must be done to each film after the shoot is complete. The picture edit, special effects, soundtrack, additional dialogue recording (ADR), sound effects, credit sequence, and so many other jobs must be completed just to get a rough edit. Shots may be missing or sub-par so pickups or reshoots might need to be scheduled. The rough edit is watched by test audiences to work out any kinks, then more changes are made. Once the edit is finalized, the trailer must be cut and most filmmakers make a website for the project. After this, the filmmaker takes the completed film to different sales agents and after weeks or months of meetings and conversations, hopefully the right representative is found.

From here, marketing materials must be created—posters, new trailers, a revamp of the website. The sales agents take the film to the markets and sell it to the distributors. They may wait a few months until the next market before making sales. Once sales are made at the market, DVD copies are made, prints or digital files are created, and the project is released in various territories.

All of this sounds easy to summarize when reading it in a book, but the process can take anything from one to three years or longer.

Any number of things can impede progress at any stage in this process, including rights issues, contract problems, budgetary shortfalls. If a film runs out of money in the post-production stage, they may have to wait months or years to find the thousands of dollars to fix something in the footage or to get the film quality up to standards that pass the quality control expectations of the sales agents and distributors.

Needless to say, when green actors hound filmmakers about a project that has taken a year or more to be released, it is not just counterproductive, but a telltale sign of that actors ignorance toward the complexities of film production and distribution.

Note: A **limited** theatrical release is when a movie is screened in between 800 and 2000 individual theatres throughout North America. A **wide** theatrical release is when a film screens in more than 2000 individual North American theatres. A release in less than 800 theatres might be referred to as being in 'selected cities'.

Why do Some Celebrity Filled Films go Straight to DVD?

If you were in a film starring Charlize Theron or Willem Dafoe you'd think that movie would come out in the theatres, and you'd probably get famous from being in it, right? Not necessarily. Did you see Willem Dafoe's *Boondock Saints*, or Charlize Theron's *Battle in Seattle*? Both are great films that ended up having just a one or two week limited run leading into what was essentially a straight to DVD release. *Boondock Saints* is probably one of the best films I've ever seen, but it's not always the quality of the film that matters.

When an independent film is pitted against bigger budget releases in theatres, few people choose to see the indie, which means theatres are not often interested in screening them. Big budget blockbusters look better on a movie screen because you can see the detail in the special effects and wide shots, which helps you feel involved in the film. Romantic comedies and dramas are still effective when watched from your couch at home. In saying that, comedies are generally more lucrative at the theatre than dramas simply because they are more fun to watch with friends and family.

Imagine for a moment that you work in an office job or doing shift work, and you are standing at the movie theatre. You're busy, so you only get to the movies maybe once a month. The movie options include *Iron Man 2*, *Shrek 4*, *Inception*, *Date Night*, and the indie film *Camille* starring James Franco and Sienna Miller. Which film would you pay fifteen dollars to see? What if you were taking a date? That's thirty dollars. Are you going to see one of the big studio films that everyone you know has seen or the low budget ($10M) indie that you haven't heard of?

When was the last time you went to the movies and ignored all the blockbusters and big budget releases to watch an indie drama starring Laura Linney or a subtitled foreign film starring Javier Bardem? You're in the industry. It's your job to watch the little artsy films. So, if *you* haven't done that lately, what are the odds that the average non-industry person has?

CHAPTER 20

FILM MARKETS

A film market is an organized event where sales agents, producers, and distributors take films to a single location to be sold to 'buyers' who work for distributors from around the world. It is literally a marketplace for films, much like when you go to a flea market on the weekend. Companies set up display booths with posters on the walls and samples of their work. Buyers walk around the market perusing the 'goods' to see if anything takes their interest and take meetings in the booths, lounges, or even at nearby restaurants or bars.

You will be amazed at how accessible filmmakers are at film markets. They are there to network and are, in many cases, more than happy to meet you. As an actor, it can be disorienting to see producers (who seem so important and intimidating in an audition room) with a DVD in hand, eager to sell their film. It really does bring home the fact that everyone has to fight to survive in this business, not just actors.

The two most notable film markets are AFM and Cannes.

AFM (The American Film Market)

AFM is held each year in Santa Monica, usually at the Loews Hotel on the beach. There is as much networking in the (free to enter) lobby, at the bar, and by the pool as there is in the closed off upper levels that cost around $250 a day to enter.

If you're in a film that's being sold at the market, use it as a reason to attend. You'll meet a ton of producers and directors. If you can, buy (or borrow) a market pass to go upstairs to see how it all works.

Cannes

Cannes is both a film festival and a film market, with separate tickets available for each. The parties and screenings are fantastic networking opportunities, and in the film market you can meet hundreds of producers and directors just by walking between the stalls. Be prepared to make ironic quips to random strangers as you look at a poster or see something a little bit different. Strike up a conversation over something arbitrary and, if the person seems friendly and receptive, introduce yourself. As an actor starting out, producers and directors will invariably respect your tenacity, especially if you are brief, professional, and personable.

CHAPTER 21

SHOOTING FORMATS

When trying to predict the probable image quality of a finished product, there are three main factors to take into consideration:

- The previous work of the DP (Director of Photography)
- The camera format
- The lenses being used

On projects over $250k (SAG-AFTRA modified low budget, low budget, and codified basic agreement), you can assume the equipment used will be professional grade. It would be a little obnoxious for an actor to ask more than who the director, DP, and other actors are. When attaching to a SAG-AFTRA Ultra Low or micro budget project, however, it is wise to also ask what type of camera they are using to get an idea of whether the finished film will be a salable project likely to get distribution.

Film vs Digital

The technical difference: 'shooting on film' means actual film is being rolled through a camera, similar to when there were film canisters in stills cameras back in the old days. Film moves past a movie camera lens at 24 'fps' (frames per second), which means the camera is taking 24 photographs every second.

Digital means the image is being captured digitally (in ones and zeros) and recorded onto a tape, computer chip, or hard drive. Digital records 30 fps in the USA (NTSC), and 25 fps in Europe (PAL). Most 'pro-sumer' (a cross between professional and consumer) and professional digital cameras have the option of recording at '24p' (24 frames per second), so the footage looks and feels more like film.

INTERESTING FACT:
Slow motion is recorded at 60 fps.

In the past, the main difference was that film recorded more information per frame of footage than digital. Digital recorded less detail in the shadows (resulting in 'crushed blacks') and the brighter areas (resulting in 'hot spots'). The difference in the size of the information is partly why TV (which needed to stream at a lower bandwidth) was shot on digital, while features (which needed to be projected onto a huge screen) were shot on film. Mostly, however, it came down to cost: shooting on film is expensive.

In recent years, HD digital cameras have advanced to the point that filmmakers are able to use digital cameras to get a filmic quality picture without the expense. Because of this, almost all films are shot on HD and film is fast becoming obsolete.

Shooting Formats

Here are the most popular shooting formats in order of quality:

Film
- 35mm
- S16mm
- 16mm

Digital
- HDSR
- HD
- Hard Drive Recording
- Digital Betacam
- DV Cam
- HDV
- Mini DV
- Video

Lenses

The lens used with each camera can drastically improve the image. Some lenses can make Mini DV look better than Digi Beta, and DV Cam look better than HD. For example, a 35mm adapter lens gives the picture a more filmic quality with a depth of field similar to that of a film camera.

As an actor you don't need to know much about lenses, but when shooting on micro or ultra low budget projects, a great lens can make the difference between a salable project and one that simply isn't shot well enough to get distribution. Ultimately, lens quality comes down to cost . . . the quality of an image shot on a $10,000 35mm lens should look much better than that of the same image shot on a cheapie video lens worth a few hundred dollars.

CHAPTER 22

CREW DEFINITIONS

K nowing what your co-worker's jobs entail is common sense, but it's also a respect thing. If you ask a grip to get you a coffee (rather than a PA) they will be insulted, and quite frankly they should be, because if a grip asked you to fetch something arbitrary you'd be feeling a little disrespected too.

For the sake of public relations, let's learn a VERY basic list of selected crew who will probably show up on any given set.

Firstly, keep in mind that on bigger budget projects these are all jobs in their own right, whereas on low budget projects you might find the producer doing the catering, the DP setting up a light, or the director moving a box of whatever with a PA. The following are the different positions you would *like* to have filled, but when budgets are restricted everyone tends to pitch in and crew take on multiple job titles.

Please also note that these positions are not all in order of authority; they are in order of job type and title so that each department is vaguely grouped together.

Executive Producer

The executive producer ('EP') provides money for a film, arranges money for a film, or introduces the filmmaker to people who have money to put into a film. An 'EP' credit is also sometimes taken by a producer who is simply overseeing a project, rather than actively producing it. Celebrities often attach their name as EP on a project that they believe in (like Oprah with *Precious*) to give it credibility. EPs aren't usually present on set but most try to visit a few times during production.

Producer

The producer oversees the production and may own part of a film. He finds the script, hires the director, hires the key crew, and brings the project to the executive producers. The producer allocates the money, allocates the ownership of backend points, assigns credits, and can overrule the director in casting choices and pretty much anything else. In most cases the producer has the right to fire any person on set, including the director (unless financing disagrees or if casting is contingent on a particular person's involvement in the project). The only people a producer answers to are the EP and the financier. Producers are not always on set during production.

Co-Producer

Contrary to common belief, 'co-producer' is not the credit given to two producers who have worked on a film together (in that instance, the producers would each take a 'producer' credit). The co-producer is hired by the producer to help produce the film, but doesn't have as much authority or involvement as a producer. Although it is still a strong producing credit, 'co-producer' is a less prominent credit than 'producer'. Co-producers are not always on set during production.

Line Producer

The line producer is essentially the 'hands on' producer, overseeing and organizing the details of pre-production and production, and responsible for things like hiring key crew and arranging location scouting. A line producer's authority in these areas depends on how involved the actual producer is on a project. The line producer allocates the budget to each department and on projects without a production accountant, may take on accounting responsibilities. He ensures the shoot is on time, on budget, running smoothly, and is the to whom one most department heads report.

Showrunner

'Showrunner' is a very important position that exists only in television ('show' being a reference to a TV show) and is essentially the TV version of

CREW DEFINITIONS • 259

a line producer. Accountable to the network, the showrunner is responsible for making sure each episode is delivered on time and on budget. Executive producers and writers often double as showrunners on TV shows.

UPM / Unit Production Manager / Production Manager

The UPM ensures a film stays on budget, reporting to the line producer and essentially micromanaging all areas for which the line producer is responsible. This includes supervising the budget, hiring the crew, approving purchase orders and timecards, and making sure all other departments are performing their jobs within the designated budget. On lower budget films, this job description is often merged with and includes the tasks of the line producer and/or unit manager.

Unit Manager

The unit manager sets up the base unit when a crew moves to a new location. Overseeing a team of PA's (and sometimes grips) to set up things like trailers, meal areas, bathrooms, and to ensure everything is where it needs to be and in working order.

Associate Producer

The associate producer aids the producer and co-producers in making a film. This title is often gifted to a PA or production office manager who has worked closely with the producers during production and has contributed greatly to the success of the shoot.

An investor who has made a financial contribution too small to justify an EP credit may be credited as an associate producer. Associate producers are not always on set during production.

Director

A director's job is to use the resources on hand (actors, crew, equipment, sets, etc.) to turn a story from a script into a movie. Everything on the set is there because the director requires it to fulfill their vision. Before a shoot, the director is expected to create a shot-list and storyboard, confer with all department heads on his vision for each scene, and to cast the film.

Once on set, the director has two main jobs: to work with the DP to visually tell the story, and to work with the actors to get the desired performances. In post, the director works with the editor and other post production crew members to assemble the footage and create a 'director's cut' of the film.

Script Supervisor / Continuity

The script supervisor is the editors eyes on set. They watch for inconsistencies in dialogue, blocking, props, costume, and anything that may not match the script or the previous takes. The script supervisor records which shots the director likes and notes when anything varies from what's written.

AD (Assistant Director)

There are many assistant director positions on set.

1st AD / 'First'

The first AD keeps the shoot on schedule and is the voice of the director for the cast and crew. The 'first' acts as an extension of the UPM, keeping the director on schedule by being aware of when each department is ready for the next shot, or when too much time has been spent trying to get a shot.

2nd AD / 'Second'

The second AD's primary goal is to keep track of everything the director needs for each shot, ensuring the props, wardrobe, locations, and actors are all ready when needed. The second AD keeps the principal actors where they need to be (whether it's on set, in makeup, or in their trailer). When you get to set, check in with the second AD and always inform a PA or AD of your whereabouts if you stray too far from your trailer.

3rd AD / Second 2nd AD / 'Third'

The third AD (or 'second-second AD' as they are often called on US TV sets) is an extension of the second AD. Among other things, the third AD is in charge of running the PAs and wrangling extras, acting as middleman between the other ADs and the PAs and extras.

DP (Director of Photography) / Cinematographer

The DP confers with the director to ensure that each scene is filmed with the framing and movement the director wants. This means manipulating the lighting, lenses, camera movement and framing. The DP has authority over the gaffers, the camera assistants, and the grips (through the key grip).

Camera Operator

A camera operator operates the camera under the strict instruction and supervision of the DP. On low budget projects the DP may operate the camera, thereby doubling as 'camera op'.

Focus Puller

Filmmakers show audiences what to look at by focusing the camera on something specific in a scene. When shooting on film or with most modern digital cameras, the focus is manually controlled by a 'focus puller'. A focus puller sometimes solely ensures that the subject is in focus for the entire shot, and sometimes 'pulls focus' from one subject to another, guiding the viewer to move their eyes from the first subject to the second.

AC (Assistant Camera / Camera Assistant)

The camera assistants work under the DP, camera operator, and focus puller. They guide the camera along the dolly tracks and change the batteries, tape, film cartridges, etc.

Gaffer

The gaffers are the lighting crew who set up things like lights, filters, and bounce boards. They report to the head gaffer, who (in turn) reports to the director of photography.

Key Grip

The key grip is the boss of all the grips, hiring the best boy and the rest of the grips and deciding (based on the script) how many grips are needed for each day of shooting. The DP, director, ADs, and UPM talk to the key grip if they need anything done, and that information is relayed through the best boy to the rest of the grips.

Best Boy

The best boy acts as a conduit between the key grip and the grips. He is an assistant to the key grip and the boss of the rest of the grips.

Grip

Grips are the on-set muscle. Grips set up scaffolding, equipment, and take care of anything physical that needs to be done. The grips report to the best boy.

Set Designer / Production Designer

The set designer works with the director and prop master to create each location in the style the director has imagined.

Set Decorator

The set decorator works alongside the prop master and the set designer to dress each set with nick nacks, curtains, paintings, and other items.

Propmaster / Props

The propmaster and props department work with the set decorator and director to provide and place every prop (item that any actor in a scene will be picking up). If weapons are involved, an armourer is brought in.

Special Effects (SFX) Makeup

SFX artists are specialists, so please don't ask them to touch up your foundation or add more eyeliner. These folks are there to do blood, guts, cool scars, swellings, bruises, and anything else out of the ordinary.

Makeup

The makeup artist does non-SFX makeup. On ultra low budget films, you will often find the makeup artist doing the actors' hair or applying SFX.

Hair

The hair department style the actors' hair.

PA / Runner

PAs (film) and runners (TV) report to the ADs, and are essentially the bottom of the 'food chain' on set. Anyone in any department can grab an AD to ask a PA to help with something. This is the person you do ask if you are stuck in makeup and need a glass of water.

Note: Most of the studio execs and filmmakers I know started out as PAs or interns. Respect the PAs. Everybody's got to start somewhere, and you'll be shocked when you see how fast these people move up the food chain and start directing or producing films. Be nice... They will invariably remember arrogant or rude actors on set.

CHAPTER 23

ON SET TERMINOLOGY

H ere are some definitions of the main terms you'll hear as an actor on a film set:

Blocking

The term 'blocking' is a reference to the movements an actor does in a scene. A 'block through' (rehearsal) is usually done prior to shooting each scene. In blocking it through, you act out the scene so the camera and lighting department can see exactly where you are going to be moving at each point, and what you will be doing when you get there. Actors usually leave the set after the block through to allow the crew to prepare for the shot. The stand-in will take your place in frame so the lighting and camera crew can set things up without you having to stand there for thirty minutes (or more).

It's important to match the blocking you did in the rehearsal during the 'master' (usually the first setup, which is a wider shot), and it is vital that you match your blocking in the master during each of the subsequent takes.

Mark

Your 'mark' is where you should end up standing or sitting at a certain point in a scene. During the block through, the scene may be paused when you stop walking so the gaffer can put down your 'mark(s)'. The mark is generally . . . well, marked, by tape in the shape of a 'T' on the floor, but can often be marked by an inanimate object, and sometimes it isn't physically marked at all. If the mark is in a 'T' shape, stand (casually) facing the top of the 'T' with one foot on either side of the line.

The mark exists because in order for the shot look a certain way, you need to be positioned in a certain place. When you do the 'walk through' (block through) of the scene and are given a specific place to stand, be aware of *how* you are standing. In tight shots, if you are even a few centimeters off, or if you change the weight of your body to the other foot, you might throw off the composition of the shot. If you are unsure, ask what your frame is and how much room you have to move.

Hitting your mark is one of the most important things you need to do as an actor. Some directors have said it should be the first thing taught in acting schools. For those of you who've never been on a set, you can practice at home by putting a mark on the floor. When you run lines, walk to that mark (without looking down at it) on a certain line of dialogue.

Note: It's important not only that you hit your mark, but that you hit it on the right line or word for the purposes of the DP timing any camera movement or focus pull, and also for continuity.

Continuity

In the majority of cases, the scenes of a script are filmed out of order, so you may shoot scene 8 on Tuesday, scene 2 on Wednesday, scene 12 on Thursday, and so on. Further to that, you might shoot the second half of scene 3 one day, and the first half of scene 3 two weeks later.

When continuity is not being properly monitored, takes or scenes may not match when pieced together in post. Wardrobe gets mixed up, hair is done differently, actors grow stubble, etc. This means that once the footage is all shot and the editor puts the takes or scenes into sequence, a character's hair or costume might change from shot to shot. If the difference is too extreme, the filmmakers may have to re-shoot the whole scene.

Be aware of how and where your body is standing and moving. If you have your hand on your hip at a certain point in one take and your arms crossed at that same point in another, the director won't be able to cut between those two takes because the way you are standing doesn't match.

Why does it matter to you if the director can't cut between takes? Isn't that their problem? Well, yes, but it's yours too. If the director has limited usable footage of you in a scene, he will have to use footage of the other actors to edit around you, which means you get less screen time and your role in the film becomes smaller.

Cheat

To 'cheat' is a blocking and camera reference. Often, you will be playing a scene on one mark for many of your takes, then the director will say something like "We're just going to cheat you over here for this one", and the exact same scene may be done from a completely different mark. It is called 'cheating' because the DP will angle the camera so that through the lens it looks like you are standing on your first mark. Cheating can also just refer to the DP cheating (moving) the camera or any other prop, scenery, or piece of equipment on set.

Beat

A beat is a moment in a scene. The term is used when directing an actor, for example: "When you play this beat, have a flicker of a smile" or "Wait a beat before you start walking." In the latter example, a beat is typically around a second and a half.

In a different context, the term is used by actors when they break a scene down into 'beats' ('bits'), which are essentially sections of the scene.

Take

The term 'take' refers to the period of time while the camera is recording footage between 'action' and 'cut'. It could be any duration from one moment, up to as long as the camera rolls before the director calls "Cut". It will usually be no longer than one scene, but again, this can vary. To shoot each scene generally requires several takes.

Frame

When you are taking a photo, everything you can see through the viewfinder is in the 'frame'. Some people say you need to make your performance larger (energy and emotion-wise) for a wider framed shot, and smaller (more internalized) for a tighter (closer) shot. Others dispute this line of thinking.

I do not believe the intensity or emotion of the acting itself should need to change in any way according to the frame of a shot. If this were the case, I'd guess that the actor may have been overacting in the wide.

The reality is you may need to slightly modify the physicality of your performance according to how tight the frame is. For example, if in the wide shot your arms were moving in a way that moved or shook your head, you're probably not going to be able to do that movement as vigorously during the close up because it may move your head too much for such a tight shot. This is partly because every centimeter your head moves in reality can turn into twenty or so when projected onto a movie screen. It is also because when the audience can't see the body movements that are causing your head to move so much, it may look odd.

Banger

'Banger' is the contract term for a trailer. You can be allocated a ⅛, ¼, ⅓, ½ or full banger, depending on your contract deal. A 'honeywagon' is the bathroom trailer, to which several ⅛ or ¼ bangers are sometimes attached.

Call Sheet

A call sheet lists the cast, crew, props, and other production needs for a specific shoot day. It also lists the location, contact details, weather forecast, and any other vital information. On set, a call sheet often comes attached to the pages of the script to be shot on that day.

Day Out of Days (DOOD)

The DOOD is a table that shows which characters are required on each day of the production.

DOOD / Call Sheet Letters

On the call sheet and DOOD, letters should be written in line with your name on any days that you're working. Here are the letters you'll most commonly see:

- S—The day you start work on the production
- W—Indicates you are working that day
- H—Indicates that you are on hold to possibly work that day
- F—The day you finish work on the production

One Line Schedule

The one-line schedule lists what scenes are scheduled to be shot each day so you know which scenes to prepare in advance. This schedule may change at any time and should be used as a guide only.

Crew / Walkie Talkie Terms

When on set, crew members use the following terms to communicate:

- "Eyes On" (can you see?) eg. "Does anyone have eyes on Alex?"
- "Ten-One" (going to pee)
- "Ten-Two" (doing a 'number two')
- "Ten-Four" (affirmative—used on walkie-talkies)
- "Twenty" (where are you?) eg: "What's your twenty?"
- "Eighty-Six it" (remove this item from set)
- "Martini" (last shot of the day)
- "MOS" (no sound is being recorded during this scene)
- "Wrap" (shooting is done for the day)

FIRST AD INSTRUCTIONS

When the 1st AD ascertains that everyone is ready for the next take, he will call for the 'first team' (actors) to take their positions from the 'second team' (stand-ins). Once the first team is on set, the AD calls out a sequence of instructions similar to the following (this can vary):

"First positions; actors set; camera set; roll sound OR roll camera; slate; action."

First Positions

Your 'first position' is where you need to be when "Action" is called at the start of the take. Your first position may be already in the frame or out of the shot waiting to enter. The camera also has a first position.

Actors Set / Camera Set

These phrases are generally only called out if the scene contains many actors or cameras. When there are a number of actors, the 'first' (1st AD) may call "Actors set" to ask the 'third' (3rd AD) whether all the actors are in position. The third will respond to the first by calling back "Set". The same may apply to calling out "Camera set" to the camera operator/s. For most setups, however, the first will be able to see that actors and cameras are set without having to ask.

Sound Speed / Speed

Once actors and camera are set, the 1st AD calls "Roll sound", which tells the production sound mixer to begin recording. The production sound mixer replies "Speed!" so the AD and AC know the tape is up to speed, levels are correct and the sound department is ready for the next take.

Roll Camera / Rolling / Camera Speed

The AD only calls "Roll camera" if the shot is 'MOS' (no sound being recorded). If sound is being recorded the AD just calls "Roll sound". The camera operator waits until the sound mixer replies "Speed" before rolling the camera on that cue. When the tape or film is up to speed and running, the camera operator responds with "Rolling" or "Camera speed".

Recording camera footage is usually more costly than recording sound, so rolling the sound first saves potentially wasting expensive film or tape stock over a sound delay.

Slate

By the time the camera is rolling, the second AC or 'clapper loader' should be in frame with a black and white 'clapper' board that shows the production name, production company name, director, director of photography, scene number and take number. The clapper loader holds the slate close to the subject in frame (so the focus puller doesn't have to adjust focus very much to see the words), then reads out the scene heading, scene number, and take number for the sound department.

The clapper loader then slaps the attached strip of wood against the body of the board, making a clapping sound.

This process serves two purposes: The information written on the board helps the editing department catalog each scene as they select takes for the final edit. The simultaneous action and sound allow the 'picture' and the sound recording to have a clear point at which to 'sync' (synchronize) so they can be linked together later in post-production. In desperation, a hand clapping in frame can double as a sync point for picture and sound.

Background Action

When background actors or moving background scenery items (like cars) are in shot, their cue to start moving is when the AD calls "Background action". This is before "Action" is called to ensure that the atmosphere in a scene is already moving by the time actors and/or camera begin the scene.

Action

When the director or 1st AD says "Action", it means the take and the main action within the scene should begin.

PART 3

Surviving LA

The Day to Day Stuff

INTRODUCTION

This section of the book is tailored towards those who are moving to LA from other cities in America, or other countries around the world. It reveals resources and tips on the basics of living and setting up a home in LA.

While much of the content does apply to anyone already living in LA, some sections are specific to international talent (eg. Visas).

Look, this stuff isn't thrilling, but it is important information and I hope your time in LA is made a little easier by having it so readily available.

CHAPTER 24

BUDGET

Day jobs in LA are hard to come by and the pay is often very low. Keep a low overhead by planning to live a very Spartan lifestyle for your first few years so you can focus on your acting work. Low rent, few expensive clubs or restaurants, no designer clothing (girls in LA LOVE outlet, second hand, and overstock stores).

It's nothing to be ashamed of . . . Jim Carrey and Sam Worthington are rumored to have spent time living in their cars, I lived in a storage room for three months, even Hillary Swank said the dress she wore to the Oscars the first year she won was worth more than her car at the time (which I think she may have also lived in at one point). Keep your costs low so you can focus on acting rather than earning money to pay for things like expensive accommodation or car payments.

Residents of many countries can come to the USA for ninety days on an 'I-9 Visa Waiver', or 'Tourist Visa'. You can't officially get a day job during those 90 days, so if you don't have a visa, you'll need to arrive with enough money or credit to survive for three months in a foreign country.

Standard Budget

For an effective ninety day (thirteen week) trial in the LA (the duration of your I-9 Visa Waiver), you'll want to have about USD $13,500 saved.

$2,400   Shared accommodation @ $800 / month.

$1,800	Rent/buy car or cabs during stay $600 / month.
$1,280	32 casting director workshops: 2–3 / week @ $40 each
$1,500	3 months of acting classes at $500 / month
$1,300	Entertainment, eating out, drinks @ $100 / week
$650	Groceries @ $50 / week
$500	Headshots, demo reel, printing
$650	Cost of gas (petrol) while you're here @ $50 / week
$270	Cell phone while you're here @ $90 / month
$150	Memberships for ActorsAccess.com, NowCasting.com, and LACasting.com
$3,000	Set aside for unexpected surprises
Total:	**$13,500 USD**

Impossibly Cheap Budget

If you have several very close friends in LA (so you can alternate couches), and you really want to give LA a shot for three months, you may be able to pull it off for as little as $5000. If you follow this budget you're literally going to have to eat Ramen noodles, fresh market vegetables, and live in the sock drawer of someone's dresser.

$1,200	Cheap accommodation (includes buying food for the host if you're staying on a friends couch)
$500	Bus money or gas money for people who drive you around
$270	Cell phone @ $90 / month
$150	Drinks at networking events
$450	Groceries @ $150 / month for 3 months
$160	Headshot reproductions and demo upload to ActorsAccess.com
$120	Three CD workshops @ $40 each
$150	Memberships for ActorsAccess.com, NowCasting.com, and LACasting.com
$2000	Set aside for unexpected surprises
Total:	$5000 USD

TIP: If your bank charges foreign transaction fees on your account when you use your card, open a US account and shift some cash into it when you get here. Most banks don't require a social security number.

CHAPTER 25

GREENCARD / VISAS

Waivers: i-94

When entering the USA for under 90 days without the intention of working, tourists from many countries can apply for the I-94W Visa Waiver. This should be done online prior to departure at: https://esta.cbp.dhs.gov and is instantly approved in most cases.

Greencard Lottery

When applications are open, sign up for the 'Greencard Lottery' at DVLottery.State.gov. Winning this lottery will save you a lot of time and money.

The US Government runs the Greencard lottery and entry is FREE. If any site asks you to pay, it is a middleman operation that is simply filling out the paperwork for you. Applying through a paid Greencard lottery site will not prioritize your application. Make sure you apply through the site listed above with the .gov web address.

Immigration Attorneys

You need a visa to work in the USA, and for this you should hire an immigration attorney. Be careful when selecting an immigration attorney. Ask people (who successfully got their visa) who they used and be wary of any red flags, like if the attorney doesn't call you back within 24 hours, makes excessive typos in emails, or seems overly confident. You're going to be spending between $2000 and $6000 with this person so make sure you trust them completely. Check the resource guide to see which lawyers other actors recommend.

Non-immigrant Visas

The term 'Non-immigrant visa' means that you are not planning to immigrate permanently. This means that according to the 'INS' (Immigration and Naturalization Service), you are planning on going home . . . eventually.

- Australia-USA Free Trade Agreement Visa (E3)
- Business and Tourist Visas (B-1 and B-2)
- Student (F and M)
- Treaty Transfer and Investor (E-1 and E-2)
- Intra-Company Transfers (L)
- Specialty Occupations, Temporary Workers and Training Programs (H-1B, H-2B, H-3)
- Exchange Programs (J)
- Aliens of Extraordinary Ability in Sciences, Arts, Education or Athletics (O)
- Entertainers and Athletes (P)
- International Cultural Exchange Programs (Q)
- Media Representatives (I)
- Religious Workers (R)
- NAFTA

Here's a more detailed look at three of the non-immigrant visas that are commonly obtained by actors.

O1 Visa

The 'O1' visa is for "Aliens of Extraordinary Ability in Sciences, Arts, Education or Athletics" and seems to be the visa most commonly obtained by actors.

The O1 can be restrictive as it only allows you to work in the industry for which you've been brought in, so you can't legally procure a non-acting day job in the USA. O1 visas are currently not being accepted by some TV networks and film studios. Don't let this fact turn you off applying for the O1, but be aware there are some restrictions with this visa.

To obtain an O1 visa, the two main requirements are to have previously worked in the film and TV industry as an actor, and to be sponsored by a production company, manager, or agent who deems it necessary to bring you into the USA. If from a production company, this sponsorship paperwork should request that you be in the country for a specific project, and should state the dates the filmmakers believe you will be required. This period can be a long time as it can include rehearsal time, shoot dates, potential pickups, and press appearances months after the intended shoot wraps.

J Visa

The J visa is a versatile work visa that allows you to work in any field you like for a year, which means you can get a day job AND get acting work in LA. Just make sure you get the visa within one year of enrolling in or graduating from full time study and if approved you'll have twelve months of absolute freedom to live and work in the USA.

E3 Visa

The E-3 Visa is a two-year USA working visa available only to citizens of Australia and their children and spouses. Applicants must have either a bachelors degree or several years of established experience in a specialty occupation. You also require a job offer from a US company prior to applying at the consulate. This visa is renewable indefinitely in two-year increments.

Immigrant Visas—Greencard

This means you're planning on permanently moving to and working in the US (i.e. immigrating).

- Family-Sponsored (this includes sponsorship by marriage)
- Investor
- Multinational Managers and Executives
- Outstanding Professors and Researchers
- Aliens of Extraordinary Ability in the Sciences, Arts Education, Business or Athletics (this is basically a 'famous person visa').
- Advanced Degree Professional/Exceptional Ability
- Professionals with Bachelor's Degrees
- Skilled Workers
- Religious Workers (EB-4)

A great list of visas is available in the resource guide or at **NextStopLAX.com**.

NextStopLAX.com

Founded in 2007, NextStopLAX is the leading immigration consultancy for entertainment professionals seeking USA work visas. After successfully navigating the transition between London and Los Angeles himself, CEO Andrew Newton-Lee created the company to help other actors hoping to make the leap. Now NextStopLAX processes clients from all over the world and employs a dedicated team of advisors.

CHAPTER 26

HOUSING AND ACCOMMODATION

L A is a transient town. There are a number of shared rentals and sub-leases that will allow you to move in for under ninety days. Rent in LA is paid *monthly* in advance.

The Most Central Area to Live for Auditions

You want to live as close as possible to the majority of your auditions. Driving in LA lives up to its reputation, so the less distance you have to cover on a daily basis, the better. Aim to live within this region:

- East of the 405 Freeway
- West of Vermont Ave
- South of Burbank Blvd
- North of Wilshire Blvd

I'd estimate that around 40% of theatrical auditions are held in or around Hollywood and West Hollywood, 30% are in the Valley, and around 30% are in less central areas. Santa Monica hosts around 85% of the commercial auditions.

Where is 'The Valley'?

The Valley is an actual valley between the Hollywood Hills and the Burbank Hills stretching West almost to Calabasas. When people in LA refer to the

"Valley" they generally mean any suburb North of the 101 freeway and South/West of the 5 freeway (until the two meet) that sits East of Westwood Blvd.

Living Alone

If you want to live alone in an average apartment, anticipate the following prices for anywhere in the Valley near the 101 (at the low end of the price range) or in Hollywood or West Hollywood:

- Studio: $800–$1400 a month.
- 1 bedroom: $1200–$2000 a month
- 2 bedroom: $1400–$3000 a month

Shared Accommodation

Sub-leasing a room in an apartment or house is definitely the most economical way to find affordable and livable accommodation. Expect to pay between $700 and $1400 a month for a room in a centrally located shared apartment or house.

Rent Control

Certain buildings in LA are on a 'rent control' restriction, which means the owners can only legally increase the rent by a maximum of 3% per year. If utilities are included in the rent, it can increase by up to 6% per year. If someone has had an apartment in a rent controlled building for several years, their rent will be much lower than the market standard for the area.

Note: Make sure you get a parking spot or a street parking permit if you are in a permit area. Parking in Hollywood or West Hollywood can be tricky and parking tickets are expensive. If not, find a parking lot with a monthly fee for your car because parking inspectors are everywhere. ladot.lacity.org/tf_Parking_permits.htm.

Backpacker Hostels

Some actors stay in backpacker hostels when they first come out here, which can work quite well if you find the good ones. My official recommend is to stay at either Banana Bungalows in West Hollywood, or USA Hostels in Hollywood, as both are centrally located and reputedly comfortable with nice facilities. Check the resource guide for more recommendations.

AirBnB.com

Whether you are coming for your first 90 days or even just for a few nights, Air BNB is a fantastic way to find accommodation in LA (and almost any city around the world). Private residents rent out spare rooms in their houses and apartments to travellers. Both tenants and hosts are verified through reviews from their friends and previous tenants, and there are a huge number of pictures listed so you know what you're getting into before you show up. The higher price is worth the hassle you save by utilizing this brilliantly designed site.

CraigsList.org

Craigslist has information on most things you'll need when moving to America. It's like those boards that used to be at the supermarket for selling something or renting out a room. Among many other things, it lists:

• Rooms for rent.
• Furniture for sale.
• Cars for sale.
• Jobs available (both legit and cash).

Check the site while budgeting your trip to get a feel for prices and availabilities of the things you're going to need out here.

Warning: I wouldn't advise sending money to ANYONE you find on Craigslist for ANYTHING. The site is great, but as with most public forums, there are con artists and bad people on there too.

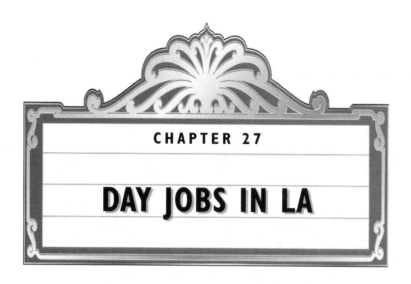

CHAPTER 27

DAY JOBS IN LA

Cash Work

While this book does not condone working illegally in any country, there are many jobs listed on Craigslist.org and Mandy.com that pay cash. You'll find anything from 'foot modeling' or handing out fliers to telemarketing or PA work. Bartending at private parties is a great way to make money fast, so ask people you meet whether they know anyone who runs a bartending service.

> **Warning:** Be very careful about answering any job ad posted on-line, as there are many predators out there. Don't answer any ads for work in remote areas, and if you do turn up for a job interview and don't like the look of the place, don't go in—just turn around and leave. No job is worth putting your safety at risk.

Surveys / Focus Groups

Focus groups are run by companies that want an 'everyman' opinion on a product they are trying to market. The company generally specifies that the focus group cannot consist of actors or people employed in the advertising industry . . . but . . . most companies do not check up on your employment history. The average session pays $80 to $150 for two or three hours, and the payment is almost always a check made out to cash or a pre-loaded card. Most recruiters will only book you to attend a focus group once every three to six months, so sign up with all of the companies listed in the resource guide.

Real Jobs

Temp agencies, job listing sites (like ServeStaff.com), and recruitment websites are listed in the resource guide. Visit restaurants and bars in your area to fill out application forms or apply through recruitment websites. If you're attractive, go in person (most bar managers in LA want pretty bar staff). Many actors also work for wait staffing companies that handle events, or with promotions companies running drink promotions or wine tastings.

LA is a normal city, so there are a myriad of typical day jobs in every industry imaginable. Many employers are used to actors, and will be more flexible than typical 9–5 bosses.

If you do get a day job, ensure that acting remains your top priority. Many actors turn down indie film roles or important auditions to keep their day job, forgetting that a day job should always come second. Your dreams and goals must be your top priority. Never forget how far you've come and how much you've given up to be in LA. Keeping savings and a low overhead will allow you to quit at short notice if acting work comes up.

UTA Job List

If you know anyone connected to a major agency, ask if they have access to the UTA job list. It is one of the best places to start when looking for assisting work at the top agencies or production companies.

CHAPTER 28

GETTING AROUND LA

In LA, your car is your lifeline. The last thing you want is to have your engine overheat or to get pulled over for some minor offense on the way to read for Mr Spielberg.

LA is easy to navigate because it is built on a grid. This is partly because there were once trams running up and down each of the main roads. Private companies reputedly bought up the tram system and replaced it with buses, which is one reason for the lack of reliance on public transportation in LA and the consequent terrible traffic conditions.

Why Not Use Public Transport?

LA has the second largest public transport system in the USA, yet due to the sprawling layout of the city many residents simply choose not to figure it out. Between the few train lines stretch miles of streets that must be navigated by bus or cab. While this can be a viable mode of transportation, the heat and walking time may cause an actor to arrive at auditions sweating and disheveled, which will not help you book roles. In short: get a car.

BASIC ROAD RULES

While you are a 'tourist' (if you are in LA but not a resident), the State will recognize the license from the country or State of which you are a resident.

Once you become a California resident, you'll need to get a California driving license. Do not drink and drive in LA. It is a criminal offense and could be grounds for jail time, or worse: denial of a Greencard or visa.

There are subtle differences between the road rules in the USA and other countries. The following is what I have been told you can do on the roads in LA and is NOT to be taken as law.

Please don't just take my word for any of this. Familiarize yourself with the local road rules through the DMV (Department of Motor Vehicles) website: DMV.gov (though DMV.org is much more user-friendly) before driving in LA.

> **TIP:** The Wrong Side of the Road: Americans drive on the wrong (right) side of the road (duh). If you are from another country, don't focus on which 'side of the road' you're supposed to be on (sounds scary, but stay with me here...). Just remember, the driver's side of the car stays in the center of the road (closest to the line dividing the two directions of traffic).

The 'Golden Lane'

You know those times when there are two lanes of traffic and one car is stopped in the middle lane waiting for a gap to turn across the oncoming traffic while twenty cars are stuck behind? That doesn't happen as often in LA thanks to a wonderful feature that I am going to call the 'Golden Lane'.

Between the lanes on most major Los Angeles streets is a "Center Left Turn Lane" lined in yellow that you must pull into while waiting to turn left so you don't block traffic. It's genius. One thing though, because this one lane is used for traffic heading both ways, watch out for cars coming towards you in the opposite direction.

The Turn Right on Red Rule

After coming to a complete stop you are allowed to turn right at a red light unless signs are posted (rare) that indicate otherwise.

The 'Turn Left on Amber' Trend

In LA, it is common practice for drivers to turn left (i.e. across the oncoming traffic) on an amber light, which means you're often completing the turn as the light goes red. While the light is green, the first two cars intending to turn left drive forward into the intersection and wait while the oncoming traffic passes by. Then, as the light turns amber, the oncoming traffic stops at the intersection, and those first two cars turn left into the cross street.

Here's the thing . . . you're not legally supposed to cross the white line at an intersection while the light is amber. However, if you are already past the white line waiting to turn and are blocking the intersection when the light turns red, you legally must clear the intersection by completing your turn. So . . . in theory, turning left on amber or red could get you a citation, but after being here for nine years, I've never heard of anyone getting busted for it.

BUYING A CAR

Car rentals are reasonably priced in the USA, so it's pretty simple: if you're staying in town for less than ninety days, rent one. More than ninety days, buy or lease one. To roam around LA in a dodgy four cylinder will cost you around fifty dollars a week in gas. If you look after it, you can sell it at a vague loss when you leave, and have had a car in LA for very little outlay.

Other than car yards, cars can be sourced in private sales from sites like Craigslist, Ebay, Recycler.com and Cars.com. Prices are much more reasonable in private sales, but some car yards offer a warranty, which can be more attractive than a discount.

The key to getting a cost-effective car is to buy a common make and model so new parts are easy to get and reasonably priced. Have a trusted mechanic inspect the car before you buy it.

> **TIP:** The Gas Buddy iPhone app shows where the cheapest gas is sold in relation to your GPS location.

Carfax.com

Carfax provides a full history of each registered vehicle in the USA according to the plates and VIN (Vehicle Identification Number). Always check the Carfax before purchasing any vehicle.

The main thing to look for on Carfax is that the car is **not a salvage title**, has not had any major accidents or water damage, and has been serviced regularly.

KellyBlueBook.com

Kelly Blue Book tracks the value of each make and model of vehicle in the

USA. It accounts for the vehicle condition, mileage, add-ons and packages. Always look for a car that is priced under or at the Kelly Blue Book value.

Check Your Oil and Water

If your car is old, learn how to check the oil and water, and do it once a month. An old, cheap car in the dry, hot climate of LA needs to stay lubricated and cool.

You check them both when the engine is cool, which means when the motor has been switched off for at least twenty minutes (preferably longer). The water (or coolant) is under a metal cap that's on top of the big grate looking thing (radiator) at the front of your engine bay. The location of the dipstick (to check the oil level) varies between vehicles, so have a mechanic show you how to check and fill the oil in your car.

Further to that: KEEP SPARE OIL AND WATER IN YOUR TRUNK so you can refill them in an emergency.

> **TIP:** If your car breaks down, you can call AAA and join on the spot for immediate assistance.

Roadside Assistance

Sign up for AAA or All State roadside assistance. They come to rescue you if your car breaks down. Useful investment in this crazy car town.

Portable Battery

Keep a pre-charged portable car battery in the trunk of your car to jump-start the engine should you ever get stuck.

California Low Cost Insurance

If your vehicle is worth less than $20,000, you have had a license for three continuous years and your household income is less than $27,075, you may qualify for California Low Cost Insurance. This means the top insurance companies must insure your vehicle for the State government low cost rate. The downside is you don't get to choose your insurer (but aren't they all pretty much the same?). Check out: insurance.ca.gov/lowcost

RENTING A CAR

Use Priceline.com, RelayRides.com or a similar site to book a cheap car rental before you land, anticipate $600/month for an economy car.

Rental Car Insurance

Rental car insurance can double the cost of renting a car. Before purchasing rental car insurance, check with both your credit card company, your existing car insurance company, and your travel insurance company. Contracts with these companies often automatically include rental car insurance. Some credit card companies (eg. AMEX) cover car insurance 'per rental' for a single low fee. This may save you the average of $15 a day that it costs to insure a low price rental car.

> **TIP:** If you use a credit card ALWAYS get a receipt. I just got charged $72 on a $12 cab fare and without my receipt I was unable to dispute the charge.

PUBLIC TRANSPORTATION

The Metro

Called the 'Metro', the LA subway (visit GoMetro.com) pales in comparison to the New York or London subway systems. In saying that, when you combine the train with the many LA buses, public transport really can get you around the sprawling suburbs of Los Angeles. The subway alone is most convenient when heading downtown or close to any of the few stops that are on the train line.

A train/bus combination can apparently get you most places, but if it's summer and you're wearing makeup for an audition, it's likely to melt off in the heat. For the guys: sweat patches under your arms, while concealable, are undoubtedly indicative that you will end up stinking up an audition room.

Taxi and Limo Services

There are seven companies that cover central LA. Currently, cabs charge a flag fee of $2.85 for the first 1/9 mile then $2.70 per mile . . . and fifty cents for every minute spent at traffic lights. When travelling *to* LAX, however, many companies offer a flat rate of between $40 and $60 (plus tip) from West Hollywood or Beverly Hills.

Here's a quick cab safety tip from the City of LA Taxi website, Taxi-CabsLA.org: *"Be sure before boarding any taxi in the city of Los Angeles that you **look for the official City of Los Angeles Taxicab Seal**. Taxicabs bearing this seal are insured, have trained drivers and are regularly inspected by the City of Los Angeles. Any cab without the seal is a bandit cab with no legal authorization to operate in the City."*

Uber
Uber is the new ride of choice in LA. It is cheaper, easier and faster than a cab, with the perks of riding in a town car. Cars are called to your location through an iPhone app through which all monies (including tips) are exchanged (rather than cash).

Lyft
Lyft is a very reasonably priced car service where the cars are driven by every day people looking for a little extra cash. They do background checks on the drivers and every car has a large pink moustache attached to the front grill. Like uber, cars are called through an iPhone app through which all monies are exchanged.

Limo
A limo costs $60 to $125 an hour, which is about how long it should take to get into Hollywood in moderate traffic. Many limo companies have a three-hour minimum booking, but some will do the airport trip for a single fee. Add a 15% to 20% tip for the driver.

Bus
Sure, it's cheap, but after sitting on a plane for thirteen hours, a bus is the last place I'd want to be. All the stops can triple the duration of the drive home and you'll still have to wrestle your bags from the bus stop to your accommodation, but if you really want to save the money, go ahead.

AIRPORT TIPS

One-Hour Delay on Arrival Time
No matter how you are planning to travel from the airport, allow a solid hour after any international flight arrival time as a buffer zone for customs

and baggage claim. This is not an exaggeration. If your flight gets in at 9AM, anticipate walking out of LAX at 10AM. Communicate this to your ride.

Airport Cheap Parking

If you are leaving town for just a few days, driving to the airport and parking near LAX saves you the trouble and cost of a friend or taxi picking you up.

There are companies near the airport (like the Mariott or other hotels) that rent parking spaces to people who don't want to pay the high overnight parking rates at LAX. Some charge as little as $6 per day, and most have free shuttles that transport you to the airport.

The same system exists for LAX, Burbank (BUR) Airport, and many other airports in the USA. Check Airport-LA.com for the best rates.

Airport-LA.com

This is the LAX website. It shows departures and arrivals of flights, delays, and even searches nearby parking lots for the best overnight parking rates.

Airport Shuttles

Shuttles are a great combination of safe, easy, fast and cheap. They pick you up from the airport arrival gate and drop you (possibly after dropping a few other passengers off) at your front door. The shuttle can also pick you up from home and take you to the airport.

Shuttles to areas outside central LA can be expensive, but to get to Hollywood or the Valley is only around $30. The two main shuttle companies are *Super Shuttle* and *Airport Shuttle*. You don't need to book ahead to get a shuttle from LAX, but if you do, book through ShuttleToLAX.com for the cheapest fares.

The Drive

If you want to avoid the freeways, simply take La Cienega South, then turn right on W Century Blvd to get to LAX, and do the opposite to get home. These roads are almost always clearer than the freeways. From Hollywood, I take Highland down to La Brea, then right on Stocker to get to La Cienega.

Getting a Ride from a Friend

The drive to LAX in rush hour from anywhere north of Wilshire is a well-known and *dreaded* drive. If your arrival time is between 7AM and 9AM or between 4PM and 7PM, please DO NOT DO THIS TO THEM. An LAX pickup in traffic can be a solid two hour round trip. These times assume the actual pickup will be one hour after your arrival time.

TIP: Southwest Rapid Rewards

For cheap last minute domestic flights, you can purchase Southwest airlines rapid rewards points from independent sellers on Craigslist.org. Most range from $250–$350 for a domestic flight within the USA.

Bus from the Airport

To catch a bus, you have to walk to the LAX city bus center which is around a 20 min walk from LAX, then catch either: the 117 and change to the 210, or the 40/42 then change to the 210.

Train from the Airport

If you have a few big bags, avoid the train. There are not many stations in LA, so you could end up faced with a long walk to your destination carting your bags with you. Carrying your passport, you'll be an easy target if you're in the wrong area at night. It costs around ten dollars for a train into Hollywood, and I advise catching a taxi from the station to your destination.

CHAPTER 29

ROADS AND TRAFFIC

TRAFFIC—PEAK / OFF PEAK HOURS

If you're unlucky enough to be traveling during peak hours in LA, anticipate your travel time being two or three times as long as usual. If you think it will take ten minutes, plan for twenty to thirty, for an hour drive, seriously leave two to three hours beforehand (though if you ask me, an hour long drive in peak hour LA traffic should just be rescheduled). This is important for auditions and going to set because the traffic in LA is not an excuse, it's a given.

Rat-running: Awesome Streets to Take in Rush Hour

- Franklin Ave: East / West from Vermont to La Brea
- Hollywood Blvd: East / West from La Brea to Fairfax
- Fountain Ave: East / West From Cahuenga to La Cienega
- Wilcox: North / South From Melrose to Franklin
- Highland: North / South from Melrose to La Brea intersect
- S La Brea: North / South from Highland intersect to Stocker
- Crescent Heights: North / South from the 10 freeway to Sunset Blvd
- Little Santa Monica: East / West from Wilshire intersect to Doheny Dr
- Carmelita or Parkway Ave: When traffic is bad on Santa Monica Blvd in Beverly Hills, drive one or two blocks North and take one of these little streets East / West.

- Elevado Ave: When traffic is bad on Sunset Blvd in Beverly Hills, drive one block South to drive East / West.
- Holloway Dr: When traffic is bad on Sunset West of La Cienega in West Hollywood.

Try to book plans between 10AM and 4PM, then after 8PM. Keep in mind, the traffic usually heads toward the central areas in the morning and away from them (toward freeway onramps) in the afternoons.

Regular Peak Hours

Morning Business Traffic
8AM to 9:30AM (triple your travel time and avoid freeways)
Traffic is travelling along all major freeways towards downtown LA.

Evening Business Traffic
5PM to 7:30PM (triple your travel time and avoid freeways)
Traffic is travelling along all major freeways away from downtown LA, and on all streets leading towards freeway on-ramps.

Fri / Sat Peak hours
8PM to 2AM (add 50% or double your travel time)
This occurs only in central Hollywood, the Sunset strip, and downtown in the warmer months. Unless there's a big event on, it really doesn't make a huge difference.

Anomalies

Events at the Staples Center
These block up the streets around Downtown LA.

Events at the Hollywood Bowl
If there's an event at the bowl, avoid all streets within a four-block radius East of La Brea, North of Hollywood, or West of Cahuenga. Never take the Highland exit or onramp from the 101 if there's something at the bowl. It's usually gridlock.

Film Premieres and Academy Awards
If Hollywood Blvd is blocked off, traffic redirects to all East / West streets. Avoid Franklin Blvd and definitely avoid Highland North of Melrose. If you're lucky, Sunset will be okay, but you'll probably have to head along Fountain to get East / West.

The LA Marathon

Don't leave the house if you're in Hollywood or WeHo. This marathon runs from Santa Monica to Downtown all the way along Santa Monica Blvd . . . just stay home, watch movies, and sleep.

MAIN ROADS

Before you come to LA, go to a mapping site (like Maps.Google.com) and enter the 'zip code' (postcode) 90028 into the search bar for a map of Hollywood and surrounding areas. Move it around until you can see Olympic Blvd at the bottom, Franklin at the top, and from Vermont to Doheny. Take a look at the main streets and you'll find the whole street system is a grid of really long roads.

Most LA locals give a street address and add a North/South street name intersecting with an East/West street name, eg: "It's near Sunset and Vine" or "Doheny and Beverly". This allows you to approximate where a small street is located so you know (before you even key it into your iPhone) approximately how far you're going to have to travel.

Top to Bottom

This is a list of East/West streets, starting at the top (Northern) one down.

- Franklin Ave
- Hollywood Blvd
- Sunset Ave
- Fountain Ave
- Santa Monica Blvd
- Melrose Ave
- Beverly Blvd
- 3rd St
- Wilshire Blvd
- Pico Blvd
- Olympic Blvd
- Venice Blvd
- Washington Blvd
- 10 Freeway

Left to Right

Streets that head from North to South, starting from the left (West) one.

- Doheny Dr
- La Cienega Blvd
- Crescent Heights Blvd
- Fairfax Ave
- La Brea Ave
- Highland Ave
- Wilcox Ave
- Cahuenga Blvd
- Vine St
- Gower St
- Wilton Pl
- Western Ave
- Normandie Ave
- Vermont Ave
- Alvarado St
- 110 Freeway

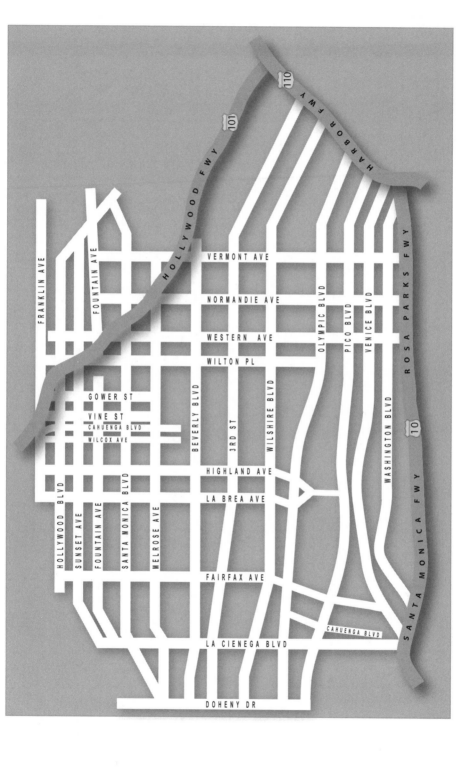

CHAPTER 30

PHONES, INTERNET, TV

Cell Phone Billing

Cell phones in America are billed by the minute across the board. It doesn't matter if you're talking to a mobile or landline, interstate or local, you get charged by the minute regardless of the type of call (unless it's overseas).

Phone companies charge for incoming calls as well as outgoing calls, so you are charged for every single minute you're on your phone. This principle applies to texts also.

When you receive an international call, you are charged by your usual rate per minute. Most phone companies charge a higher rate for outgoing international texts and calls.

Cell Phone Companies

The phone companies all have their pros and cons . . . check the resource guide for an overview of the main ones. I highly recommend T-Mobile pre-paid for anyone staying under ninety days. Home phones are usually added to a cable or cell phone plan.

Skype.com

Skype is a great way to stay in touch with friends and family back home. If you can teach your parents to use the internet, you'll be able to video chat with them for free online.

International Calling Cards

Any convenience store should have pre-paid international calling cards. You simply buy the card, call a local number in the USA, and then enter the overseas number of your choice into the system.

> **TIP: Get a Local Number**
>
> When you get a phone, ensure that you get an 'area' code that is in Los Angeles, because some CDs will not bring in actors with a non-local phone number. Ensure that you request a number that starts with **310**, **323**, or **818**. That's (generally) Beverly Hills, Hollywood, and the Valley, respectively.

iPhone Apps

HeyTell

HeyTell is like the love child of a walkie-talkie and a voice message system. At any time you can send a voice message to a friend's account, and it is stored so they can listen to it and respond at their leisure. It's like the voice version of text messaging, and is a free way to communicate internationally.

WhatsApp

WhatsApp is a popular iPhone app for sending free texts internationally.

Viber

Viber provides free calls, texts, photos, and location sharing.

MagicJack.com

A Magic Jack is a small USB device that you plug into a computer in the USA and it is assigned a permanent USA phone number. Mail or take your Magic Jack back to your family overseas and plug it into their computer, then plug their phone into the Magic Jack. Their home phone is then able to

> **TIP: *67 Blocks Your Number**
>
> To call from a blocked (private) number, type *67 prior to entering the phone number.

make calls from and accept calls to that USA phone number, which means calling between USA and another country through a Magic Jack becomes a LOCAL CALL. Awesome.

Cable and Direct TV

The two major companies are Warner Horizon for cable TV, and Direct TV for direct digital television.

Internet

Most people get internet through a phone company, cable company, or Direct-TV provider.

Phone Services

- Emergency   911
- Information   411
- Dialing out of the USA   011

RANDOM TIP: Automated Phone Systems

Most automated phone systems have a default button where if you want to skip the automated questions and get to a real person, just press '0'.

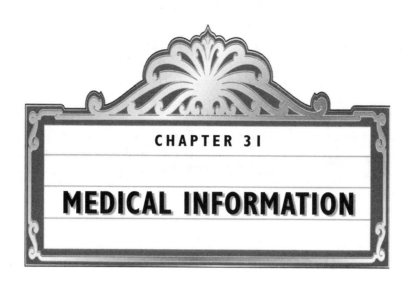

CHAPTER 31

MEDICAL INFORMATION

Doctors

Doctors charge an up front fee in the USA. Free STD tests are available at Planned Parenthood. There are free clinics around town (Women's Clinic, Saban Clinic) but if you can afford to pay, check the list of reasonably priced doctors on Yelp.com. Whatever you do, try to avoid ambulances and the emergency room as they can cost a fortune.

Health Insurance

Decent health insurance in the USA can cost hundreds of dollars a month. This is why jobs with a good health plan are so appealing to American workers. If you are coming out on a ninety-day visa waiver, it may be best to secure travel insurance that covers injuries obtained while overseas. If you are living in LA, check the resource guide for a list of reasonably priced insurance providers.

Bill AB 774

This bill restricts how much hospitals are allowed to charge you for each service. If you do end up with a hefty hospital bill, find out if your yearly

income is less than 350% of the Federal Poverty Level. If so, bill AB 774 may apply to you.
(Ref: OSHPD.ca.gov/hid/products/hospitals/fairpricing/index.html)

Dentists

If you need a dentist in an emergency but don't have the cash, UCLA has a dental clinic as part of the University where the students observe the procedures. You end up paying around a third of the price of going to a dentist. Check Yelp.com for a list of recommended dentists in LA.

CHAPTER 32

GROCERIES IN LA

In LA, there are a number of grocery stores, each with a unique selection of foods and household products. These are the main grocery companies in LA:

- Trader Joes (cheap healthy stuff and great organic food)
- Fresh and Easy (fantastic, cheap grocery store)
- Food4Less (normal CHEAP grocery store)
- Wholefoods (expensive organic food)
- Ralphs (normal expensive grocery store with big brands)
- Vons (normal grocery store with big brands)
- Jons (cheap groceries and produce)
- Gelsons and/or Albertsons (expensive grocery store with organic selection)
- Bristol Farms (high end, super expensive organic grocery store)
- Farmers Market at the Grove (great for fresh fruit and veggies, baked goods, and deli)
- Yucca Market (produce store in Hollywood with cheap fruit and veg)

Bulk Grocery Stores

Costco and Smart & Final only sell in bulk quantities, so head there for toilet paper, hand towels, cheap alcohol, food, drinks, or junk food. Costco is a much bigger 'members only' store that sells furniture, electronic, and white goods as well as food, drink and household products. Membership is attained by paying a monthly fee. Smart & Final is much smaller, has no membership program, and stocks mostly food, drink, and household products.

Organic vs Non-Organic Veggies

Vegetables seem to be generally cheaper in America than in other first world countries. The prices can be kept low because the majority of veggies here are grown in huge quantities and are bred to grow much larger and faster than their organic counterparts. This unfortunately causes the soil depletion which is responsible for a massive decrease in the nutrients in non-organic produce.

Organic vegetables in the USA are often cheaper than even low priced veggies in other countries, so rather than saving the money on nutrient deprived goods that look like vegetables, most of the people I know stick to the real thing and eat organic produce while in LA.

CHAPTER 33

OTHER HELPFUL INFORMATION

Tipping

Tip when you are receiving a service, like a waitress bringing your drink or a concierge carrying your bags. You don't need to tip at a fast food place because the person taking your order doesn't have to bring the food to you.

At a café where you pay at the counter, are assigned a number, then the waiter brings your food to your table, you might put a dollar in the tip jar or 10% on the credit card tab but it's definitely not rude if you don't.

The main people who should be tipped are:

- Waiters and Waitresses   10% of pre-tax total if service is bad, 15% if service is good, 20% if service is excellent
- Bartenders $1 per drink up to around $3 for more than 3
- Café or Coffee Shop Server $1 or $2 on the check or in the tip jar
- Taxi Drivers   10% of the fare is fine, or more if the driver helps with heavy bags
- Limo Drivers   10% to 15% of the ride cost (this is often pre-paid on the bill if a car is booked for you)
- Concierge at Hotels $2 per large bag

- Beautician / Masseuse
10% to 20% depending on the bill or quality of service
- House cleaner
10% to 20% at your discretion

You can always tip more, but these are the standard tip levels that will keep you from being scowled at by angry service industry folk who think you're being rude.

Places you do not tip are:
- Grocery stores and retail outlets
- Gas stations
- Fast food joints
- Dermatologists or doctors
- Mechanics, plumbers or other maintenance services

Taxes
There is a tax rate of almost 10% on every sale that is made in the USA. This means if you have a $30 dinner, you'll pay just under $3 in tax. Add a 20% tip of $6 and your $30 meal turns into a $39 one.

Claiming Expenses on Your Tax Return
Actors are able to claim a variety of expenses on their yearly tax return. Ensure you keep receipts for all expenditures. While using your credit card statement to find the totals is a great time saving tool, you will need the receipts to back up these figures should an audit occur.

Note: The following list is intended as a guide only. Please double check these suggestions with your tax professional. My research indicates actors are able to claim the following expenses:

- Entertainment: Movies, theater shows, music concerts, film festivals
- Meals: Business breakfasts, lunches and dinners are 50% deductible. Must be dining with other actors, representation, filmmakers, CDs, etc. and should be documented as meeting for business
- Clothing: Deduct ONLY clothing used for an audition or role that is not appropriate for every day wear. This mostly applies to costumes.
- Mileage: Keep a mileage log. Any miles travelled to and from auditions or jobs, going to see your agent, going to class, etc., are claimable. This includes taxis, Uber, Lyft, and public transport
- Education: Acting classes, classes attaining skills for a specific role

- Makeup / Hair: Any theatrical makeup purchased specifically for auditions (not every day wear) or hair alterations done specifically for a role
- Office supplies: items purchased for your acting career
- Postage: mail sent relating to your acting career
- Gifts: $25 per person per year
- Marketing: Printing headshots, postcards, business cards, resumes, headshot sessions, demo reel taping services, self submission sites
- Tools and Equipment: items specific to the job like microphones, printers, computers, etc. The purchase cost is fully claimable up to a certain figure, beyond which each item has the depreciation 'written off' over 5–7 years
- Home office: If you have a room that you use exclusively as a home office, it may qualify as a business deduction. This enables you to deduct any rental costs, mortgage interest, insurance, repairs, utilities, taxes, etc.

Getting Over Jetlag

You'll be barely functional for two days, tangibly damaged for around a week and subtle impairments (that you probably won't even notice) stick around for up to two weeks.

In my experience, the most important action you can take to get over jetlag is to stay awake the whole day when you first arrive. NO NAPS! No exceptions. If you can stay up till around 8PM the day you land, then sleep a solid twelve to fourteen hours, you'll be back to normal in no time.

The other key is to drink lots of water. In fact, it's so important, I'm giving it an entire section:

Drink More Water

"Why am I so tired?" It may not just be jetlag . . . you're probably dehydrated. LA is in a desert. It averages less than forty days of rain per year. There is so little moisture in the air and so much pollution that you simply have to be conscious of staying hydrated all the time.

I recommend avoiding LA tap water . . . many people say it's fine, but I have my doubts. To avoid buying bottles, I have a PUR™ water filter attached to the tap (I buy the filter cartridges online for half the store price).

Humidifier

The Crane™ COOL mist humidifier changed my world. It comes in the shape of a frog, penguin, and a myriad of other animal folk (no, I don't have the dragon AND the elephant . . . that would be childish). Seriously . . . get a humidifier. Run it every night and it will help rescue you from nosebleeds, dry skin, wrinkles, and overall dehydration.

Avoiding Feast / Famine Spending

It can be overwhelming to receive a procession of huge paychecks after not working for six months . . . and it's easy to forget those checks only last as long as the job (residuals can be unpredictable). The solution is to save and invest, but the temptation for many is to blow it all on shoes and dinners.

If allocating money wisely isn't your strong suit, when you get a big pay-check I recommend immediately paying off any high interest debt first (e.g. credit cards and car loans). The next priority is to pre-pay the 'survival' bills that you will definitely have to pay at some point. Good bills to pre-pay are those like rent, utilities, cell phone bills, car payments, car insurance, union dues, and cable bills.

When I get a decent paycheck, I do allocate a portion to blow on random fun stuff (otherwise what's point of it all?), but only AFTER I pre-pay all my bills for three months. I also stock up on a few months worth of non-perishable things like toothpaste, face creams, water filters, and printer toner cartridges. You could even buy an "emergency" gift card to your favorite grocery store to set aside for a rainy day. It all sounds a little crazy, but when the cash reserves run low it's nice to know your basic living essentials are taken care of for a few months.

Banking in LA

You can open a bank account in the USA on a tourist visa without being a US Citizen and without having a proven permanent residence in the USA. What you will need is your passport, foreign driving license, and a USA phone and address. They'll just enter a bunch of zeros into the system as your social security number and you'll be good to go. The main banks are:

- Chase
- Bank Of America
- Wells Fargo
- HSBC
- Cincinati National (entertainment bank)
- Citibank

Credit Unions

A credit union is a not for profit, member-run organization that works in a very similar way to a bank, only with lower fees and less morally questionable business practices. If you don't want to support the big banks, and want to avoid big fees, credit unions (eg. the AFTRA-SAG Federal Credit Union) are a great place to store your hard earned dollars.

Cash Passport / Travel Visa

Cash Passport™ or a 'Travel Visa' is a prepaid Visa™ or MasterCard™. You load it up with a currency and it allows you to safely travel with only the funds you choose to put onto the card. It saves you from paying currency conversion fees on a foreign credit card, and since it is not linked to your bank account, it is a safer way to carry money overseas. See CashPassport.com or your bank website for details.

Second Hand Clothing

Some actors earn big chunks of money, spend it, then run low on cash and need money. To accommodate this, there are second hand stores that buy your designer clothing back from you:
• Buffalo Exchange
• Crossroads
• Out of the Closet
• Urban Wasteland

Overstock Stores

When stores or manufacturers can't sell their left over stock they sell it to overstock stores at a HUGE discount. These stores are GREAT for finding discounted brand names and cheap outfits for auditions or theatre shows:
• Ross
• Marshalls
• TJ Maxx
• JCPenney

CHAPTER 34

CHECKLIST FOR 90 DAYS IN LA

H ere's what I would do if I were arriving in LA for my first ninety-day stay:

Before Leaving Your Hometown or Home Country

❑ Join a Facebook group that is specific to your region (eg. Texans in LA) and keep an eye out for cars and rooms to rent.

❑ Sign up for paid ActorsAccess.com and NowCasting.com accounts a week before you land. Have your profiles fully set up, and start submitting on projects three or four days before you get here.

❑ Format your resume and other marketing tools.

❑ Join the HSG mailing list and chat room.

❑ PERFECT YOUR STANDARD AMERICAN ACCENT

❑ Ask your hometown representation to refer you to any agents and managers they have relationships with in LA.

When You Arrive

❑ Rent a car or take the shuttle from the airport.

❑ If you don't have a place to stay or a friend's couch, book your first week in town in a backpackers hostel while you arrange something more permanent.

❑ Find a sub-let room rental through Facebook, AirBNB or Craigslist for around $650 a month.

❏ Get a pre-paid phone from T-Mobile.
❏ Go to Trader Joes and get groceries.
❏ Go to Smart & Final for household products and bulk food.
❏ Check the online casting websites twice daily and submit accordingly.

When the Jetlag Has Faded

❏ Audition for a casting workshop and buy packages of workshops to get a lower rate. Attend as often as possible (I used to do 5 a week).
❏ Meet with potential visa attorneys.
❏ Keep track of any producers you meet, as they may be willing to sponsor you into the country.
❏ Say YES to every invitation.
❏ Buy coffee or lunch as payment to pick the brains of anyone you know in the industry.
❏ Ask everyone you know to refer you to anyone who might be able to give you advice or help you.
❏ Against my advice, send your cover letters and headshots (or emails with them attached plus a demo link) to any of the agents or managers in town that you're interested in working with . . . because you're in Hollywood now, and in Hollywood anything can happen!

CONCLUSION

Los Angeles is smoggy and dirty, with cracked roads and an ever-present feeling of desperation, insecurity, and broken dreams. It's the loneliest town I've ever lived in and you'll be shocked to see that the glamour of Hollywood takes place mere feet away from poverty and homelessness. The town is abundant with temptation and people who are controlled by their vices, willing to abandon their morals and dignity for any chance of success.

Hollywood is like a drug, an addiction you can't shake. Any day you could make it, any day you could get that phone call saying "You got the part" and that's it, you've finally got a shot at the big time. It's like a million people wake up every day with a lottery ticket and all they have to do to stay in the running is be in LA hoping for the big prize of fame, fortune, and success in the film and TV industry.

Along with the fantasy comes the legitimate potential for real success, the kind you work strategically and methodically for years to achieve. There are many passionate people here with a strong work ethic, clear goals, and unwavering focus. There is a real underdog feeling, like we're all battlers trying to win a war against anonymity.

Contrary to common belief, there is a strong camaraderie between the actors in Hollywood and an overwhelming willingness to help one another. If you look hard enough, you'll find likeminded friends who share in the quest to be successful in this career path and art form that so passionately wraps its arms around you and eternally maintains a warm, but firm embrace upon your life and your heart.

When you peek past LA's seemingly impenetrable veneer, you'll find a throbbing epicenter of art, music, passion, and creativity. Filmmakers and actors share the desire to maintain a ritual that humans have played out for thousands of years, since tribesmen drew pictures on the walls of their caves and the ancients told tales to their children. The art of telling stories that change lives and define entire generations, stories that can now educate, inspire, and entertain billions of people around the world.

To tell stories. That is what all the fame, money, and craziness of Hollywood is ultimately about, which is why you must chase your dreams across the world to find those precious few stories you know in your heart it is your destiny to tell.

STAY IN TOUCH!

Website: www.TheHollywoodSurvivalGuide.com

Your thoughts, questions, and comments about this book are important to me. Please let me know via:

Email: Kym@TheHollywoodSurvivalGuide.com

Kym's Twitter: @AussieGirly

Hollywood Survival Guide's Twitter: @HollywoodSGuide

INDEX

stand-in, 27, 267
Stanislavski, 9
star names only, 90
starmeter, 41, 42, 62
Stella Adler, 9
student films, 138, 141, 203–
204
studio films, 21, 38, 98, 136–138,
202, 239
stunt casting, 93
stunt coordinator, 69, 185
stunts, 11, 47, 68–69, 184–185
submission (role), 21, 37, 44,
48, 50, 55, 57, 75–76, 80,
82–84, 90, 93, 99, 100, 123,
153, 163, 309
Summit, 137
Sundance film festival, 177–178
supporting role, 19, 20, 25, 31,
44, 75, 90, 92, 98, 139, 188,
201

table read, 93, 94, 182
taft hartley, 120–122
tax incentives, 137, 149–150
television (TV), 14, 24, 26,
50–51, 84, 93–94, 98, 111,
119, 123, 130, 132–133,
146–147, 202, 211, 236,
238, 258–259, 301
tentpole movie, 240–241
test audience, 237–238
test deal, 114
thank you gifts, 80–82, 85, 103
The Group Theatre, 9
The Harold, 10
The Pilot Report, 203

The Weinstein Company, 137
theatrical release (limited), 139,
249
theatrical release (wide), 24, 54,
139, 147, 249
theatrical agent, 14, 19, 47, 51,
59, 61–63, 67–68
TMA (Talent Managers Association), 52, 57, 59
top LA agents, 63
top LA managers, 65
top of show, 29
Toronto Film Festival, 177, 211
Tribeca film festival, 177
turnaround, 232
Twitter, xvii, 32, 44
type (character), 14–16, 20, 35,
39, 54–55, 62–63, 69, 71,
153–154, 157

UCB, 10
union dues, 122, 310
upfronts, 237
Universal, 136

Venice film festival, 177
Viber, 300
Vimeo.com, 33, 39, 117, 151
visa, 3, 23, 43, 51, 99, 104, 153,
192, 208, 209, 211, 218,
273, 275–278, 286, 303,
310–311, 314
VistaPrint.com, 50
VOD (video on demand), 130,
139, 201, 244
voice-over, 65–67, 155, 204
VP of casting, 74

Μιχαήλ Καβέλος